CH

D1024813

The *Energy Healing* Experiments

The *Energy Healing* Experiments

Science Reveals Our Natural Power to Heal

Gary E. Schwartz, PhD

with William L. Simon

ATRIA BOOKS

NEW YORK • LONDON • TORONTO • SYDNEY

ATRIA BOOKS

1230 Avenue of the Americas
New York, NY 10020

In some cases, the names of people who participated in an experiment or
incident have been changed. Also, some details have been modified to further insure anonymity.

Library of Congress Cataloging-in-Publication Data
Schwartz, Gary E.
The energy healing experiments : science reveals our natural
power to heal / by Gary E. Schwartz, with William L. Simon.—
1st Atria Books hardcover ed.
      p. cm.
   Includes index.
   1. Energy medicine. 2. Healing. I. Simon, William L. II. Title.
RZ421.S39 2007
615.5'3—dc22   2006101302

ISBN-13: 978-0-7432-9237-5
ISBN-10:   0-7432-9237-5

First Atria Books hardcover edition August 2007

10 9 8 7 6 5 4 3 2 1

ATRIA BOOKS is an imprint of Simon & Schuster, Inc.

Manufactured in the United States of America

For information about special discounts for bulk purchases,
please contact Simon & Schuster Special Sales at 1-800-456-6798
or business@simonandschuster.com.

For Jim, Natalie, Rhonda, Marcia, Mel, Jerry, Susy, and Sam

And for Arynne, Victoria, and David, Sheldon, Merrilee, Vincent, and Elena

We may therefore regard matter as being constituted by the regions of space in which the [energy] field is extremely intense . . . There is no place in this new kind of physics both for the field and matter, for the field is the only reality.

—ALBERT EINSTEIN

Contents

Foreword

The Energy Healing Experiments is a thought-provoking, innovative, and much needed scientific review of an often overlooked, poorly understood, and perplexing area of energy medicine. It might also be entitled Scientific Journeys into the Twilight Zone! There are few traditional health care or medical practitioners who have not been challenged by a phenomenon that they witnessed but could not explain in terms of their allopathic or Western medical education. Often these observations are dismissed, marginalized, described as placebo effects, or rejected because they don't fit into our own unintended and poorly recognized biases.

This realization began for me as a young child when I witnessed my grandmother and other select senior family members and friends employing herbs, "laying on of the hands," and spiritual interventions. These practices were all part of my Hispanic heritage and undoubtedly were transmitted from generation to generation. I certainly was "clueless" at the time. However, years later in retrospective analysis these experiences gave me valuable insight into what today we would term complementary medicine. My grandmother might be compelled to comment about the arrogance of Western medicine in calling these practices alternative or complementary, since they were clearly mainstream for her, her ancestors, and most of the world even today!

In addition, as a young man and Army Special Forces Medic traveling the world in war and peace, I also lived among diverse cultures and witnessed their healing practices. I observed a variety of healers practicing their crafts, sometimes with success and sometimes without, just as happens with Western medicine.

In Southeast Asia I lived with the indigenous tribes called Montagnards. Physically strong and healthy but of small stature, they are a

1

hunter-gatherer/farmer society. I witnessed the practices of tribal medicine by mind, body, and spirit healers. I watched herbal remedies dispensed, procedures performed with primitive handmade instruments, and energy exchanged physically and spiritually during various rituals designed to treat disease or foster health and wellness.

Many years later as a physician working with Native American tribes in the Southwest, I again witnessed similar healers and practices, in cultures that had been "Americanized," but whose people passionately tried to retain their native culture and heritage. These practices around the world appeared effective, although I could not explain them in terms of my Western allopathic education as a medic, registered nurse, physician's assistant, scientist, or physician.

Seeing patients being operated on with acupuncture or hypnosis instead of any anesthesia makes one wonder how this is possible. Neither the Yin and Yang nor Chinese energy meridians are in our traditional medical vocabularies. As physicians, most of us can nevertheless attest to the value of the patient/doctor relationship and the way the sense of touch plays a big part in that. Most of us recognize that, although not presently quantifiable, there is healing value in that touch, and ensuing relationship. Patients who go to surgery with a positive mind, body, and spirit generally have better outcomes.

Years ago, Norman Cousins attempted to capture the value of many unrecognized therapies, including laughter, in healing and improved immunity in his seminal book, *Anatomy of an Illness As Perceived by the Patient.* In *The Energy Healing Experiments,* Dr. Schwartz takes us on a journey where allopathic medicine does not generally travel. Take the trip with him; it is well worth it.

Open your mind, set your biases and preconceived notions aside. We do not have all the answers and there is clearly more that we do not know and need to learn. Where the science supports these integrative concepts of energy medicine, let's use them. Where there is not enough science, let the studies begin and continue.

During my tenure as the 17th Surgeon General of the United States, I had the privilege to be a part of the team that strongly advocated for the formation of The National Center for Alternative and Complementary Medicine at the National Institutes of Health (NIH). This Center's challenge is to study all forms of complementary and alternative medicine, including energy medicine, so as to develop an evidence base for utilizing or rejecting various modalities. In my new position at Canyon Ranch I have the unique opportunity to continue with the Surgeon General's initiatives of health and wellness while working in one of the finest integrative health environments in the world. Practitioners and the public alike should approach energy medicine with an open mind. Allow the science to guide you to logical conclusions. "The Power of Possibility" is before us!

Richard Carmona, MD, MPH, FACS

17th Surgeon General of the United States

Vice Chairman, Canyon Ranch—CEO, Canyon Ranch Health

Distinguished Professor of Public Health, The Mel and Enid Zuckerman College of Public Health at the University of Arizona

May the story captivate us, the science awaken
us, and the truth transform us.

—JAMES LEVIN, MD

Preface

What you are about to read is a personal journey of discovery and awakening. You will partake in my adventures—and witness my transformations—as I explore the world of energy healing as a scientist, clinician, and human being.

This book presents reports—gathered for the first time in one place—of a wealth of novel experiments, conducted by my colleagues and me, that point inexorably to a new vision of healing. You will travel with me as I discover that Western science and society have been viewing the world through the illusion of materialism rather than seeing what might be called "the emerging reality of energy-ism" (accurate, even if a little clunky). That is, we've been seeing the world only in its material form and ignoring the essential reality: that energy, not matter, underlies all and plays a major role in health and healing.

With my writing partner, William Simon, I have attempted to create an integrative and bridging book that connects stories with science, explorations with experiments, and feelings with facts. Our challenge has been to strike a balance between presenting the larger story and conveying the science that inspires it.

Some readers will be more interested in the exciting adventures and what the new findings mean for health and life; others will be more interested in the details of the basic experiments themselves. Personal preferences aside, we hope that all readers will celebrate the larger vision as expressed by Dr. James Levin in the quote above. The story told in these pages captivated me, the science awakened me, and the truth has indeed transformed me. My wish is that the same will happen for you.

This book focuses on more than a decade of experiments conducted in my laboratory at the University of Arizona that were supported primarily by a Biofield Center grant and individual research grants from the National Center for Complementary and Alternative Medicine (NCCAM) of the National Institutes of Health (NIH), as well as by gifts from the Canyon Ranch Institute. The views you are about to read reflect those of the author, not the funding sources.

You are about to enter a world of possibility, where energy becomes the vibrant bridge that connects mind with matter, the spiritual with the physical. As you will discover, fields of energy are not only fundamental and far-reaching, they are also great fun.

Part I

Everything Has Energy and Conscious Intention

*I'm not saying that [a particular unlikely event]
is possible; I'm saying that it happens.*

—SIR WILLIAM CROOKES

Chapter 1

My Eyes Are Opened

Would you believe that a healer removed the pain of a broken wrist and bone in fifteen minutes?

Would you believe that another healer removed an ovarian tumor in a matter of weeks?

Would you believe that a third healer regenerated the nerves of a broken spine in a few months, remotely, on a person thousands of miles away?

As thoroughly unlikely as these examples may sound, I have personally witnessed such healings at first hand. They seem like miracles—yet they really did happen. The question is, how? The answer to this question involves a new understanding of energy and consciousness.

I'm a Harvard PhD, a former Yale professor of psychology and psychiatry and director of the Yale Psychophysiology Center. I'm currently a professor of psychology, surgery, medicine, neurology, and psychiatry at the University of Arizona. I was awarded one of two NIH grants to establish a Center for Frontier Medicine in Biofield Science. Though I was originally taught that such healing miracles do not and can not happen, the fact is that they do. Science can now help us to understand and celebrate them.

Pain That Disappears

The first energy healing I ever experienced was completely unexpected. In the summer of 1994, I was visiting a colleague on the East Coast, a psychotherapist I will call Suzanne.

Her father had been a distinguished physician and scientist who, though conventionally trained, was open to alternative therapies. After his death, Suzanne developed an interest in energy healing and was taking advanced courses in what's called healing touch.

While I was visiting with her, Suzanne received an emergency phone call from one of her counseling patients. In tears, the patient explained that her husband had been repairing the roof and had fallen off. He was rushed to the hospital in extreme pain. The lady pleaded with Suzanne to meet her at the emergency room and help her cope with this stress. Suzanne agreed to go, and I went as well.

We found her husband, Robert, apparently in excruciating pain, with his right wrist bent at an unlikely angle. I stepped out of the room so Suzanne could attempt healing. Curious about the process, I snuck a quick peek over her shoulder before I left. I saw Robert lying with his eyes closed while Suzanne waved her hands a few inches above his arm and wrist. I realized she was being circumspect: the hospital staff would not have been pleased about these goings-on, which they probably would have thought closely akin to voodoo.

After about fifteen minutes, Suzanne asked us to return. We found Robert with his eyes wide open and smiling like a surprised Cheshire cat. He said he had no idea what had just transpired, but to his amazement the severe pain in his wrist and arm was virtually gone. And no, he had not been given any pain medications.

He still couldn't move his limb, and X-rays would confirm he had a fractured wrist. Nonetheless, he was unexpectedly pain free and greatly relieved. So was his wife.

As for me, I was frankly in shock. If this was a placebo response—if Robert had believed Suzanne could relieve his pain, and his belief had tricked his body into making the pain disappear—then it was certainly a dramatic example. Could the elimination of Robert's pain be explained solely as the power of his mind over his body?

Or had something more occurred, something to do with healing that Suzanne had induced? Had I witnessed my first energy healing?

A Tumor Vanishes

Several years ago, a New Yorker I'll call Jane was diagnosed using ultrasound as having a large tumor on her right ovary. Refusing an immediate biopsy, she announced that she wanted to take a month to try alternative healing techniques.

She focused on two modalities—herbs, prescribed by a psychiatrist, and energy healing, to be performed by her husband, Mark, who happened to be a psychologist as well as a budding healer. He used the technique called Reiki, a form of energy healing that originated in Japan and has become popular in the United States and worldwide. Mark took a week off before the second ultrasound and spent four hours a day sending his wife loving energy. At times she would work at her computer and he would sit in a chair in the corner sending Reiki energy across the room. They focused on success, but what happened was not at all what they could have expected.

When the doctor repeated the ultrasound, he was astonished to find that the tumor had vanished. It had quite literally disappeared. I was shown the initial and follow-up ultrasound pictures, so was able to confirm the report for myself: a large tumor in the initial pictures, a complete absence of any tumor in the follow-up. The radiologist who took the pictures said he was completely baffled—he had never witnessed such a thing before.

In rare cases, tumors have been known to disappear by spontaneous remission. Perhaps that's what happened here. Or did it happen primarily through the combination of herbs and Mark's loving attention? Did his intentions and energies play a significant if not synergistic role as well?

The aftermath was less happy. After Jane and Mark divorced a few years later, she again developed tumors. This time she chose to have them surgically removed.

Help for a Permanently Disabled Man

A friend of mine in California, whom I will call Michael, asked me if I knew someone who could do a long-distance medical intuition diagnosis for his friend James. Medical intuition is a controversial process in which psychics—also known as intuitives—claim to receive information about a person's medical problems that includes energetic, emotional, and spiritual components. These diagnoses are often made long-distance, without the diagnostician ever meeting the patient.

James had been injured in an accident that left him paralyzed from the neck down. His neurologists came to the conclusion that his condition was incurable. Patients with this kind of injury frequently die within three years. Michael said that James was not receiving physical therapy. Since his case was hopeless, there seemed to be no point in any treatment.

I told Michael about an Arizona medical intuitive and energy healer, Lynn, who had made some surprisingly accurate long-distance diagnoses in my presence, and I gave him her phone number. Since conventional medicine had failed to help, there was nothing to lose in giving alternative medicine a try.

Lynn not only provided an accurate medical diagnosis but accepted James as a patient, holding more than sixty therapy sessions with him over the ensuing eight months. All of the sessions were conducted long-distance, most over the telephone, along with a few via meditation.

Despite the predictions of conventional medicine, James began to regain much of his functioning. He regained use of his abdominal muscles and regained bladder control. He developed sensation in his legs, and then was able to move his legs and toes to the point where it was possible for him to start physical therapy. He even regained the ability to have sex. His doctors in San Diego were baffled because his MRIs indicated that his nerves were clearly regenerating, something they had never seen before.

Just a miracle? Or was there something more going on here? Was Lynn's long-distance spiritual energy healing actually responsible?

Any reputable scientist will tell you that a story of an individual, isolated experience—referred to as "anecdotal evidence"—is invalid, essentially meaningless. However, a collection of independently observed experiences begins to suggest that something real is going on and deserves scientific examination.

Exploring Energy Healing

What you are about to read will probably stretch your mind as it tugs at your heart. You will accompany me in the laboratory and clinic as I gather evidence, slowly but surely, that energy healing is real and can play a vital role in human existence, offering the tantalizing potential of improving the quality of life for every one of us. You will experience the challenges I faced as a scientist as I struggled to make sense of findings I was not prepared to discover. The evidence typically took me beyond my personal comfort level.

Medicine and science are in the throes of a dramatic evolution—which some might call a revolution. We live in a time of a profound change in thinking that is absolutely fundamental. The messages of contemporary physics tell us that our everyday sensory experience of the world is extremely limited, and that reality is far more interesting and mysterious than most of us are yet aware of.

The first sections of this book present a wide-ranging set of human energy experiments, mostly with nonhealers—from young undergraduate students at the University of Arizona in their late teens and early twenties to mature former students at Harvard University in their mid-sixties. The experiments address fundamental and far-reaching issues such as:

- Whether our bodies register invisible fields of energy, including TV and radio signals
- Whether we sense the energies of people, animals, and even plants
- Whether the energies generated by our bodies can be measured by electronic devices
- Whether our energies affect the physiology and behavior of diverse living systems—bacteria, animals, plants, and even other people—and can be used by us to foster healing and health

As you witness my personal scientific journey and ponder the discoveries my colleagues and I have made, consider the following: if all this, and more, is real, then as Dr. James Levin puts it, not only are we all "energy beings," we all have the inherent ability to be energy *healers*— to others, but most important, to ourselves.

Since research has solidly established that we can use our minds to help heal ourselves, and the physical body is actually a dynamic organization of energy and fields, it therefore follows that we are all potential energy healers as well. Further, because energy radiates beyond the body, in principle (and in fact, as I discuss in this book) energy healing can extend from your mind to others' bodies.

If you find the evidence of this book compelling, be ready to claim your natural power to heal.

Most of the things worth doing in the world had
been declared impossible before they were done.

—LOUIS D. BRANDEIS

Chapter 2

Examining Energy Healing

Sometimes we experience the seemingly impossible. That happened to me in the late 1990s when I witnessed and participated in another healing event, an incident that left me bewildered and stunned. I now look on it as a perfect representation of both the typical as well as seemingly magical aspects of energy healing.

The event took place not in a clinic or a doctor's office but in a family home, on the spur of the moment at a small dinner party in San Diego hosted by a couple who had been married for more than forty years: Philip, a retired businessman turned philanthropist, and Joan, a lawyer who assisted nonprofit organizations. Drinks had been served and people were mingling when there was a small commotion on one side of the room. Our host had suddenly developed a severe migraine. His pain and dizziness were so intense that he went to his bedroom to lie down.

I had been speaking to a well-known La Jolla, California, internist whom I'll call Dr. Elizabeth Adams. She had recently started learning energy-healing techniques from a gifted practitioner and claimed to have a natural affinity for it. Standing apart from the other guests, Dr. Adams and I had been quietly sharing some of our experiences when Philip's headache struck.

Joan asked Dr. Adams if she could help. The doctor explained that the basic energy-healing techniques she had been learning could occasionally result in rapid symptomatic relief for her medical patients. Joan was eager for her to try, and Philip agreed. The doctor invited me to assist her, and Joan and Philip both welcomed my support.

To help you appreciate what happened, I would like you to imagine that you are Philip. As you put yourself in Philip's shoes, so to speak, remember that the healing I'm about to recount actually happened. Imagine that you are tall, about six feet two. You are fit and distinguished looking, and you are experiencing a grueling headache accompanied by painful pulsating sensations in your eyes and at the back of your head. You are feeling extraordinarily dizzy—the world seems like it is revolving around you. You can hardly stand or talk.

As you lie on your bed, your head is propped up with two pillows, so your face is pointing across the room, and your eyes are closed.

Dr. Adams says she will attempt to sense areas of heat and coldness in your energy field. Holding her hands six to twelve inches above you, she slowly scans your energy field from face to feet. She does not say a word. You have no idea what she is about to do, and given the way you are feeling, you are in no state to pay close attention.

Suddenly you are startled by a dramatic increase in pain; because your eyes are closed, you're unaware that the doctor has placed her hands slightly above your face, in the area between your eyes (the area sometimes called the "third eye"). Then the pain lessens; unbeknownst to you, the doctor has moved her hands away from your forehead to near your jaw. Next you again experience an increase in the pain and report this to her; this time she has moved about three feet toward the foot of the bed and has extended her hands into the line projecting from the space between your eyes. She then moves six feet away and repeats the process. When her hands enter this region, the pain again increases. It's not until Dr. Adams moves more than nine feet away that you no longer experience a greater pain when she extends her hands.

To determine whether these changes in pain level are caused by something unique to Dr. Adams, I ask you whether you would allow me to repeat the procedure, and you agree. To my utter amazement, you report increased pain even when I stand more than nine feet away and place my hands in the hot area in line with your forehead. Dr. Adams later shared with me her understanding that patients who are having a migraine sometimes experience an increase in pain when healers "enter their energy field" in this region above and between the eyes, and this effect can extend some distance from the patient. It is sometimes called "spiking."

Returning to Philip, the doctor then begins her healing attempt. She explains that she will be using her index finger and gently clearing the energy around your eyes. For approximately five minutes, she moves her finger in a clockwise motion, as if drilling holes. She also "wipes away" the area around your eyes and head, as if attempting to displace the energy field. You cannot see this, but you can feel subtle changes in temperature. You notice that the dizziness is decreasing dramatically, and your pain has dulled to a throbbing.

After explaining what she's about to do, she holds the back of your head with one hand while gently covering your eyes with the other. Her hands feel warm and comforting. Every now and again, she moves her hands slightly as if in response to some kind of subtle shifts inside you. She does this for about ten minutes, and you begin experiencing substantial relief.

Your migraines usually last about twenty-four hours, but now the pain has almost completely subsided. You start getting groggy. Dr. Adams suggests that you might wish to take a nap; everyone leaves the room as you effortlessly drift off to sleep.

After about forty minutes, Joan returns and gently awakens you. You're surprised to discover that your headache is virtually gone. You are experiencing no dizziness, and you feel relatively refreshed. You are able to return to the dinner party and enjoy the rest of the evening. You recount the story of your unexpected and seemingly miraculous healing at dinner. This triggers a memorable conversation about what might account for this seemingly unaccountable healing.

Possible Explanations

What could have happened here? Consider these three main possibilities:

Explanation 1: What Philip actually had was an anomalous headache—something out of the ordinary—and it disappeared by itself. In medical terms this is called "spontaneous remission."

Explanation 2: Suffering severe pain, Philip was strongly motivated to get rid of the symptoms because of the dinner party, and trusted Joan and Dr. Adams to help him. It was his beliefs and expectations that resulted in the headache disappearing, coupled with the gentle touch of Dr. Adams's hands for the last ten minutes of the treatment. This is called a "mind-body" effect; it is sometimes termed a "placebo effect."

Explanation 3: As a budding and talented energy healer in training, Dr. Adams can actually sense energy, and she somehow treated Philip's energy so as to cancel the unexpected migraine process and returned him to his former healthy state. This would be an energy-healing effect.

Anyone who knows little about energy healing would be inclined to believe that the explanation is either a spontaneous remission (explanation 1) and/or a placebo effect (explanation 2). But how to explain Philip's weird experience of somehow sensing, through increases in his pain, when Dr. Adams was placing her hands in the area between and slightly above his eyes—and that he could sense this halfway across the room? Or the fact that the same thing happened when I repeated Dr. Adams's procedure? Explanations 1 and 2 cannot address this phenomenon.

Could Philip really have been sensing, directly or indirectly, the energy of Dr. Adams's hands and my hands? His eyes were closed; he did not see this as it happened. Another possibility is that Philip could have been picking up some sort of electromagnetic fields generated by the doctor's hands and mine.

Even if Philip had been sensing energy fields created by our hands, could these fields actually have been responsible for his pain relief?

The Cardiologist and the Healer

When Dr. James Levin, a dear colleague and friend, read the first draft of this chapter, he told me a remarkable incident that Philip's experience brought to mind.

In brief, a cardiologist who was a successful, responsible, and careful physician was doing volunteer work at a children's hospital outside Bangalore, India. He had just finished assisting a cardiac surgeon in the repair of a congenital heart deficit (called tetralogy of Fallot) in a young boy, aged three or four. If the patient's heart rate drops too low following surgery, it's often necessary to implant a cardiac pacemaker to maintain a healthy heart rhythm. The young boy's heart rate was dropping, it was fifty going on forty, and the cardiologist was about to install the pacemaker, when an unanticipated meeting occurred.

A distinguished Indian spiritual leader, famed internationally as a Hindu wisdom keeper, or avatar, came up to him and asked what he was doing. When the cardiologist explained the child's condition, the avatar asked, "What can I do to help?"

The physician, doubtful yet open because of the other man's renown, asked, "Can you increase his heart rate?"

The avatar answered with a question: "What heart rate would you like?"

The cardiologist replied, "Seventy beats per minute."

"Let me see what I can do," the Indian answered. He gently took the child's wrist in his hands. In a few minutes, as the cardiologist watched, astonished, the EKG monitor showed that the child's heart rate had settled at a steady seventy-plus beats per minute.

Seeing this, the cardiologist asked, "Can you make it eighty?" A few minutes went by, and the patient's heart rate climbed to just over eighty beats per minute. When it was clear that the child's heart rate was holding, the cardiologist recognized that the youngster no longer needed a pacemaker.

Is this incident some kind of fantasy? Many would assume so. Is it worth exploring whether such things are really possible? When the source of the information is credible, my answer has been an unqualified yes.

As you read this book, I hope you'll manage to keep in mind Philip's experience and this little boy's healing. Though only a subset of patients who have benefited from dramatic symptomatic relief in a single session, these incidents are prototypical of the kinds of dramatic healings that are regularly witnessed by practicing energy healers, including responsible physicians and nurses.

Both these accounts raise fundamental and far-reaching questions that underlie the subject of this book:

Are energy fields real?

Do our bodies register energy fields?

Can we learn to sense energy fields?

Do energy fields play a role in how our bodies normally function?

Do energy fields connect us with one another as well as with animals, plants, nature, and the universe as a whole?

Can these energy fields actually be used for healing and health?

If energy is the rule and not the exception in the universe, and therefore all material systems, including the human body, are energy systems, then is all healing ultimately energy healing, and are we all natural energy healers?

> *The field is the only reality.*
>
> —ALBERT EINSTEIN

Chapter 3

Unlocking the Mystery of Invisible Energy Fields

Before we can talk about healing energy, we need to talk about energy in the broader physical sense.

One of the greatest mysteries and miracles in the known universe is the existence of what physicists call "fields." These are completely invisible structures that are nonmaterial—meaning that they do not have mass. In the abstract, fields are described by equations that physicists use to understand the existence and organization of energy and matter.

Though physics can describe fields mathematically, the truth is that the nature of fields is a profound mystery—no one, and I mean no one, truly understands the pervasive existence of these ephemeral "no-things." The fact is that although fields are not matter, they certainly matter. Fields are in a deep sense the essence of matter. No fields, no matter. It's that simple.

When I think of fields, I first think of my cell phone and how the tiny antenna picks up invisible fields that can connect me with devices and people across the hall, across the city, or around the world. And not only for conversations but also for exchanging digital photos and e-mails, and for searching the Web.

The invisible fields that carry these signals are *everywhere.* Even when we're in a place where they are too weak to connect us, the fields are nonetheless present. Common examples of invisible fields include magnetic fields, gravitational fields, and nuclear fields.

According to physics, in principle fields extend infinitely in the vacuum of space. The words "infinite" and "vacuum" are important to appreciate and ponder. How far is "infinite"? By definition, fields extend farther than the mind can imagine. Is the "vacuum of space" really *empty*? Quite the opposite—the so-called vacuum is actually filled with fields. And not simply filled but virtually *infinitely* filled—which is, by definition, more filled than the mind can imagine. So space may indeed be empty of matter, but it isn't empty of fields.

(If you happen to be interested in a technical discussion of fields and energy, especially biofields and bioenergy, you can find a review article at our Web site, www.drgaryschwartz.com.)

I have a deep feeling and respect for fields. I had my first scientific mystical experience with fields when I was a young child, and it forever transformed my consciousness. Even today, as I write these words, I relive the amazement and awe that I experienced when I first realized that I, and everyone else, communicate with fields.

The Human Antenna: A Childhood "Aha" Experience

It was the early 1950s, and I was six or seven years old. My family had an old AM radio housed in a wooden case that used a single wire as an antenna. Our household also had a black-and-white television set with a rabbit-ears antenna sitting on top of the set.

My fascination with the antennas began when I discovered—as did most people who enjoyed radios and TVs in that era—that the clarity of the sound and picture varied depending upon where the antenna was placed and how close people (or animals) were to it. When I approached the TV to change the channel—there were no remote controls in those days—the picture sometimes became distorted or showed ghost images—double images of everything on the screen.

One day, I disconnected the antenna from the TV and watched the picture disappear. But to my surprise and delight, I discovered that if I touched the screw terminals in the back of the TV where the antenna connected, the picture reappeared.

I did this again and again. *It's one thing to imagine this event; it's another to experience it first hand as a child.* The idea that I could function like rabbit ears seemed positively miraculous. I was hooked.

Since then I've learned that human beings actually are antennas. Wherever we go, whatever we do, we silently and invisibly pick up radio and TV signals—and numerous other electromagnetic frequencies— just like a rabbit-ears antenna.

These fields don't simply pass through us: we *resonate* with them. We focus and amplify the fields just as antennas do.

Think about this. As you are reading these words, you are picking up hundreds if not thousands of radio and television shows, as well as many thousands of cell-phone calls—all at the same time. Though you have no conscious awareness of this fact, it's actually happening. You are serving as an antenna for satellite transmissions from DISH Network TV and XM Radio, as well as Verizon calls and who knows what else (secret government communications?).

A Mystical Satellite Radio Antenna Experience in New Mexico

I will never forget my first experience with digital satellite radio. In 2004, heading for an appointment in a little town about forty miles outside of Santa Fe in a rental car equipped with satellite radio, I found a station called Watercolors that plays smooth jazz twenty-four/seven with no commercials. I happen to have a special passion for that style of music. I was, so to speak, driving in smooth jazz heaven.

As I drove farther into open country, my cell phone lost its signal but the satellite-radio signal remained absolutely crystal clear. I realized that a little antenna the size of a quarter was picking up these signals and that the air was literally filled with music relayed from a satellite in space that I could only hear with a satellite radio. Remembering my early childhood experience when I first discovered that I functioned as a TV antenna, I now imagined that I was also serving as a digital antenna for hundreds of radio signals playing simultaneously.

I pondered the fact of the universe being structured in such a way that invisible fields of energy could completely and reliably convey patterns of information expressing the soul of composers and the artistry of musicians. The reality and beauty of these invisible fields impressed me profoundly. I wondered not only about the invisible fields that were manipulated by humankind but about other invisible fields, including more cosmic music fields that might reflect what Pythagoras called "the music of the spheres." I realized that everything on the earth was being bathed not only in fields of information and energy beamed from man-made satellites, but by universe-made structures whose fields and signals we had yet to comprehend, develop, and enjoy.

As you read these words, the molecules in your body are vibrating to the tunes of hundreds of melodies and harmonies all being performed simultaneously. Your molecules are literally in tune with these vibrations. Can you imagine how they are dancing?

To Move Is to Manifest and Modify Electromagnetic Fields of Energy

Our bodies generate patterns of electromagnetic fields of energy and information that are extraordinarily more complex than the most sophisticated man-made satellites in the sky. We are not only, so to speak, walking antennas and satellite dishes; we are walking generators and satellite transmitters as well.

A simple example will demonstrate what biophysics refers to as electrostatic body motion effects. Imagine you are moving your hand up and down as if you were gently and lovingly patting a child on its head. Do you think this action is generating a measurable electromagnetic field? If so, would the child pick up the invisible magnetic field you are generating, even before you touch his head?

If you answered yes to both, you're right.

These are not speculations or hypotheses. They are completely replicable effects that most people are either unaware of or do not understand; that's unfortunately also true of most physicians, who typically assume fields are not important to the body's functioning. (The technically inclined reader will find a formal write-up of the first experiments we performed on these phenomena at www.drgaryschwartz.com.)

The overview that follows will I hope be sufficient to transform your consciousness forever about our dual roles as transmitters and receivers of fields of energy and information.

In fact, the magnetic fields caused by movement can be measured and plotted. In the lab, we recorded measurements of the up-and-down hand movement in the patting-the-head gesture. For these graphs, the patting-the-head gesture was made from about one foot to a few inches, up and down, above an electroencephalogram (EEG) electrode box that was serving as the antenna. Plots of two of these tests are shown in figure 3.1.

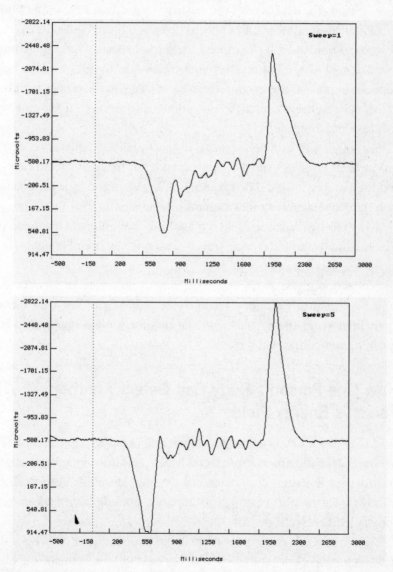

Figure. 3.1 Plots of the Magnetic Fields Generated by Up-and-Down Hand Movements

The spikes are caused by the generation of electromagnetic fields that result from the person moving his hand up and down in space. The graphs are arranged so that when you move your hand down, the spike on the plot goes down, and vice versa. These effects are based on the fact that all biological systems have a charge, called an "electrostatic charge." You may at times have experienced a shock when you touched a door-knob, causing the discharge of the electrostatic field carried by your body.

When an electrostatically charged object—a piece of plastic, a plank of wood, a human limb—is moved in physical space, a field is created; the size and shape/pattern/form/information conveyed by the field depends in part on the magnitude of the charge on the object, which is influenced by the material composition of the object itself and the nature of the movement.

As you would probably expect, distance makes a difference. If the experimenter moves even a couple of feet away from the electrode box and then moves his hand down and up, the size of the spike associated with the movement becomes significantly smaller.

The electromagnetic field created by the moving electrostatic charge extends out into space, traveling away at the speed of light—in a vacuum, 186,000 miles per second.

Think about this. Every time you move, you create an electromagnetic field that travels into space at the speed of light. Yes, your movement field is relatively small, but it's definitely measurable. And it's worth remembering that it exists.

How One Person's Body Can Detect Another Person's Energy Fields

Now that you know how the movement of a charged object creates a field, let's take the process one step further. This time, imagine that you are the experimenter, and instead of working alone, you are working with an assistant who is sitting at the table, holding her hand an inch above the EEG electrode box.

You now gently move your hand up and down, above the assistant's head, getting as close as an inch from her hair without actually touching it. Your hand is now not getting as close to the electrodes as in the previous experiment, but instead comes no closer than a couple of feet from the electrode box. The instruments will show a less intense spike—right?

Wrong. The assistant's body acts as an antenna, amplifying your hand motion and producing a clearly visible large spike on the screen. Unexpected and remarkable: the body acts an antenna.

The truth is, we are all interconnected by electromagnetic fields, including the fields we create when we move. As I'm writing these words, I can see a flurry of ten to twenty finches and sparrows enjoying the thistle seeds I put out for them. As they flutter their wings, I image the flurry of electromagnetic signals that are passing through the window, bathing my face and body with their excited energies.

When a Puppy Wags His Tail: The Electrostatics of Love?

Feathers and hair, including fur, can carry sizable electrostatic charges—so when feathers and hair move in space, they create sizable electromagnetic fields.

One day I was testing a portable EEG device to see if it could detect electrostatic body motion effects. A former colleague, Dr. Linda Russek, serving as my subject, was seated ten feet away from me. On my instruction, she would move her head, which of course moved her hair. With my hand over the EEG electrodes, clearly visible spikes appeared on the computer screen when she moved.

Unexpectedly but fortuitously, her small West Highland white terrier, Freudy II, entered my study. I noticed that the EEG amplifier went crazy. The line tracings literally rose off the screen as the amplifier became momentarily overloaded; to use an electronics term, it became saturated.

I said, quietly yet somewhat forcefully, "Freudy, please sit down." And being a dog person, I unthinkingly added an explanation: "You're overloading the amplifier."

Freudy reluctantly honored my request. He sat down with his tail still wagging. To my amazement—and absolute joy—I saw on the screen a waving line that paralleled the movements of his tail!

I sat in awe as I experienced myself being an antenna for Freudy's wagging tail.

This unexpected Freudy-tailwagging Aha moment transformed my consciousness. I immediately realized that dogs, cats, and other furry creatures are literally huge generators of electromagnetic fields. Under the right circumstances, the effect is exaggerated. For example, when a dog is happy, it wags every part of its body—not just its tail. The synchronized movements of an animal's billions of hairs generate coordinated electromagnetic fields. And when we stroke a dog or cat, we are creating an intimate and dynamic human-animal energy system of complex interacting electromagnetic fields.

Feathers and fur. I wondered, are they designed in part to create electromagnetic movement fields? Could this be a mechanism of nature for energetically interconnecting the animal kingdom and the larger ecosystem as a whole?

Perhaps the movements of plants in the garden create electromagnetic fields as well. Maybe even the moving of waves on the beach. Or clouds in the sky. Possibly all of these are part of some great cosmic energetic communication network or matrix, in which fields of energy interconnect every physical—and *non*-physical—thing in the universe.

Or . . . there is a possibility even more startling: that these fields, which interconnect all things, might be functioning as *healing* fields. They might be part of the natural power of the universe that provides us—and everything else—with the capacity to heal.

For me, the challenge was to remain open enough to explore this question and responsible enough to follow where the research would lead. The story of where the research has led begins with the following chapter.

> *Man's mind, once stretched by a new idea, never regains its original dimensions.*
>
> —OLIVER WENDELL HOLMES, SR.

Chapter 4

Experiencing Human Energy Fields

Physics tells us that everything has energy. The invisible fields of energy are everywhere in the universe, and they convey information about the structure of everything, from subatomic particles and cells to planets and galaxies, and beyond.

Our bodies are also teeming with energies and frequencies. You can feel this energy if you pay attention to it. A simple experiment will help you experience this at first hand. I can tell you about an orange or a sunset but there is no substitute for tasting the orange or seeing the sunset for yourself. Sensations must be experienced directly in order for you truly to understand.

Relax your left hand (or for left-handed people, your right hand) and hold it with your palm facing upward. Point the index finger of your writing hand toward the palm about one inch away. Slowly move your index finger in a circular motion, tracing an invisible circle on your palm. As you do this, pay close attention to whatever sensations you feel in your palm or your index finger. Do this for about a minute.

If you experienced any sensation, you are in the majority—at least by the standards of formal studies as well as classroom demonstrations I've conducted with thousands of college students. Approximately 60 percent of randomly selected college students report having one or more sensations of warmth, pressure, tingling, or pulling. Most who reported this said the sensation followed the movement of the index finger. I find it fascinating that virtually 100 percent of people who call themselves healers report having such sensations.

The question arises, where do these sensations come from? Are they simply imaginary, a creation of our expectations, of our minds? Or do they reflect the exquisite sensitivity of our hands to electromagnetic energies?

Detecting Other People's Energies

When healers claim that they can sense other people's energies with their hands, how do we know if this is true? As a scientist, I wondered whether it was possible to test such statements scientifically and determine if they were correct.

It turns out that this is remarkably easy to examine in the laboratory. If you choose, you can replicate the experiment I'm about to describe. You'll need the assistance of another person, even a child. Blindfold your helper and have him sit as described earlier, with palms facing up.

Place your right hand (left hand for southpaws) a few inches above either of the subject's hands and hold it there for about half a minute. Ask the subject to guess left or right and then to rate the confidence of his guess, from zero, meaning no confidence that his guess was correct, to ten, meaning complete confidence. Repeat this a number of times, each time writing down the correct answer, what the subject guessed, and his confidence. Make sure that your order of lefts and rights is random and that you use the same number of right-hand trials as left.

If there is nothing but chance at play, the proportion of correct answers will of course be close to 50 percent.

I began doing hand-energy detection experiments like this in 1995. In our initial experiments, we ran twenty-four trials per subject—twelve left-hand trials and twelve right-hand. Initially I was the subject and Justin Beltran, then an undergraduate student working with me, served as the experimenter. At the time Justin had no formal training in energy healing, and neither did I.

Justin created the counterbalanced order of trials. During the twenty-four trials, I frankly felt nothing. In fact, my ratings of confidence using the zero to ten scale ranged between zero and one, leaving me quite convinced that I had demonstrated the hypothesis was invalid—at least for me.

However, to my great surprise—and Justin's—I got nineteen out of twenty-four correct. This is almost 80 percent accuracy. Statistics tell us that this level of accuracy is likely not due to chance. The probability of getting nineteen out of twenty-four correct by chance (guessing) alone is less than three out of one hundred. In science, getting a probability of anything below five out of one hundred is considered to be statistically significant.

How could I have been statistically accurate in detecting Justin's hand energy when I had no conscious awareness of what was happening? What exactly was I picking up? And was this observation unique to me?

It turns out that what I did is quite common. The fact is that many of us have no idea that we can actually detect someone else's energy. This talent is typically latent in all of us, waiting to be discovered and developed.

Research on Detecting Hand Energy

In the Laboratory for Advances in Consciousness and Health (formerly called the Human Energy Systems Laboratory) at the University of Arizona, we have conducted numerous experiments examining whether undergraduate students can detect a person's hand energy. In our first experiment, I trained Justin to be the experimenter. Twenty college students in their late teens and early twenties volunteered to participate in the experiment. During the testing they were blindfolded and sat with their eyes closed. They rested their forearms gently on their laps, palms up.

The participants were each given twenty-four trials, following the same routine Justin and I had originally used. Between trials, Justin placed his hands together to keep his hand temperature relatively constant.

In a second set of experiments, we expanded the number of tests, using twenty-one different experimenters trained by Justin and forty-one participants. Otherwise, the procedures were identical. The goal was to determine whether the effects observed in the first experiment were unique to Justin or could be observed in others.

Across the two experiments, there were eleven male and eleven female experimenters and twenty-four male and thirty-seven female participants.

The results were fascinating: 59 percent accuracy in experiment 1, increasing to 70 percent in experiment 2. Statistically, the average hand-energy detection in both experiments was significantly greater than chance.

As in my own case, the students' estimates of their performance were lower than their actual performance scores: they estimated their performance at 46 percent in experiment 1 and 55 percent in experiment 2.

Unmasking the Superstars

It sometimes happens that experimental data contains fascinating extra information, if the experimenter thinks of asking the right questions. We analyzed the data from these experiments by looking at the results on the basis of performance, sorting the results into four performance subgroups: poor (42 percent average detection; fourteen students), low (58 percent average detection; seven students), medium (70 percent average detection; twenty-seven students), and high detection (85 percent average; thirteen students).

Students in the poor and low categories actually did a good job of estimating how well they did, while the medium and high subjects underestimated their performance (figure 4.1). Clearly, the "superstars" in these two experiments were not aware that they had a talent for detecting hand energy.

However, a closer examination of the individual confidence ratings reveals an even more surprising discovery. As you can see in figure 4.2, it turned out that on the individual trials that they happened to guess correctly, the students' confidence ratings were higher than on the trials they got wrong. Moreover, all four performance groups showed this intuitive sense of their own accuracy in a given trial.

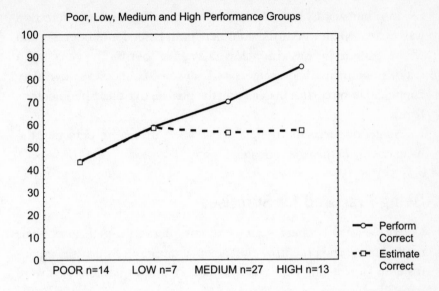

Figure 4.1 Performance and Subjects' Estimates of Performance for Poor, Low, Medium, and High Detection Groups

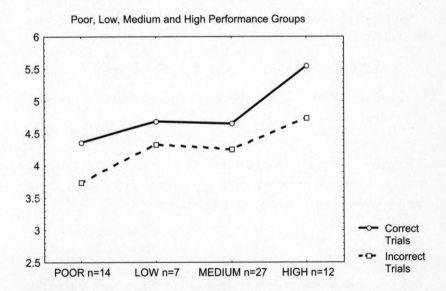

Figure 4.2 Confidence in Correct and Incorrect Trials in Poor, Low, Medium, and High Detection Groups

In other words, even the students whose hand-energy detection was below 50 percent (the fourteen poor-detection students), and whose confidence was clearly low (averaging four on the zero to ten scale) nonetheless had an increased sense of confidence when they happened to be correct in detecting the presence of the experimenter's hand.

Somehow even the duffers knew when they were detecting the hand energy of the experimenter.

Being Prepared for Surprises

One of the joys of doing research is discovering surprises that inspire us to pose novel and potentially fundamental questions, which sometimes result in far-reaching implications. Here are a few questions that were raised by this research:

Is it possible that all of us have the potential to detect another person's energy fields, whether we are aware of this fact or not?

Though some of us may be more skilled or have more talent than others, can all of us learn in some degree to detect human energy fields?

Is energy detection the rule rather than the exception in nature?

Are our bodies designed to be exquisitely sensitive to the energy around us?

Where this journey took me next reminded me once again of the most important lesson I've learned through ten years of conducting energy-healing experiments: Be prepared for surprises.

Note for the technical reader: If we are to be precise, mass does not *have* energy, but rather it *is* energy, since $E = mc^2$. Also, strictly speaking, energy does not convey information; rather, frequencies and signals are modulations in the field. In fact, technically speaking, a more accurate term than energy healing would be "field healing."

> *Our intention creates our reality.*
>
> —WAYNE DYER

Chapter 5

Perceiving a Person's Intention

So far we've examined energy and fields to explore whether energy plays a role in healing. We've seen that yes, the human body acts like an antenna and receiver as well as transmitter of electromagnetic fields (chapter 3). And yes, humans can detect apparent energy fields emitted by the human hand, though they may not be aware that they are doing so (chapter 4).

This line of reasoning also suggests another question, more challenging and by far more controversial: Is it possible that our bodies are responsive not only to the invisible energies around us, but also to the *conscious intentions* of people around us?

Recall that the young student experimenters who participated in our early energy-detection research were carefully trained to follow the instructions of the research protocol. On each trial they first silently read instructions and then consciously and deliberately placed their hand over the receiver's left or right hand. So the experimenters were not simply moving their hands near the receivers' hands, they were first having the conscious intention to move their hands in this fashion. A decision of the mind preceded a movement of the hand.

This insight is important and worth repeating: Their thoughts preceded their movements.

Recognizing this requires us to at least entertain the possibility that the receivers were not only detecting the physical energies, such as

infrared heat, and electromagnetic fields, such as magnetic signals generated by the muscles in the fingers, emitted by the experimenters'
hands, *but that they were also unknowingly detecting the conscious
intentions, thoughts, and even emotions of the student experimenter.*

In early 2000, I decided to explore this possibility.

Exploring Energy and Intention

With Lonnie Nelson, then a graduate student at the University of Arizona and now a PhD, I designed a series of experiments to test one possible though highly unlikely premise: that the conscious intention of an
experimenter could influence the outcome of hand-energy experiments
like the ones we had been doing.

Lonnie and I used six different tasks. Two were labeled "proximal"
tasks, in which the experimenter's hand was only a few inches from the
subject's body, as in the earlier experiments. The other four were
labeled "distal" tasks, in which the experimenter was a few feet from the
subject's body; of these four, two would be done with "intense" intention, and two with "gentle" intention, involving virtually no physical
movement. Each of the six tasks had trials repeated ten times for a total
of sixty trials; in all but one, the subject was blindfolded.

The Proximal Tasks—Hand and Ear Sensing

One of the proximal tasks replicated the hand-detection experiments
done earlier: the experimenter, seated in front of the subject, places his
dominant hand a few inches away from the subject's right or left hand,
and the subject says which hand he thinks is being covered.

For the other proximal task—called ear detection—the experimenter, seated behind the subject, places his or her dominant hand a
few inches away from the subject's right or left ear. The subject says
which ear he thinks the experimenter's hand is close to.

The human hand generates multiple electromagnetic fields simultaneously, including electrostatic hand-motion fields, infrared (heat)
fields, electromyographic (muscle) fields, and even skin-potential fields.
The experiment was designed to shed light on whether the subjects
could sense any or all of these fields.

The Two Intense Distal Tasks

These tasks involved focused and intense staring on the part of the experimenters. One—called "face/stomach discrimination"—involves the experimenter standing a few feet in front of the subject and deliberately staring at the subject's face or stomach; the subject says which he thinks the experimenter is staring at.

In the other intense-intention distal task—called "head/back discrimination"—the experimenter stands a few feet in back of the subject and deliberately stares at the subject's head or back; again, the subject says which he thinks is the subject of the experimenter's focus. For both these tasks, the experimenter's hands remain at his sides.

The Gentle Distal Tasks

The last two distal tasks were more gentle and subtle. One—an established experimental practice called "staring sensing"—involved the experimenter standing a few feet in back of the subject and either purposely staring at the subject's back or gazing elsewhere; the subject's task was to guess whether the experimenter was staring at his back.

For the final task—called "movement anticipation sensing without a blindfold"—the experimenter stands a few feet in front of the subject with his eyes closed and mentally focuses his attention on one of his own hands. The subject guesses which hand the experimenter is focusing on.

Simple Predictions, Surprising Findings

We anticipated that if the subjects were primarily detecting the proximal electromagnetic fields of the experimenter's hands, they would do best on the two proximal tasks, and do poorly, if not fail completely, on the four distal tasks. Unless, that is, the subjects were detecting the conscious intentions of the experimenter as well as his energy fields; in that unlikely case, they might perform equally well on all six tasks.

Lonnie and I conducted two experiments. The first involved eighty-six undergraduate students; the second, twenty-seven students.

The results showed that the students' average detection performance was around 58 percent; when compared to chance (50 percent), this performance was highly statistically significant. To my surprise, the subjects' average performance was comparable for the proximal and distal tasks when they were analyzed separately. Both male and female subjects showed this effect.

Replicating the findings from the experiments discussed in chapter 4, the subjects underestimated their actual sensing performance in all six tasks—they guessed that their accuracy was only 51 percent (chance).

Then, when we separated the subjects into poor, average, good, and excellent performers based on their average performance, we found that the subjects who did very well on the proximal tasks also did very well on the distal tasks, and the subjects who did poorly on the proximal tasks also did poorly on the distal tasks. The best subjects averaged 75 percent to 80 percent accuracy on each of the six tasks; the worst subjects averaged approximately 45 percent accuracy on each of the six tasks. Some people have a talent for this kind of sensing—both energy fields and conscious intention—and others do not.

Moreover, in this experiment we asked the subjects to rate the extent to which they thought they were energy sensitive. Again we found that the subjects who believed that they were energy sensitive not only estimated their performance as higher, they also actually performed better—that is, their energy detection and their intention detection were higher—than subjects who believed that they were energy insensitive.

I cannot help wondering if further research might show that people sensitive to the intentions of others can, like a martial arts master, recognize when an aggressive or angry person is about to strike out at them. Will we find that people with this ability can also intuit the responses of a loved one at a distance—sensing a child who has just been injured or a father suffering a heart attack? I hope further studies will be conducted soon.

The Influence of Beliefs and Experience

Sometimes a scientist pursues a question simply to rule out an unlikely possibility. I wondered whether certain beliefs and experiences with the spiritual and metaphysical might have any influence on the results of individual subjects. We devised a questionnaire asking the subjects to what extent they *believed* in God, ghosts, angels, prayer, and extrasensory perception (ESP), and then to what extent they believed they had actually *experienced* God, ghosts, angels, prayer, and ESP.

It turned out that the subjects' ratings of their experiences of ESP significantly predicted their estimates of their performance, their ratings of energy sensitivity, and their actual behavioral performance—that is, their ability to sense not only energy but even intention. In other words, subjects who reported having had strong ESP experiences (as opposed to just beliefs) not only rated themselves as being energy sensitive and estimated their performance as higher, but *performed* better as well.

If we accept—at least for the sake of discussion—that these experiments were done correctly and that the subjects and experimenters were not cheating, we are left with the remarkable conclusion that somehow, in some way, the majority of the subjects could detect the conscious intentions of the experimenters. If the detection had only been biophysical, the subjects would have done worse on the distal tasks compared to the proximal tasks. This controversial research takes us beyond basic biophysics and biology and brings us to topics that are typically labeled paranormal and psychic.

It appears that people can sense not only a person's biophysical energies and associated fields but their conscious intentions as well.

For scientists who label themselves parapsychologists, both of these conclusions are neither unique nor surprising. Sophisticated parapsychologists such as Rupert Sheldrake (author of *The Sense of Being Stared At* and *Dogs That Know When Their Owners Are Coming Home*) and Dean Radin (*The Conscious Universe* and *Entangled Minds*)—after having conducted numerous experiments themselves as well as carefully reviewing the findings of other scientists—have reached the firm (though controversial) conclusion that the minds of humans and even animals have the power to sense both energy and intention. Moreover, they have concluded, and I paraphrase, that just as some people have a great ear for music, some people have a great "ear" for sensing energy and even detecting the conscious intentions of others.

About Sensing

You may be wondering why I'm continuing to separate the process of energy sensing from the process of intention sensing. Given the experiments discussed so far, you might ask, why bring up energy sensing at all? Didn't the subjects do just as well in the distal tasks as they did on the proximal tasks? Maybe all the subjects were doing was sensing conscious intention, period.

There are three reasons for us to continue to distinguish between energy detection as a process and intention detection as a process. They are: wise caution, theory discernment, and actual experimental possibility.

Concerning wise caution, readers of my previous books will know that I like to quote a phrase popular with emergency-room physicians: "When you hear hoofbeats, don't think zebras." If an ER doctor has a patient who could be dying, he or she needs to make quick decisions that could mean life or death. The best way to do this is to consider the most probable explanation for the patient's symptoms first and then rule this explanation in or out.

When you hear hoofbeats (unless you're living in certain parts of Africa), the most probable explanation is a horse. If the horse explanation doesn't fit, we would then consider various pony, donkey, or mule explanations before we would entertain zebra, camel, or hippopotamus explanations.

The same idea can be applied to science. It's one thing to explain the findings of these experiments as being the detection of an electromagnetic field—the horse explanation. It's another to explain the findings as being the detection of conscious intentions—the zebra explanation. (Some superskeptical disbelievers might sarcastically call this the "unicorn" explanation.)

Wise caution suggests that we continue to accept the most probable explanation—the energy-field hypothesis—even as we entertain the possibility of the more controversial explanation—the conscious-intention hypothesis.

It's because I tend to follow the hoofbeats philosophy that I initially expected the subjects might perform successfully on the proximal tasks and would probably fail on the distal tasks.

A Note for the Technical Reader

Because the energy and intention explanations involve different levels of theoretical constructs, it's essential to discern their differences. Note that electromagnetic fields can be interpreted in terms of conventional biophysics as well as quantum physics. Whereas conventional biophysics focuses on field effects that decrease with distance and do not involve consciousness, quantum physics recognizes quantum field effects that do not decrease with distance, termed "nonlocal" effects, which are modified by the observer, including the experimenter, and therefore directly involve consciousness. In fact, quantum physics is becoming a powerful theoretical framework for understanding key aspects of the effects of consciousness on energy, matter, living systems, and healing. Dean Radin's book *Entangled Minds* presents in a reader-friendly way some of the challenging and enticing connections between contemporary quantum physics, consciousness science, and parapsychology.

However, to a laboratory scientist, the bottom line is the experiment and what the findings reveal. For me, what matters most is what happens in the laboratory. I am, so to speak, a scientist from the Show-Me State, Missouri (though in fact I grew up in New York). Caution is certainly important, and theoretical discernment is clearly essential, but experimental evidence is what ultimately matters to me. And here the ultimate question is, What can experiments show us about the nature of these phenomena, whether we are prepared to accept the truth of the findings or not?

The Influence of Personal Relationships and Stress

In chapter 4, we observed that when the experimenters knew the subjects—in the second experiment the subjects were family members or friends of the experimenters—the energy-detection performance of the sample as a whole was higher. And in the two experiments reported in this chapter, the subjects were again family members or friends of the experimenters.

We used family members and friends for practical as well as theoretical reasons. The practical reason was that it was easier to collect a large amount of data in a relatively short period of time by training multiple people to serve as experimenters and have them work with people close to them. The theoretical reason was that not only would the findings be more applicable if they could be replicated across many different experimenters—females, males, Caucasians, Hispanics, and so forth—but also we thought that if the subjects knew the experimenters, they might be more motivated to succeed, they might feel more relaxed doing the tasks, and they might be more "energetically connected" with the experimenters.

I wondered, what would happen with the six tasks if subjects did not know the experimenters? What would happen if this experiment was less intimate and significantly more stressful? As part of doctoral candidate Lonnie Nelson's dissertation, he and I created a replication and extension of the experiment discussed above—repeating the six detection tasks, this time using two experimenters who were trained in techniques for measuring EEG (the electromagnetic signals of the brain) and EKG (the electromagnetic signals of the heart). Nineteen channels of EEG plus the EKG were continuously recorded from each of twenty subjects as they performed the six detection tasks.

What might happen in this experiment? There were a number of possible outcomes. The most cautious and conservative expectation might be that given the stress and distraction of wearing a tight-fitting EEG electrode cap, having to sit very still (for the sake of the EEG recordings), not knowing the experimenter, and so on, the subjects' performance might decrease on all six tasks, possibly to chance levels.

The second possible outcome might be that despite the stress of the experiment, the subjects would replicate the previous experiments and achieve statistically significant results on all six tasks.

However, it was the third possible outcome that was the most interesting theoretically. If energy detection involves the sensing of actual electromagnetic fields, whereas intention detection involves the sensing of a person's consciousness (which is presumably more subtle), then the combination of the increased stress involved in the experiment, plus the lack of connection between the experimenter and subject, might impair the four distal tasks more than the two proximal tasks. In other words, the energy-sensing process might be more robust and replicable than the intention-sensing process.

This third possible outcome was the prediction most consistent with research in contemporary quantum physics and consciousness science that addresses so-called paranormal phenomena.

When we analyzed the data, the findings actually fit the third outcome. In fact, the subjects' performance on the two proximal tasks completely replicated the previous experiment's proximal findings (approximately 58 percent), whereas the subjects' performance on the distal tasks declined and reached chance levels (approximately 51 percent).

The scope of the research for Lonnie's dissertation didn't provide the opportunity to determine how important personal relationships are in this setting—factors such as the degree of openness, caring, and love—nor the influence of the stress and distraction involved in the experiment. Future research can systematically study these alternative factors. What Lonnie's findings do is encourage us to continue exploring these challenging possibilities.

In any case, it was clear that energy-detection experiments can be misleading, since the results can be influenced by intentions. What we call "energy detection" can involve intention detection as well.

I believe anyone who has not encountered this before will find startling the idea that some people can actually sense the *intentions* of another person. It appears that the mind has the power to connect with the physical world and with consciousness itself beyond what conventional Western science currently acknowledges. This is what the emerging research tells us—if we are open enough to listen and prepared to accept the evidence.

When the Laboratory Mirrors the Clinic

These basic-science explorations lay the groundwork for experiments that reveal the true nature of energy healing and therefore have meaningful implications for our ultimate understanding of healers and healing.

Healers tell us that their ability to sense the energies and intentions of their patients and clients depends upon their ability to create connections with the people they serve. Healers mostly come from a place of caring, compassion, and love. They approach their patients and clients with open minds and hearts. They use various personal techniques to relax themselves so they can be fully present and aware of energies and intentions coming not only from the people they are attempting to heal, but from energies and intentions they believe come from the universe and a larger spiritual reality. Healers claim that the better they can relax their patients and clients, the better they can connect with them for the sake of healing and transformation. Healers even do energy healing on themselves in order to work optimally with their clients.

Healing is a complex art. What is remarkable to me is how laboratory experiments can sometimes, in a fundamental microscopic way, mirror what happens in the complex macroscopic context of real-life human healing.

Do all of us have the inherent ability to detect electromagnetic fields? In principle, yes. Do all of us have the intrinsic ability to detect the conscious intentions of others? Again, in principle, yes.

Given this, can we all learn how to detect the energy and intentions of others? Science offers answers to that question as well.

> *The only thing that interferes with my learning is my education.*
>
> —ALBERT EINSTEIN

Chapter 6

Learning to Detect Energy and Consciousness

We accept without question that we humans can learn to speak, play sports, use computers, build buildings, invent airplanes, create music, and devise a way to search the Web from our portable PDA cell phones.

But if you tell someone you've just read in a book written by a scientist that humans can learn to sense subtle energy fields around a human body, and even detect people's intentions, they might think you had just gone off the deep end. Until fairly recently, I would have thought that way myself about anybody making such claims. My Western education in physics, psychology, and medicine dissuaded me from even entertaining this possibility.

As Einstein said, sometimes our education gets in the way of our learning.

In light of what I've presented already about detecting energy and detecting intentions, it seems prudent for us to go one step further. If everything is ultimately energy—the fundamental premise of this book—and we are all potentially energy healers—the core implication of this book—then it becomes essential to determine if we can learn to develop, and even master, the capacity to sense energy and intentions and use this ability for healing and health.

45

The Lesson from Wine Tasters, Musicians, Radiologists, and Perfumers

My experiences in life have brought me to the firm conclusion that the human capacity for sensory discrimination and discernment should never be underestimated. Evidence supporting this conclusion is all around us.

Consider wine tasting. People can learn to become extraordinarily gifted in discriminating different qualities, regions, and years of wines. To the untrained palate, wine is wine. They all taste more or less the same. To the connoisseur, the world of wine contains a vast variety of possibilities. They find some wines crisp, others sharp, some predominantly nutty, others mostly fruity, some thin, others full-flavored. With advanced experience comes a dramatic magnification of distinctions and individualities among wines.

I never became a wine connoisseur, but I did spend a couple of years in my mid-twenties tasting different wines. I remember having dinners in Cambridge and Boston at which a group of us would compare and contrast three different years of a fine wine like a Château Latour, or three different wines of the same year like a 1964 Château Latour, Château Margaux, and Château Lafite Rothschild. With time I came to distinguish and appreciate some of the differences, and I even developed preferences for certain vintages and years.

Consider music. To the untrained ear, jazz is jazz. Improvisations may sound more or less the same. To the sophisticated jazz musician, the world of jazz contains a seemingly infinite variety of possibilities. As a professional jazz guitarist, I learned to discriminate subtle points of sliding, plucking, and making tonal adjustments on my guitar and amplifier, including combinations of sound pickups (my guitar had three), plus variations in treble, bass, and echo. As a new drummer in training, I'm currently learning to discern fine points in striking a cymbal or tapping a tom-tom. It's a common experience among musicians that the more you learn about how to play a given instrument, the more sensitive you become to the richness and complexity of what, to the untrained ear, may sound like a lot of similar notes and noises.

Another example concerns X-rays and ultrasounds. To the untrained eye, an X-ray is an X-ray, and an ultrasound is an ultrasound. The blurry images may look more or less the same. To the radiology oncologist or echocardiologist, a world of information can be discerned, providing the details for making critical decisions about cancer or heart disease.

Probably the most amazing sensory discernment, at least to me, involves the creation of perfume. Just as the vintner knows how to bring out the best flavor in his wines, the perfumer has an uncanny sensitivity for bringing out the best fragrances.

In the mid-1980s I met the master perfumer who invented the men's fragrance Polo. He told me that after he was given the task of creating this new fragrance, one day an olfactory image came to him that contained more than thirty different ingredients. He wrote them down in a list, with their associated amounts, and had his assistant mix them. He then smelled the mixture, decided it was not quite right, adjusted the formula, and had his assistant prepare another mix. He repeated this procedure, over and over, and eventually settled on a unique combination of ingredients that ultimately became a best-selling cologne.

Try as I might, I find it extraordinarily difficult to image how he does this. I have lived my life with a more or less constantly stuffy nose—my sense of smell is typically limited at best.

However, a dear friend of mine, Krishna Madappa, is a master creator of healing fragrances. Krishna not only creates exceptional aromatherapies, but he is a gifted energy healer as well. Though my sense of smell is crude (to put it mildly), when I sniff Krishna's fragrances, I can't help breaking out in smiles of joy. His mixtures are simply delicious; some of them I would call out of this world.

The human eye can discriminate millions of shades of colors. Retinal cells in the eye can detect single photons of light. Is it so far-fetched to imagine the possibility that people can learn to sense and discriminate images and feelings that many of us are as yet unaware of?

If we listen to what gifted healers are telling us, there exists a world of energy experience, latent in all of us, that can enrich our lives immensely.

Awareness without Awareness

It's well established in contemporary psychological science that people can respond to information that they can't consciously perceive and can even remember information received at the subconscious level. Scientists use the terms "implicit perception" and "implicit memories" when referring to these phenomena.

Studies on implicit memory, originally conducted at the University of Arizona and Harvard University by Dr. Daniel Schacter and colleagues, have demonstrated that people who are presented with auditory information while they are unconscious—either asleep or under anesthesia during surgery—later respond to this information as if they recognize it. They show evidence of implicit memory even though they have no conscious awareness of having heard the information.

In my psychophysiology laboratories at Yale University and the University of Arizona, we have conducted a series of EEG studies examining the brain's responses to odors presented at subliminal concentrations. Subjects were presented with pairs of bottles to smell; both contained a solvent, and one also contained an amount of a molecule—isoamyl acetate—that smells like banana. If the concentration of the molecule was high enough, the subjects could correctly determine which of the two bottles contained the extra substance.

In some tests, we reduced the concentration of the molecule to the point where the subjects' ability to detect which bottle contained the banana aroma was at chance—50 percent.

Here's the surprising part: Even when people thought they were guessing, our measurements of their EEG showed that their brains were correctly discriminating between the two bottles.

Moreover, when people rated the confidence of their guesses, even though they were guessing at 50 percent chance accuracy, they would rate the confidence of their guess higher when they smelled the bottle containing the molecule!

In other words, even though they were not consciously aware that they had smelled the molecule, their brain detected its presence, and they intuitively sensed the fact, as demonstrated by increases in their confidence ratings. They were, so to speak, intuitively (implicitly) aware of the presence of the molecule without being consciously (explicitly) aware of the molecule.

What this tells us is that the new discoveries reported in chapters 4 and 5 involving energy and intention detection are actually not as strange or anomalous as they might first appear. Psychological science has now firmly established the existence of implicit unconscious perception and memory for conventional senses such as vision, audition, and olfaction. (For more details, you can read some scientific articles at the Web site for this book, www.drgaryschwartz.com.)

It's important to understand that the sensation of light and sound— and yes, even odor—involves the processing of energy and information. All sensation, and ultimately all information detection, involves the registration and processing of energy fields that are vibrating in specific patterned ways. These specific patterned fields of energies are what convey detailed information that we ultimately experience as sight, hearing, or olfaction.

When I served as the first pilot subject in our initial hand-energy-sensing experiment (described in chapter 4), while my score was close to 80 percent, I rated my confidence level as near zero—showing that I was at some level clearly "aware" of Justin's hand energy, even though I was not consciously aware that I was aware.

The questions arise: Can I be taught to become more explicitly aware of my apparent implicit awareness? Can healers, undergraduate students, even children be taught to become aware of other people's energies and intentions? Are some people better able than others to learn these discriminations?

If our latent energy- and intention-detection talents can be developed, then who knows how far each of us can improve our abilities to become skilled energy-healing beings—at least for our self-healing, ideally for our loved ones, and possibly for others as well.

A Health-Care Experiment with Unexpected Results

Dr. Andrew Weil and a team of physicians at the University of Arizona have created a postgraduate training program for interested doctors to learn how to integrate conventional, complementary, and alternative medicine. To reach as many physicians as possible, they have developed an associate fellowship program that allows participants to receive much of their education via distance learning. The fellows convene in Tucson on a regular basis for in-person lectures and workshops led by health-care providers skilled in complementary and alternative medicine modalities, including nutrition, herbal medicine, acupuncture, massage, osteopathy, and energy healing. Participants can also choose to participate in an intensive five-day workshop experience with gifted practitioners and healers. Often the workshops are open to other health-care providers, including nurses and psychologists. One of the healers who has offered a number of intensive workshops to the fellows is Rosalyn Bruyere, the author of *Wheels of Light,* a book that describes her unique approach to energy and spiritual healing.

For five years I served on the faculty of the Program in Integrative Medicine, giving lectures on biofield science and energy healing to the fellows. One group of fellows and other health-care providers who signed up for the intensive workshop with Ms. Bruyere decided that they wanted to be tested to see if any changes could be measured in their energy-detection abilities as a result of her training.

Twenty-seven of these health-care providers—twenty-four women and three men—not only volunteered to be pretested prior to the workshop and posttested immediately afterward, but they each personally contributed funds to help cover the costs of the laboratory tests. They were clearly motivated to obtain this knowledge. Fourteen were physicians; the remaining thirteen were primarily psychologists and nurses.

The participants filled out a battery of questionnaires before and after the workshop. They also worked in pairs, taking turns serving as experimenter and subject, testing each other's ability to sense hand energy. They conducted a total of twenty-four hand-energy sensing trials, using the same procedures described earlier. We were able to collect posttest data on twenty-two of the participants.

To help interpret the meaning of any postworkshop increases in hand-energy sensing, we included among the pretest questionnaires an instrument that measures individual differences in what is termed "absorption."

The Tellegen Absorption Scale, developed at the University of Min-

A Note for the Technical Reader

Because it was not feasible to implement a randomized controlled design in this experiment, the findings must be viewed as exploratory. We were not in position financially to obtain a matched control group of health-care providers who would be pre- and posttested in the same way. Ideally participants in such a matched control would either not receive healing-energy training with Ms. Bruyere (called a "no treatment" control) or they would receive five days of intensive training in some other alternative-medicine modality, such as herbal medicine, that did not involve training in energy healing.

Lacking a matched control group, if we observed increases in hand-energy sensing following the workshop, we could not be completely sure that the increases were caused only by the workshop training. Increases in hand-energy detection might also have occurred for other reasons, such as the participants being initially stressed due to traveling to Tucson, getting over jet lag, and so forth, or the participants becoming more familiar with the laboratory and testing procedures and therefore more comfortable or in some other way better prepared during the posttesting as compared to the pretesting.

nesota by Dr. A. Tellegen and colleagues, assesses the extent to which people experience a connection with stimuli in their environment by asking questions about how often they lose track of time while listening to music, how much they identify with characters while reading a novel, whether they get lost in a sunset or become immersed in the plot of a movie. People who score high in absorption tend to be highly hypnotizable, are more likely to seek alternative-medicine procedures for treatment and prevention, and also report having increased paranormal and spiritual experiences.

There are thirty-three yes-no items in the absorption scale; in principle people can receive total scores from zero to thirty-three. The participants in the Bruyere workshop had total absorption scores that ranged from a low of ten to a high of thirty-two. We predicted that participants who were sensitive to energy and became absorbed in stimuli—people with high absorption scores—might gain more from the workshop and therefore show larger increases in sensing hand energy following the workshop.

Consistent with the premise that energy-healing training can improve actual hand-energy detection, we found that, on average, subjects did indeed increase their ability to sense hand energy following the workshop. Though the average increase was relatively small (5.5 percent), it was statistically significant. Since we only included a proximal hand-energy task, we don't know if their ability to sense intention also increased following the workshop as well.

The more important and meaningful finding that emerged from this experiment was that *the participant's pretest absorption scores predicted how much their hand-energy sensing would increase following the workshop.*

For the low absorbers, there was no overall increase in hand-energy sensing observed following the workshop, but those in the high-absorption group showed an average increase of 10 percent. Moreover, four of the high absorbers generated an increase of 20 percent or more in their energy-sensing accuracy.

These findings were published in a special issue on energy healing in the *Journal of Alternative and Complementary Medicine* in 2004. The paper describing the findings was significant because this was the first laboratory experiment ever conducted that investigated whether evidence for improvements in hand-energy sensing could be obtained in real-life health-care providers (as opposed to university undergraduates) who were obtaining state-of-the-art clinical training in energy-health techniques.

Moreover, this was the first experiment to explore the possibility that individual differences in sensitivity and openness to experiencing energy could predict aptitude for learning energy healing among health-care professionals.

A Call for Future Research on Energy-Detection Training

I look forward to the time when the National Institutes of Health will provide funding for research to examine energy and intention detection in healers and laymen, to explore the role of energy and intention awareness in healing and health, and to develop methods for training health-care professionals in learning to sense energy and intention. At the present time the government is not funding research in these areas.

Despite the fact that the capacity of people to sense energy and intention is fundamental to the practice of energy healing, this potentially valuable area has been largely ignored by biomedical and behavioral investigators. This state of affairs needs to change.

One of my goals in writing this book is not only to help awaken readers to their natural capacity to become energy healers for themselves and others, but also to awaken open-minded biomedical and behavioral scientists to the great opportunity for conducting essential, seminal research in these areas in the years to come.

Chapter 7

Sensing the Energy of Minerals and Crystals

When you were a child, did you ever play with a crystal radio? When I was around eleven years old, I spent many wonder-filled hours listening to Long Island and New York City radio stations with my toy crystal radio set.

The words "wonder filled" do not capture the rapture and awe that I experienced as I carefully placed the little wire probe on segments of a tiny quartz crystal. I was able to discover the hot spots on the crystal that made it possible for me to hear faint voices and music coming through the headphones.

How could a little shiny rock—the quartz crystal—connected to a wire antenna tune in and amplify invisible signals that brought programs like Murray the K, a famous disc jockey of the 1950s? There was clearly more to minerals and crystals than their external structure and beauty.

Native Americans and other indigenous peoples believe that minerals and crystals have energy. That minerals and crystals can sense our energies and the energies of their environments. That minerals and crystals generate specific patterns of frequencies, which when used by a skilled medicine woman or shaman can contribute to healing and health. That these creations of nature are as alive as plants and animals.

And that, moreover, if we are trained to listen to them, we can learn to communicate with them. To native peoples, rocks are not inanimate objects—they are gifts of spirits placed here for our health, education, and evolution.

Though my early experience with crystal radios awakened me to the possibility that there was more to rocks than met the eye, I treated as legend the idea that humans could actually detect specific energies or signatures of minerals and crystals. I considered Native American folklore to be just that—folklore, not fact. Until a few years ago, my interpretation of so-called crystal healings was that if they occurred, they were an expression of belief and expectation, not energies and frequencies. As far as the healing process was concerned, crystals were just another form of placebo.

The White Crow of Sensing Crystal Energies

One of my favorite quotes, as readers of my earlier books know, is from William James, MD, the distinguished professor of psychology at Harvard in the late nineteenth century. James was fond of saying, and I paraphrase slightly, "In order to disprove the law that all crows are black, you need only find one white crow."

In the late 1990s, a young undergraduate walked into my office at the University of Arizona with a very strange request. To protect his anonymity, I'll call him Jason. He wanted to find a way to prove to the scientific world that people could detect the energies of specific crystals with their hands. He knew that I directed what was then called the Human Energy Systems Laboratory and that I conducted research in biofield science and energy healing. He surmised, correctly, that if any scientist on campus would be open to investigating his claims, it would be me.

My first impression of Jason was that he was, so to speak, a strange bird. The possibility didn't even occur to me that he might prove himself to be a white crow of crystal-energy detection.

His history, as he recounted it at that first meeting, was unusual. Part Hopi, he grew up among family members who claimed to have psychic and intuitive gifts, including the ability to communicate with animals, plants, and even minerals and crystals. Jason said he spent thousands of hours as a child and adolescent playing and working with minerals and crystals. He had a huge collection of stones, many of which (perhaps he would prefer it if I wrote "many of *whom*") he considered to be his friends. He would "ask" individual stones if they wanted to play with him or be used for specific healing purposes. He even claimed that his cat had favorite crystals and could discriminate between them even if they were hidden from view.

Was Jason sane and well grounded? I wasn't sure. He seemed to be an extraordinarily playful and open-minded individual. But children have wonderful imaginations; were his claims a product of lingering childhood fantasies? Or a combination of superstition plus self-deception?

Or was he perhaps recounting real events about a genuine phenomenon that could be observed and documented in the laboratory?

To test Jason's devotion to this work, I suggested that he first produce a compendium of the various minerals and crystals he had, plus others, and carefully describe their histories in terms of purported personalities, healing properties, and human sensory effects. For example, some crystals are believed to have sedative effects, while others are thought to be stimulating.

Jason came back a few months later with a tome of organized information. No question about it, he was a hard worker, well organized, thorough, and devoted. His crystal and mineral volume was scholarly and comprehensive. The totality of information he showed me, which I thought was probably mostly fictional, frankly gave me a headache when I realized he knew most of it by heart.

He claimed that he could sense the qualities of different minerals and crystals, even if he could not see them or touch them. When I approach a scientific question, I begin at the simplest level. The conversations went something like this. I asked Jason, "Could you detect whether a stone was present or not?"

He said, "Of course. That's easy." Anybody can make an outlandish claim; could he back it up in the lab?

I asked, "If we placed a series of stones in enclosed containers so you couldn't see them, could you sense whether or not a stone was present in each?"

He said, "Sure."

"So if we built ten containers and put stones at random in five of them, you think you could determine which boxes held the stones," I said.

He replied "Why not?" Again, this might seem like a no-brainer to him, but I seriously wondered whether he was deluding himself. Or trying to delude me.

Over the course of a few meetings, we designed and had built ten wooden boxes. They were approximately twelve inches by twelve inches at the base and sixteen inches tall. Each had a silk-cloth front so that Jason could put his hand inside without being able to see whether a stone was present. The bottom of the box was lined with silk upon which a stone could be placed. A silk cloth with little holes was secured about four inches from the bottom of the box, which prevented him from reaching down to feel whether a stone was present but still purportedly allowed the energy to come through.

One of the many questions that arose was how the minerals and crystals should be selected. You can imagine my surprise at Jason's response: he suggested that he ask his stones which of them wanted to participate in the research. Given that Jason was the "expert," and I wanted him to feel comfortable with the process, I said, "Good idea." Later on, and if he succeeded with this first test, we could always test his ability to detect specific stones. We could even determine in future experiments if it really made a difference whether the stones "agreed" to participate in the research or not.

The experiment was designed as follows. A research assistant, Shirley, would place stones in five of the boxes and then set them out at random on a table in two rows of five boxes each. Jason would then be invited to enter the room, place his hand inside each box—not touching the sides of the box or the stretched silk cloth within the box—and attempt to sense the presence or absence of a stone. He could take up to a minute to make each determination. Shirley would record his responses.

After completing the ten boxes, Jason would leave the room. Shirley would then select a new random set of numbers (a random order of the numbers one through ten calculated by statisticians) and rearrange the boxes accordingly. Jason would be invited back into the room and go from box to box, making his determinations. This procedure would be repeated ten times. Since there were ten boxes and ten sets of trials, this generated a hundred trials of information.

If Jason was deluding himself and he could not in reality sense the presence of the stones, his accuracy would hover around 50 percent. Statistics tells us that out of a hundred trials, if he got 65 percent correct, his performance would be statistically significant—this is a probability level of $p < 0.05$ (five out of a hundred), which is one out of twenty by chance. If he got 75 percent correct, his performance would be highly statistically significant—this is a probability level of $p < 0.0004$ (four out of ten thousand), which is one of twenty-five hundred by chance.

How did Jason do? No question about it, he appeared to be a white crow. Jason averaged above 95 percent accuracy. *Ninety-five percent!* This is extraordinarily statistically significant, a probability level far beyond one in a million by chance. Not only did he average above 95 percent accuracy—detecting when a stone was present and when it was absent—but his performance was in the low to high nineties for *each* of the ten boxes.

My initial thought was, Something must be wrong here. Could the assistant be helping him cheat? Could Jason be somehow shaking the boxes? I requested that they repeat the experiment with five new stones (again, Jason was permitted to let the stones "agree" to participate). Moreover, I requested that someone else conduct the experiment. Shirley's mother, who was highly skeptical of Jason's crystal claims, agreed to serve as the research assistant. Driven by her suspicions, she would be watching closely to see if she could catch Jason doing anything improper. The experiment would be videotaped. A total of one hundred trials would again be conducted. Would the findings be replicated?

To my surprise, Jason's performance continued to average around 95 percent accuracy.

We then repeated the experiment a third time. Another hundred trials were collected. The results were the same. It appeared that Jason could do what he claimed he could do.

Imagine the situation for Jason—growing up exposed to Native American beliefs and practices and accepting them as his own. Playing and working with minerals and crystals and making them into "friends." Reaching the point where these experiences seemed second nature to him but were viewed as weird, if not crazy, by his peers and teachers. Regularly communicating with his stones. And then, this professor asks him to do an experiment, over and over, where he must blindly detect whether one of his friends is in a box or not. How would you feel doing these simplistic experiments?

Jason appreciated my need to start from the beginning. He understood my need to establish definitively that at least one white crow of mineral and crystal detection existed and could be studied in the laboratory. If there was one white crow, there were probably others. Moreover, in theory it was a possibility worth investigating that people— including you and me—could be taught to detect the presence of stones, and even the energy signatures of stones, just as people can be taught to detect the presence of fractures in X-rays, and even the signatures and particulars of the fractures.

More Crystal Experiments

Jason and I did many mineral- and crystal-sensing experiments. One of my favorites—and the most important—concerned his claim that natural crystals had stronger energies and were more "alive" than man-made or synthetic crystals.

Moreover, Jason discovered that he did not actually have to put his hands inside the box. He claimed it was easier to sense the difference between natural versus synthetic quartz crystals if he kept his hands outside the box—the wood actually served as a subtle filter that facilitated the distinction between natural and man-made.

We always used ten boxes. This time, three of the boxes contained fairly large—two to three inches long—natural quartz crystals. Three other boxes contained even larger—three to four inches long—synthetic quartz crystals. And four boxes contained no crystals. A total of a hundred trials constituted a single experiment.

The findings were basically as follows. When Jason's hands were outside the box, his performance for natural-crystal detection fell from 95 percent to approximately 75 percent. In other words, 25 percent of the time he said there was no stone when a natural quartz crystal was present. Not as impressive, but still highly statistically significant.

At the same time, his accuracy in detecting the absence of stones also fell from 95 percent to 75 percent. Instead of reporting 5 percent of the time that a stone was present when it was not, he reported this 25 percent of the time. Not only were his hands farther from the stones—inside the box his hands were five to six inches away from the stones, outside they were seventeen to eighteen inches away—but the wood on top was serving as a subtle filter or shield for the energies.

The important question was, given these experimental conditions, what would be his ability to detect the man-made quartz crystals? What we discovered was that when his hands were outside the box, his ability to detect whether there was a man-made crystal in a particular box plummeted to 50 percent, pure chance.

In other words, we confirmed both of Jason's claims. First, he could detect above chance the presence of a natural stone even if his hands were outside the box. And secondly, man-made quartz did not generate the same level or dynamics of energy as did natural quartz, so he often thought that a box containing a man-made crystal had no stone in it.

Presuming for the moment that this experiment was valid—and I'm convinced that it was—these questions arise: What does it mean? Is natural quartz more "alive" than synthetic quartz? Does natural quartz emit stronger and more dynamic energies than a synthetic crystal?

Is the natural quartz possibly even detecting the presence of Jason's energies, if not his consciousness, and responding in kind? This prediction comes from what is called "dynamical systems theory"—the idea that atoms, molecules, cells, and so on exchange information and energy to various degrees. Is this a two-way street—a communication process between Jason and his crystal "friends"?

Later in this book, we'll explore the idea that science provides a firm foundation for theorizing and documenting the dynamics of energy communication within and between all things—both visible and invisible—from the extraordinarily tiny to the infinitely large.

A Sad Yet Potentially Evidential Postscript

An unanticipated and untoward circumstance led to the conclusion that what Jason was demonstrating in our mineral- and crystal-sensing experiments was probably beyond reproach.

You may be wondering if Jason was somehow cheating, consciously or unconsciously, in these experiments. Could he have somehow fooled me, Shirley, her mother, and perhaps even himself into believing that he could sense the energies of minerals and crystals?

Not long after those experiments, Jason underwent major surgery. The anesthesia used caused him to develop epileptic seizures, and both the seizures and the medication prescribed to control them affected his cognitive function. A side effect of these complications was that Jason's attention and sensitivity was hampered somewhat, and he could no longer interact with his minerals and crystals as he once did. He reported feeling as if he had lost contact with his earth friends.

Meanwhile, his cat continued to find the special crystals he and Shirley (who was by then his wife) hid in the house.

If Jason had been consciously cheating—for example, subtly shaking the boxes—he would probably be able to continue fooling us in experiments today. However, if his skills had been genuine—as they appeared to be—his unfortunate medical complications could have interfered with them.

Energy healers, medical intuitives, and psychics of various sorts report that their ability to receive information and practice their crafts is impaired by fatigue, pain, and illness. Like any performer practicing a complex skill—be it music, painting, athletics, or whatever—a healer must be in peak shape to practice his or her craft optimally.

I have spent a little time seeing if I could detect various minerals and crystals. My performance level thus far has been metaphorically more like playing "Chopsticks" on the piano than playing "Rhapsody in Blue" as Jason did. However, when I'm relaxed and not fatigued, I can often perform statistically above chance. The truth is, no one yet knows who the great musicians of mineral and crystal sensing are. One of them might be you.

At this point, energy sensing abilities—be they of people, animals, plants, even minerals and crystals—are relatively unknown. However, the research conducted to date is completely consistent with the idea that humans have an inherent talent to sense energy.

As we have said, everything has energy. Everything is energy. Everything senses energy. And that includes us. Our bodies contain cells that are supersensitive to energy and information. As mentioned previously, our eyes contain retinal cells that can detect single photons of light.

The apparatus exists within us to sense the supersubtle; it's up to each of us to discover and use this apparatus to its fullest potential.

To see or not to see, that is the question.

Part II

Our Energy Fields Connect Us with Everything

The heart is the first feature of working minds.
　　　　　　　　—FRANK LLOYD WRIGHT

Chapter 8

Interplay—The Heart and the Brain

Since everything has energy and is energy, and since energy extends out in all directions, then everything potentially affects everything else to various degrees. This logic is inescapable.

In physics, energy is described as "the capacity to do work and overcome resistance." It follows that if something not only has energy but is energy, then it has the capacity (the ability, the potential) to do work and overcome resistance. So energy by definition has the capacity to affect something else.

The heart and brain each generate energy and therefore, according to physics, have the inherent capacity to do work and overcome resistance. The heart and brain have the potential not only to affect each other energetically but to affect every other organ, cell, and molecule in the body to various degrees as well.

So the heart and brain can affect not only each other through neural and chemical means, which is the standard medical/physical model, but also energetically by means of electromagnetic fields—the emerging explanation that uses what is called the bioelectromagnetic/biophysical model. This implies that your heart can affect your brain energetically, and vice versa, by the electromagnetic fields they each generate.

But before we consider why this is so, and how we can measure fields, it will be helpful to begin with a brief exploration of the understanding scientists currently hold about energy and fields and the way that fields affect one another.

Invisible Spheres of Fields

One of the first people to deeply appreciate the universality of energy and fields was Sir Isaac Newton, the scientist and mystic who first recognized the fundamental qualities of the gravitational field. Newton came to the conclusion that an object that had mass would have a gravitational field that extended out from it in all directions like an expanding three-dimensional sphere. In a deep sense, the gravitational field is a pulsating field sphere.

According to contemporary physics, this three-dimensional field sphere extends into space at the speed of light, and has the potential to reach to infinity. This can be a difficult concept to accept: that the diameter of the field sphere has the potential to be *infinite*. The greater the mass of the object, the stronger the expanding gravitational field sphere.

Though the magnitude of the field sphere depends upon the mass of the object, the distance the field extends into space does not. Weaker fields extend just as far as stronger fields. Even though the strength of the field weakens with distance, it theoretically does not disappear.

Consequently, imagine this: The universe is presumed by the majority of today's physicists to be approximately 13.7 billion years old. Certain physical objects that have mass—from subatomic particles to atoms—have existed for most of that time. This means that their fields have been extending out into space for billions and billions of years.

Imagine that a mass the size of a basketball is "born" and begins to extend its gravitational field. In one second, the field will have extended approximately 186,000 miles into space, in all directions—left-right, up-down, front-back. The size of this field sphere would now be 372,000 miles large. In one year, the field would have extended approximately 5.9 trillion miles into space, in all directions. The size of this field sphere would now be 11.7 trillion miles gigantic.

Now think about how big that gravitational field sphere would be if the original basketball-sized object had come into existence more than 13 billion years ago. The answer would contain a great many zeros.

If this isn't incomprehensible enough, imagine that the universe is 13.7 billion years old and contains billions and billions of galaxies. Each contains billions and billions of stars, plus billions and billions of smaller objects—planets, moons, and asteroids, and many others. Each of these objects has a gravitational field sphere that extends out into space, and the pulsating field spheres all overlap. We're talking about billions of billions of billions of billions of overlapping spheres of fields.

These fields are crossing in space, in all directions, not merely as lines of force, but as three-dimensional spheres of force. And they are all affecting one another to various degrees.

If thinking about this gives you a headache, welcome to the club. Though astrophysicists have gotten pretty good at figuring out how two or three large objects can affect one another via their gravitational fields, the challenge of calculating the multibody problem—say, the effects nine planets (now eight—goodbye, Pluto) of various sizes and orbits influencing one another as they revolve around the sun (the current model of our solar system)—is as yet unmanageable.

Since these gravitation field spheres are invisible, we have to infer their existence by the motion of objects we can see. We infer that these invisible fields exist because they provide an accurate explanation that makes sense of the orderliness of how objects seem to move in space.

Just because fields are merely inferred does not mean that they are unreal. Our senses are limited, but our minds can conceive beyond what our senses provide. As Einstein said, "Imagination is more important than knowledge." Yes, with our minds we can imagine things that are not real, but we can also imagine things that are. The challenge is to discern what is real and what is not.

Remembering the need for wise caution, I use the word "real" here in the Missouri sense—meaning that if a concept helps me make sense of what I experience and if it works in practice, then I will use it. Physicists presume that fields are real because the concept works.

I have come to the conclusion that humans can detect energetic fields and even detect conscious intentions because when I design experiments to examine these possibilities, the experiments produce results that are consistent with this explanation. Carefully conducted, the experiments do replicate and extend one another.

Measuring Heart and Brain Fields

Since the heart and brain each have mass, they each generate pulsating electromagnetic fields that we can visualize and document in the laboratory. They are in constant communication electromagnetically. Some years ago, scientists began to explore what effect the fields from the heart have on the brain and what effect the fields from the brain have on the heart.

The electromagnetic fields from the heart are the fields being measured when electrodes are placed on the chest to record an electrocardiogram, or EKG. The electromagnetic fields from the brain are the fields being measured when electrodes are placed on the scalp to record an electroencephalogram, or EEG.

The heart and brain generate other kinds of fields as well. For example, using what is termed a SQUID—a magnetic field detector (the acronym stands for "superconducting quantum interference device")—we can measure magnetic fields generated by the heart; they're revealed in a magnetocardiogram, or MCG. We can also measure similar fields generated by the brain, which are revealed in a magnetoencephalogram, or MEG. We can even quantify changes in blood flow in the heart and brain using state-of-the-art functional magnetic resonance imaging techniques, called fMRI. These techniques work by taking advantage of the magnetic fields generated by the nuclei in atoms; tracking the movement of water molecules via their magnetic fields allows the fMRI instrument to monitor changes in blood flow, in three-dimensional space, on a moment-to-moment basis.

Most people, including cardiologists and neurologists, don't ponder the possible health consequences of the electromagnetic fields constantly being generated by the heart and brain—fields that are, by biological standards, relatively large, and travel throughout the body, interacting to various degrees with every cell and molecule in the body.

Heart and Brain Interacting

Are the heart and brain affecting each other energetically? And if so, what role might their apparently intimate energetic connections play in healing and health? These challenging questions have been examined in some depth by a small group of visionary scientists and healers at the Institute of HeartMath (www.heartmath.org). My former colleague Dr. Linda Russek, my former graduate student Dr. Linda Song, and I have also examined these questions and have conducted a number of experiments that address them (for example, in the Song, Schwartz, and Russek paper published in *Alternative Therapies in Health and Medicine,* 1999). The basic notion is easy to explain.

Each time the heart beats, it generates a pattern of electrical charges that extend out from it in all directions—up-down, left-right, and front-back. Scientists and doctors give names to the various parts of this heartbeat signature. The heart has two chambers, the atria (left and right) and the ventricles (also left and right); the atria receive blood from veins and send the blood to the ventricles, which pump the blood through the lungs and the body as a whole. A small bump in the EKG signature, called the P wave, is the electrical pulse associated with the contraction of the atria. The P wave is followed by a substantially larger spike, the R spike, which is associated with contraction of the ventricles. Smaller Q and S waves bracket the R spike.

Next comes the T wave, which is typically taller and longer-lasting than the P wave but still substantially smaller than the R spike. After a pause, this five-waved PQRST pattern is repeated, over and over.

This five-waved electrical pattern travels through the bloodstream and other fluids in the body, reaching every cell of the body—from the top of the scalp to the bottom of the feet and the tips of the fingers. This isn't difficult to prove. It's possible to record the EKG from electrodes placed on any part of the body, so long as one electrode is on one side of the heart and the second electrode is on the other side— above and below, or left and right, or front and back. The electrical pattern revealed by the EKG is literally everywhere.

Every cell of the body—be it a neuron, white blood cell, skin cell, or brain cell—is bathed in the heart's electrical fields.

Meanwhile, the electrical waves being generated by the brain, the EEG waves, travel though the body just as the heart's electrical waves do. So the EEG can be recorded from any part of the body, too, so long as one electrode is placed above and the second electrode is placed below the brain.

Which organ do you think generates a larger electrical signal, the heart or the brain? It turns out that the heart's EKG is substantially bigger than the brain's EEG. The difference is even greater when the magnetic fields are considered. The magnetic field of the heart, the MCG, can be five hundred to five thousand times bigger than the magnetic field of the brain, the MEG.

Revealing the Heart's EKG in the Brain's EEG

A cardiologist is interested in examining the signals from the heart, not the brain. A neurologist is interested in examining the signals from the brain, not the heart. However, if what I said above is true—and it is— then how is it possible to record the EKG separately from the EEG?

Here's how it works. Since the EKG is bigger than the EEG, when the EKG signal reaches the brain, it will normally overpower the EEG signal, unless the EKG signal is somehow subtracted. Neurologists connect a pair of electrodes to the scalp, to pick up the signals from the brain, and a pair of electrodes to the ears (termed a "linked ears" electrode placement) to pick up the EKG from the heart; by electronically subtracting the EKG from the scalp signal, the neurologist is able to see the EEG alone.

(When we talk about the EKG being subtracted from the EEG, we're talking about something going on in an electronic device sitting in the lab; in the brain of the subject being tested, the EKG signal and the EEG signal are of course still interacting.)

The same logic applies to EEG waves reaching the heart. If one electrode is placed above the heart and another electrode below the heart, and the top electrode is subtracted from the bottom electrode, the EEG that travels to and through, as well as around the heart can be electronically removed, leaving a heart EKG signal free of any signal from the brain.

How can we prove this? Easily. If we place one electrode on the scalp and the second electrode below the heart, what do you think we will see? The answer is straightforward. Since the EKG and EEG are actually mixing in the bloodstream and other aqueous fluids of the body, what we will see is the EEG riding on the top of the EKG. In other words, the brain waves, which are smaller than the heart's wave, will be vibrating at a higher frequency—for example, the alpha frequency, which is 8 to 12 cycles per second—while moving up and down along the heart's waves, whose frequency is much slower.

Think about this. Your EKG is mixing with your EEG, and your EEG is mixing with your EKG. Remember, these are physical energies and fields, and energy is defined as the capacity to do work and overcome resistance. Therefore, the EKG and the EEG can each potentially affect any cells and molecules that they come in contact with. So every cell in the body can be thought of as being an antenna/receiver of EKG and EEG signals.

How the Mind Affects the Brain's Registration of the Heart's EKG

It's one thing to demonstrate that the EKG, the heart wave, can be observed in the EEG of the brain; it's another to determine whether the brain is actually detecting the heart wave and possibly responding to it. Thanks to the vision and motivation of Dr. Linda Song, we were able to address this intriguing and possibly highly significant question in the laboratory.

When Linda Song came to the University of Arizona from China, she had completed the equivalent of an MD in Western medicine plus an MD in Chinese medicine. Because of her background in Qigong, a Chinese form of energy exercise and healing, she had a special interest in the energies of the heart and how they might influence the mind.

As part of her master's thesis, Linda decided to attempt to determine if a subject's intention to experience the beating of his or her heart amplified the brain's registration of the heart wave.

For the experiment, we attached nineteen electrodes to each volunteer's head, all wired to the EEG machine, so that we could record nineteen separate channels of brain waves. We also attached an EKG to the EEG machine to record heart waves simultaneously with the EEG. Each volunteer was asked to sit quietly with her eyes closed. We explained that the purpose of the experiment was to examine possible brain and heart changes that accompany paying attention to different parts of the body. For a given two-minute trial, she was asked either to focus her

A Note for the Technical Reader

Feel free to skim or skip this if you are not interested in the details of how it's possible to measure the presence of the EKG in the EEG—the heart's energy in the brain, which I call "the ARC in the SEA."

It's possible, using state-of-the-art computers, to design software that reveals to what extent the EKG is influencing the EEG. I designed a software package when I was a professor at Yale University, originally called the ARC-SEA, that made this kind of analysis possible. ARC stands for "averaged repetitive cycle" and SEA stands for "synchronized event averages." The simple way to understand how this works is to imagine a boat, the ARC, floating in the water, the SEA.

Imagine you are on the boat, and each time a wave reaches you, your boat rides the wave—it rises and falls as each wave reaches you and then moves past. If we had a computer that tracked the rise and fall of each wave under your boat and then averaged the waves—which would be like placing each waveform one on top of the other—we would generate a graph that displayed what the average wave looked like.

If the primary wave, in this case, was the R spike of the EKG, and your boat was rising and falling with each PQRST wave pattern, we could draw a graph that displayed what the average EKG wave pattern looked like over 120 repetitive beats. This would be the averaged repetitive cycle of the EKG, or EKG-ARC.

Now imagine that you are back on the boat and you are looking out in various directions. You are wondering which waves in the ocean, if any, are synchronized with your boat—that is, are correlated with the specific waves that are causing your boat to rise and fall. In other words, you are looking to see which, if any, parts of the SEA are synchronized with your ARC. If we extend the computer program to average at the same time specific areas in the SEA and determine which areas, if any, create an average that is synchronized with your ARC, we can then look for specific EEG-SEAs that might be synchronized with your EKG-ARC.

If the waves in the SEA were randomly related to your boat, the ARC, and you average them with respect to the ARC, what you would see was essentially a flat line, because some waves would be going up, and others would be going down, and they would cancel each other out. However, if the waves in the SEA were not random and were somehow synchronized with respect to the ARC, then those waves that were synchronized would add up, while those that were not would cancel out. What would happen is that the synchronized signals would grow in clarity, while the nonsynchronized signals would decrease into the noise. In other words, the signal-to-noise ratio would grow.

Imagine that you have been hooked up to a nineteen-channel EEG device that is recording your brain waves from electrodes placed on nineteen different locations on your scalp, while your EKG is being simultaneously recorded. We use the ARC-SEA software implemented so that your EKG is the ARC and your nineteen channels of EEG create nineteen potential SEAs. What do you think we will see? Will your nineteen EEG-SEA waveforms be flat, or random? Or will we see a pattern of SEA waveforms that are synchronized with your EKG-ARC?

Figure 8.2 presents an average of twenty subjects recorded in this way. The graphs focus on the QRS portion of the EKG wave signature. The first nineteen EEG-SEA graphs represent the different electrode locations on the subjects' heads. The graphs are arranged as if we were looking down at the top of the head. The upper two graphs were recorded from the front of the head (called the frontal region), the lower two graphs were measured from the back of the head (called the occipital region). The single graph at the bottom reflects the average of the EKG R spike—in other words, the EKG-ARC. (As presented in the figure, the EKG-ARC looks to be the same magnitude as the nineteen EEG-SEAs; this is actually not the case. Because the EKG-ARC is so much larger, these charts in the figure are reduced by a factor of a thousand in order to display them on the same scale. Also, recall that the EKG has been subtracted from the EEG.)

We have computed EKG-ARCs and EEG-SEAs from men in their mid-sixties and from male and female college students in their early twenties. The ARC-SEA patterns are virtually the same in all three groups. You can see in the figure that the EEG-SEAs that are synchronized with the R spike (shown as the EKG-ARC) are largest in the back of the head, are smallest in the front of the head, and tend to be larger on the right front side compared to left front side. Also, the EEG-SEA is somewhat smaller in the middle of the head than on either side.

Why the brain displays this particular pattern of EEG-SEA waves is not important here. What is important to take away from this somewhat complicated graph is that the EKG can be discovered in the EEG, even when the actual recording procedure attempts to subtract the EKG from the EEG.

Simply stated, the heart's energy field can be picked up in the brain's energy field, and the resulting pattern is synchronized, not random. If you doubted whether the heart's energy can be observed in the brain, I hope your doubts have been dispelled.

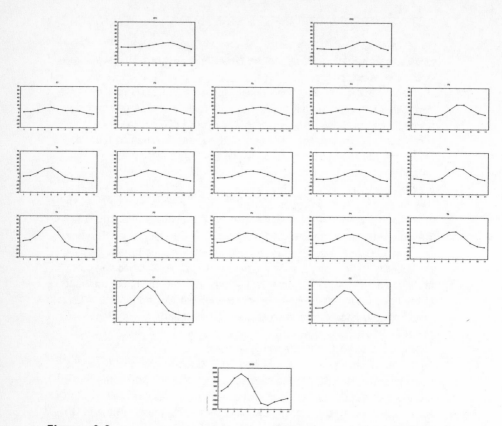

Figure 8.2. Nineteen Synchronized Average Event Brain Waveforms (EEG-SEAs) and the Corresponding Average Repetitive Cycle of the Heart (EKG-ARC)

attention on the beating of her heart or the movements of her eyes, and to silently count the beats or movements. To increase her ability to sense her heartbeats or eye movements, on some trials she was allowed to place her fingers on her wrist to better sense her heartbeat or place her fingers on her closed eyelids to better sense her eye movements. At the end of each trial, she was asked to report how many heartbeats or eye movements she sensed.

Not surprisingly, people reported sensing more heartbeats or eye movements when they were allowed to feel pulsations in their wrist or movements through their eyelids.

After the testing was finished, we did computer analyses (EKG-ARC and EEG-SEA) for each of the four types of trials: (1) paying attention to heartbeats without touching the wrist; (2) paying attention to heartbeats augmented by touching the wrist; (3) paying attention to eye movements without touching the eyelids; and (4) paying attention to eye movements augmented by touching the eyelids.

We had two primary hypotheses. The high-probability prediction was that the size of the T spike in the heart wave as detected in the brain-wave analysis (EEG-SEA) would be increased when subjects were paying attention to their heartbeats and touching their wrists, as compared to the other three trials when they were not touching their wrists.

This prediction was physiological, not electromagnetic, and therefore wasn't controversial. When the ventricle contracts, blood is expelled from the heart and quickly travels down the arteries. With the subject's fingers pressed to the wrist, the movement of blood is sensed in the fingertips, just as a doctor or nurse senses the movement when taking a pulse count. This information is transmitted rapidly to the brain, where it is experienced subjectively as heart pulsations. By the time these neural impulses reach the brain and result in conscious awareness of the pulsation, the heart has reached its T-wave period. That would mean the brain was indeed sensing the information from fingertips-on-wrist and responding to it. The brain was processing the signals generated by the fingertips following each heartbeat and expressing this processing as an electrical bump on the chart.

In the lab, we conducted these tests in 1997 with college students. We found that when subjects were sensing their heart pulsations with their fingers, the computer analysis (ARC-SEA) revealed an increase in the brain wave that was indeed synchronized with the T wave of the heart. The high-probability prediction was confirmed.

However, the low-probability prediction—which was electromagnetic—was quite controversial. If the student concentrates on trying to experience his/her heartbeat, would we be able to detect an increase of the heart-wave component in the brain wave? If so, it would tend to confirm that the brain is not merely receiving the heart-wave signals but actually detecting the heart wave and possibly responding to it.

When the ventricles contract, they force blood out of the heart and through the body, but when the atria contract, they merely move blood from the atrial chambers to the ventricles. If we observed an increase of heart signal in the brain wave at the moment of atrial contraction (P wave), it would be evidence that the brain was responding to an *electromagnetic* signal—since all heart actions represented by spikes in the EKG are triggered by electromagnetic pulses, the P wave included.

If the brain was indeed sensing the electromagnetic P-wave signal from the heart when subjects were intending to sense their heartbeats, their brains would be showing increased registration of the heart's P waves in their EEGs. To my surprise—and delight—we found that the computer analysis revealed an increase in the brain wave that was synchronized with the P wave of the EKG. The low-probability prediction was also confirmed.

Think about this. Our hearts and brains generate electrical signals sent throughout the body that we don't experience consciously. But when we focus our attention on our hearts, our brains amplify the electrical fields coming from our hearts even during those moments—the P-wave periods—when sensations from the heart have yet to reach our brains. Stated another way, our brains have implicit perception of our heart energies.

So energy from the heart reaches and interacts with the energy within the brain. That simple fact has profound significance for energy healing.

When science is at its best, it not only answers specific questions, but also raises new ones that challenge and expand our understanding of nature and the universe. This research has suggested a slew of fascinating questions waiting to be researched.

For example, do people vary in their brain's ability to detect and process electromagnetic signals coming from their heart? Are individuals who are loving and compassionate more heart-brain connected, not just physiologically, but energetically as well? Do certain kinds of meditation foster increased heart-brain synchronization? Does stress, and especially anger, potentially diminish the brain's capacity to register and respond to electromagnetic fields coming from the heart? Are repression and self-deception associated with decreased heart-brain synchronization? Is increased health and vitality associated with increased heart-brain synchronization?

The heart and brain are inherently connected electromagnetically. We should not forget this fact. The energy and information is clearly there, available for the brain and heart to detect, process, and use.

The Heart as Conductor of the Symphonic Body, and the Brain as the Score

It has been estimated that the body has at least 60 trillion cells. Each cell has its own nucleus, its own DNA, and its own functions. How does this outrageously complex network of cells ever function as an organized whole?

The word "health" comes from an Old English word meaning "whole." To be healthy is to function as a whole. Where does the holistic organization come from? How do the cells coordinate their unique activities? As yet, no one really knows.

However, here is a hypothesis that follows directly from the vision that the body is ultimately an organized energy system interconnected by a network or matrix of electromagnetic (and other) fields.

Imagine that we had a huge symphony composed of numerous instruments and musicians. Each musician, with her or his particular instrument, plays a particular part in the score. How does such an orchestra ever play as an organized whole?

Sure: the orchestra has a conductor. His task goes beyond what's apparent to the observer in the audience. I happen to know about this at first hand, because I took conducting lessons when I was a teenager attending music camps. The conductor does three things. Besides providing the downbeat as the cue to start, and providing the tempo, he also provides information about dynamics or amplitude. The conductor can make bigger movements or smaller movements and thereby modulate the intensity of the sound and the attack on a section or on specific notes—for the whole orchestra at one moment, for a selected section or an individual player at another. A good conductor can inspire an orchestra and skillfully bring the music to life.

If we were to look for a possible conductor inside the body, we'd seek out an organ that was centrally located, that generated a huge "downbeat" signal reaching every cell within the body, and whose signal conveyed essential information. The answer becomes obvious. The conducting organ would be the heart, not the brain. In fact, even if the brain happens to cease functioning—after an accident or some other trauma—the heart can potentially keep on beating and, with proper nutrition, the body can continue to survive.

Think about this. The magnitude of the heart's QRS wave, when the ventricles contract, can be tens of thousands or hundreds of thousands of times larger than the size of an individual cell's electromagnetic field. Is this simply an artifact of the size of the heart? Or is the heart, electromagnetically speaking, playing a fundamental role in helping the body function as a beautiful orchestra?

Of course, no matter how good a given conductor is, the ultimate success of the orchestra depends upon the intentions and skills of each individual musician. They must be willing and able to play together for the sake of the whole if the orchestra is to be successful.

Just as an orchestra relies not just on a conductor to provide guidance but also on a score that presents the composer's music, the body needs both a conducting heart, and a composing brain that provides a healthy score. The heart and brain must work together—not just physiologically, but energetically—if the body is to function as a whole.

The truth is probably more complex than this because the "score" comes not only from the brain, but from other organs as well, and not just from inside the body, but also from outside.

Do our hearts and brains send signals beyond our bodies? If we take the evidence of physics seriously, the answer is absolutely yes. Does this make life, and health, more complicated and more magnificent? The journey continues.

> *The only lasting beauty is the beauty of the heart.*
>
> —RUMI

Chapter 9

How Your Heart's Energy Can Affect Another Person's Brain

Here's an unlikely statement to consider: "Your heart's energy can influence another person's brain from a distance." That doesn't sound very probable, does it?

It suggests a whole collection of unlikely possibilities: That the heart is in a deep sense like a beating sun, spreading life-fostering energies beyond the skin. That we can literally touch one another from a distance with our heart energies, not only across a room, but even across a continent. That we might be able to recognize our loved one's heart-energy signatures.

For me, it also raised a question about whether we might be more open to registering the heart energies of others if we were raised by loving, caring parents.

Are possibilities such as these merely new-age musings of an aging researcher, or are there convincing scientific theories and data that make such conjectures not only plausible but potentially probable as well?

It turns out that the biophysics of the heart, combined with fundamental properties of magnetic resonance, provide a strong reason to entertain the possibility that humans and animals are genetically wired to detect, even from a distance, the heart energies of others, especially the fields of their family and loved ones. Moreover, research using magnetic resonance imaging makes it possible to address these questions in the laboratory.

Envisioning the Extended Heart

As discussed in the previous chapter, the heart generates electrical signals that can be revealed by the EKG, and magnetic signals that can be revealed by the MCG. Recall that the EKG electrodes are placed on the person's skin and the SQUID detector for the MCG is placed a few inches off the skin.

Consider the following questions: Do the heart's electromagnetic fields stop at the skin or a few inches beyond it? Or do they extend into space just as gravitational fields and light do?

Another way to formulate this question is to ask, Why would the heart's electromagnetic fields cease at the skin? Is the body encased in an electromagnetic shield? Clearly it's not. Once the heart's electrical and magnetic fields reach the skin, nothing prevents them from continuing. *Nothing.* As a result, they naturally and effortlessly extend out into space.

As we observed earlier, electromagnetic fields travel in space at the speed of light, so that approximately one second after your heart has beat, its electromagnetic wave will have traveled approximately 186,000 miles into space. Yes, the magnitude of your cardiac electrical and magnetic fields will be extraordinarily tiny. But the physics of electromagnetic fields is very clear about the fact that, in principle, our electromagnetic fields extend into space. And once they are in space, like the Energizer Bunny they keep going and going and going.

What's more immediately significant in everyday life is whether our heart signals travel a few feet across a room. If they do, can a loved one nearby serve as an antenna/receiver, registering our heart energies? Can we serve as an antenna/receiver for our loved one's heart fields? Given that our brains can register our own heart's energy fields, as described in the previous chapter, these questions logically follow.

If we can resonate with our own heart's fields, it follows that in principle we should be able to resonate with our loved one's heart fields as well. And, yes, with other people's heart fields, including those of complete strangers.

However, like any antenna/receiver, theoretically we may have to be open to registering and processing the signals. Our antennas may need to be pointed in the right direction and our amplifiers may need to be turned on and tuned correctly to receive the heart signals in question.

How would we explore this hypothesis in the laboratory? The answer is ARC-SEA: ARC, the averaged repetitive cycle of the EKG; SEA, the synchronized event average of the EEG.

Imagine using two sets of EEG and EKG amplifiers—one to record heart and brain electrical fields from person A, the other to record heart and brain electrical fields from person B. You could be person A, your loved one (or a friend, or even a stranger) could be person B.

We have already established (in an earlier technical section) that a person's EKG signal can be used as the synchronizing trigger (called the ARC, the averaged repetitive cycle) to calculate their synchronized EEG waves (called the SEA, or synchronized event average). You can think of the EKG-ARC as being a heart "boat" floating in the water, and the EEG-SEA as being brain "waves" that are some distance from the boat. In this instance we're looking for the presence of one person's heart waves (EKG-ARC) in the other person's brain waves (EEG-SEA)—A's heart waves in B's brain waves and B's heart waves in A's brain waves.

To do this, we switch ARCs and SEAs, and we program the software to use person A's EKG as the synchronizing trigger to calculate person B's EEG-SEAs and person B's EKG as the synchronizing trigger to calculate person's A's EEG-SEAs. In both of these instances, we would be looking for the presence of one person's heart signals in the other person's brain signals.

Collecting the data was a bit of a challenge. I had to run two computers simultaneously, one with each hand. And the data analysis was extremely time-consuming, especially using MS-DOS ARC-SEA programs that were not user-friendly. However, my fascination with the body's capacity to be an antenna/receiver for TV and radio signals had never left me. I had a burning passion to determine scientifically whether one person's brain could serve as an antenna/receiver for another person's heart.

A Note for the Technical Reader

When I first envisioned this possibility in the mid 1990s, the available EEG and EKG hardware and software systems used the original Microsoft operating system, MS-DOS, on a 386 or 486 Intel chip. In order to collect two people's EEGs and EKGs simultaneously, I had to use two computers simultaneously, one for each person. I recorded nineteen channels of EEG and the EKG using Lexicor Neurosearch-24 systems. I used two Lexicor systems, one for each person.

You might wonder, if each computer was separate, how did I synchronize the two? The procedure for calculating ARC-SEAs requires precise timing of the EKGs with the SEAs. The solution was made possible by the Lexicor hardware. It actually contained twenty-four amplifiers, four of which could be used for non-EEG signals.

What I did was wire the Lexicors in such a way that for person A's Lexicor, I recorded person A's EEG, person A's EKG, and person B's EKG. For person B's Lexicor, I recorded person B's EEG, person B's EKG, and person A's EKG. Each computer therefore recorded one brain and two hearts. Later, after the experiment was completed, I could perform ARC-SEA analysis using either EKG A or EKG B as ARC triggers to average EEG A, and using either EKG B or EKG A as ARC triggers to average EEG B.

Thanks to my former colleague Dr. Linda Russek, it was possible for me to extend the ARC-SEA system to two people and then collect data to test the hypothesis. In her own way, Linda was as committed to addressing this question as I was. She had the devotion and the funds; I had the motivation and the skills. Together we were able to address a controversial question that offered a low probability of working but if successful would definitely have a high payoff of great theoretical and practical significance.

Background: The Harvard Mastery of Stress Study

In one of my earlier books with Bill Simon, *The Afterlife Experiments* (Atria, 2002), I recounted the history of the Harvard Mastery of Stress

Study. With apologies to readers of that earlier book, I want to present the information again to show how it relates to the current subject.

In the early 1950s, a study was conducted on healthy Harvard male undergraduates to examine physiological responses to laboratory stressors such as loud noises and electric shocks. The investigators summarized their findings in a 1957 book titled *Mastery of Stress.* With her father, the distinguished cardiologist Dr. Henry Russek, Linda Russek decided that it would be valuable to follow up this study to see if measures of stress in college carried any predictions of the men's physical and psychological health when they were in their fifties. Though their findings were somewhat complicated, they essentially discovered that certain measures of anxiety and stress collected when the men were at Harvard predicted their health status in midlife.

When I met Linda in 1994, her father had just died, and she wanted to do a further follow-up study in his honor. We were both interested in the electromagnetic fields of the heart and the possibility of a heart-brain connection. As part of this forty-two-year follow-up, we decided that I would record nineteen channels of EEG and EKG from Linda, as the interviewer, and from the subjects, who were now in their mid-sixties.

We were able to enlist the participation of twenty men from the original sample. Some of the interviews were performed in New York City, the rest in Boston. The men flew in at their own expense to contribute to the research.

The data were collected in soundproof recording studios, with chairs arranged so the subjects were facing the interviewer and about three feet from her. Psychophysiological studies require the collection of frequent baseline data from the subject while he sits quietly, resting with his eyes closed. Before Linda began her lengthy list of interview questions, I had her and the subject sit quietly with their eyes closed for two minutes while I collected their EEGs and EKGs on their respective computers.

Unbeknownst to the subjects, there was a potential high payoff built into this initial resting baseline condition. Since the interviewer was facing the interviewee, it was possible for me to later measure not only the presence of the interviewee's EKG (heart waves) in his EEG (brain waves), but the possibility of the interviewer's EKG waves in his EEG waves, as well. Using the resting data was important because it was the purest experimental condition, uncontaminated by any emotional parts in the interview about to take place.

Unlike the experiment described in the previous chapter, this time the ARC-SEA software was triggered by the EKG of the interviewer instead of the EKG of the subject—so that we could see if one person's heart could be detected in another person's brain.

One of the most stunning outcomes from our study concerned how the subjects, when they were in college, felt about the love they had received from their parents and how those responses predicted their health all these years later.

They had been asked to rate their mothers and fathers on a numerical scale, in six positive traits: loving, just, fair, clever, hard-working, and strong. We called this the Harvard Parental Caring Scale. Eleven of the men rated their mothers and fathers high on these items, and nine of them rated their mothers and fathers low.

When I looked at the current health of the men forty-two years later, I found that among the men who in college rated their parents high in parental caring, only four of the eleven, or 36 percent, had a current physical or emotional diagnosed condition (such as high blood pressure, cancer, drug addiction). However, among those who had rated their parents low in parental caring, eight of the nine, or 89 percent, had a current physical or emotional diagnosed condition.

That in itself was an extraordinary finding. We then went on to wonder, if perceptions of parental love and caring, assessed in college, could predict future health with some degree of accuracy, was it also possible that perceptions of parental love and caring might influence the extent to which the men, unconsciously, were registering the presence of the interviewer's heart in their brains? That became one of the questions I explored in the new study.

Parental Love and Heart-Energy Registration

In the follow-up data collected in 1994, I computed the ARC-SEA analyses for the level of the interviewer's EKG in the subjects' EEG separately for the high- and low-parental-caring subjects. The results were frankly amazing.

What I found was that among the subjects who ranked their parental caring as high, there was clear evidence of waves in the EEG-SEAs of the subjects that were synchronized with the interviewer's EKG. In other words, if the subjects perceived their parents as loving when they were in college, they registered the presence of the interviewer's heart waves in their brain waves when they were mature adults.

In contrast, among the low-parental-caring subjects, the brain waves synchronized with the interviewer's EKG were both attenuated and delayed. In other words, it was as if the low-parental-caring subjects—who were physically and emotionally less healthy—weren't as receptive to the interviewer's heart EKG as the high-parental-caring subjects.

The EEG-SEA patterns were a bit weird, and I admit that at first I was somewhat dumbfounded. Recall that when we examined what a subject's heart waves looked like in the subject's brain waves, we observed that the waves were biggest in the back of the head and smallest in the front of the head. However, when I studied what the interviewer's heart waves looked like in the subject's brain waves, I observed that waves were biggest in the front of the head and smallest in the back of the head—exactly the opposite of the earlier results.

What could be going on here? This gets a little complicated, and it involves what is called "vector cardiology." Simply put, the heart does not generate a simple sphere of electrical signals like those gravitation-field spheres we imagined emerging around stars and planets. The three-dimensional form of the dynamically pulsating cardiac field is shaped more like an egg tilted on its side.

One explanation for why the person's EKG in their own EEG is larger in the back of their head than the front may relate to how the cardiac vectors are pointed, possibly oriented more toward the back of the head than toward the front. If this is the case, then when a person is facing us, for example, her or his physical heart is facing us. It's logical that if another person's cardiac vectors are like our cardiac vectors—and this seems to be the case—then from this vantage point, the effect of their heart waves on our brain waves would be reversed from the effect of our own heart waves on our brain waves.

There are two ways to test this theory—one completely impractical in the real world, the other eminently doable. The completely impractical procedure would be to rotate your head 180 degrees and see if the pattern of your EEG-SEAs reversed. Of course, you'd have to break your neck to do this, and you might not figure it was worth that. The eminently doable procedure would be to have the person facing you turn around and see if the pattern of their EKG-triggered effects on your EEG-SEAs reversed. That experiment is waiting to be done.

It's important not to lose the forest for the trees. The forest here is that one person's EKG waves can potentially be detected in another person's EEG waves. Though the effects are somewhat small, and individual differences seem to matter—such as one's perception of parental love and caring—the effects appear to be evident.

I believe that these effects are real partly because they were independently replicated by scientists at the Institute of HeartMath. A bottom line in science is for independent laboratories to conduct research; if a phenomenon found by one lab is real, other labs will be able to replicate the results, providing corroboration.

One More Surprising Finding—Recognizing Our Unique Heart's Signature

It turned out that each interview took two to three hours. As a result, I ended up watching two computers collecting EEGs and EKGs from two people simultaneously for hours at a time. Because I was recording both the interviewer's and the interviewee's EKGs simultaneously on both computers, I could see every heartbeat that both people experienced as two consecutive lines on each screen. Because the interviewer (Linda) was the same with each subject, I ended up becoming familiar with the shape of her EKG waves as contrasted with the subjects' EKG waves, which differed subtly from person to person.

Just as a musician learns with practice to discriminate ever finer subtleties in music and a radiologist learns to discriminate ever finer subtleties in X-rays, I was learning to discriminate ever finer subtleties in EKG waves. What I came to discover completely and utterly surprised me.

To my originally untrained eye, the EKGs all looked similar. However, by the time I had finished watching the tenth session comparing the interviewer's heart with the tenth interviewee's heart, my eye was becoming trained to discern the differences. The EKG waves were beginning to look more different than similar. I found that I could tell people apart by the precise pattern of their PQRST wave shapes. Yes, every healthy heartbeat has a PQRST waveform pattern. In one sense, every EKG looks the same. However, the relative shapes, sizes, durations, and ratios of the P waves, the QRS waves, and the T waves differed in a characteristic way from person to person.

Watching the PQRST wave patterns reminded me of watching faces. In one sense, all faces look the same. Every healthy face has two eyes, a nose, a mouth, yet each face is unique. Even identical twins have subtle differences in the relative shapes, sizes, and ratios of their eyes, noses, and mouths.

If our eyes can readily recognize faces, especially of our loved ones and the people we know best, who is to say that our bodies' energy systems can't recognize the cardiac-field forms of our loved ones and the people we know best—even if we can't put into words what we're detecting. This level of energy-pattern recognition may exist in most if not all of us.

In the same way that I didn't know I could detect, above chance, the presence of Justin's hand (chapter 4), it may be the case that I'm not aware that I can actually detect, above chance, the presence of my loved one's heart-field forms. Implicit energy perception, recognition, and memory may be the rule in nature, not the exception.

It's worth remembering that not too long ago, humans were unaware of the existence of what today we know as radio waves and TV waves. Until the twentieth century, our species had no idea that we were personally acting as antennas for these frequencies of electromagnetic fields that occurred spontaneously in nature and in the cosmos.

Let's entertain the possibility that this basic premise is true. Let's assume that all of us, to various degrees, have the natural abilities of implicit electromagnetic perception, recognition, and memory. Now, consider the first nine of months of our life. We all exist as a fetus in the womb of our mother. Our mother's EKG waves are bathing our emerging organism, beginning with the very act of creation when the egg and sperm join. As we grow from one cell to two cells to four cells to eight cells and ultimately to trillions of cells, our cells are constantly bathed in the electromagnetic fields generated by our mother's heart.

The claim that our cells are bathed in our mother's EKG waves is not speculation. It's fact. When a neonatal cardiologist attempts to record the fetus's EKG waves *in utero,* she does not see one being's EKG waves, but two, because the EKG waves of the mother travel through her fluids to the fetus, and conversely, the fetus's EKG waves travel through the mother's fluid and even reach the mother's brain.

Though I have not conducted this experiment, it's virtually 100 percent guaranteed that if we extended the ARC-SEA procedure and used the fetus's EKG as the ARC trigger, and the mother's EEG as the SEA, we would discover the presence of the fetus's EKG waves in the mother's EEG waves.

Think of a loving mother who really wants her baby, who has great love for the baby she is carrying, who spends time every day paying attention to her abdomen and even singing to her unborn child. Would we find that this mother's EEG waves were more strongly registering the EKG waves of her baby? Do mothers and babies create heart-brain energetic bonds with each other in the profound fluid intimacy of the mother's body?

The fact is that the intimate electromagnetic connection between the mother and baby often does not stop at birth. Mothers who breast-feed their babies hold them close. The sharing of heart energies is obviously amplified when mother and infant are in direct physical contact.

I remember the day it hit me that when two people hold hands and an EKG machine is placed between them, what we would see with the EKG machine is a combination of their EKG waves in the same channel. This happens 100 percent of the time. The fact is, when we make physical contact with a person—or an animal—there is increased conductivity of our electrical fields and our heart energies literally swim with each other.

If three people hold hands and complete a circuit, their three EKG waves mix together. You do not need a sophisticated ARC-SEA averaging system to witness this. It can be seen with the naked and untrained eye using a standard EKG machine.

One of the joys of doing research is envisioning experiments yet to be conducted. Imagine the following. We have two mothers and two daughters. We can call them mother A and daughter A, and mother B and daughter B. Let's assume that the A's have not met the B's. Also let's assume that both mothers have a loving and healthy relationship with their daughters.

Imagine that the mothers and daughters are blindfolded and kept in separate rooms. For the duration of the experiment, the subjects are not allowed to speak. To rule out odor as a possible sensory cue, imagine that the subjects will be wearing oxygen masks for the duration of the experiment. The subjects will be tested in pairs, sitting three feet from each other, while their EEGs and EKGs are monitored. Mother A will be tested with daughter A, daughter B, and also with mother B. Daughter A will be tested with mother A and with daughter B and mother B. ARC-SEAs will then be computed for all possible combinations.

Will we discover that mother A's EEG-SEAs will respond more strongly to her daughter's EKG-ARC than to daughter B's EKG-ARC or mother B's EKG-ARC? Will we find that mother B's EEG-SEAs will respond more strongly to her daughter's EKG-ARC than to daughter A's EKG-ARC or mother A's EKG-ARC?

I haven't done this experiment; as far as I know, no one has—it begs to be conducted. However, let's imagine that some version of this experiment has been conducted and that positive findings were obtained. Imagine that we have found that a loving mother's brain actually has the potential to implicitly recognize and respond to her loving daughter's heart energies. And let's not be sexist here. Let's imagine that this ability applies to loving sons and even, yes, loving fathers.

Would such findings make you smile? Would such findings open your mind and heart to the inspiring conclusion that we are all energetically interconnected to various degrees, not simply by electrostatic body-motion effects, but by our hearts' and even brains' electromagnetic fields?

We Experience the Heartbeats of All Things

If everything we call "matter"—the material world—is not simply generating and registering energy but is ultimately energy itself, it follows that then we humans are ultimately and fundamentally energy ourselves. Experiencing ourselves as living energy beings transforms our awareness of virtually everything.

As I write this, it's about 5:30 p.m. in Tucson and the evening sky is cloudy. Because I happen to love birds and also Native American art—which uses bird feathers extensively—I tend to use bird examples a lot. My attention is drawn once again by the half-dozen finches and sparrows busily jumping around my two thistle feeders.

Though I can't consciously sense their heartbeats, I now know that, in principle, their heartbeats are with me, just as my heartbeats are with them. We are, so to speak, swimming electromagnetically in one another's EKG energy fields.

If this simple exercise reminds you of what Native Americans and shamans have been saying for thousands of years about our natural relationship with animals, it's a memory worth cherishing.

There may be much more to our heart than its function as a mechanical pump.

> *If at first the idea is not absurd, then there is no
> hope for it.*
>
> —ALBERT EINSTEIN

Chapter 10

Your Body Can Affect TV Satellite Dishes

Though the idea from the previous chapter that your heart may affect someone else's brain might have seemed a bit far-fetched to you on first hearing, the idea that your heart—or more broadly, your body—might affect someone else's satellite dish may seem like the kind of absurd idea Einstein was referring to in the quote above.

But is it in fact possible that our energy fields interact with—and perhaps in some sense even communicate with—the energy fields not only of animals, plants, minerals, and crystals, but also of machines and technological devices?

And if that is actually happening, then perhaps it might follow that energetic interaction and communication is a fundamental, universal process of connection that occurs within every level of nature—from subatomic particles, through cells and biological beings, to planets, galaxies, and beyond.

In a limited sense, we now take part of this for granted every time we use a cell phone. We understand that these devices are intentionally designed to accurately register our voices—which are frequencies of sounds (energies)—and that these sound vibrations are converted into electromagnetic signals that are transmitted over wires, fiberoptic cables, and through space for the sake of human communication. In fact, the existence of two-way communications between the earth and "outer space" is not only accepted by astrophysics, it's a mainstay of telecommunications through the medium of satellite technology.

But it begins to sound absurd if we take this to the next step by asking, for example, Are we, in some way, in direct communication with satellite dishes themselves? If electromagnetic communication is really the rule and not the exception in the universe, then could we be in energetic communication with our TV technology?

You probably recognize that I would not raise such a ridiculous idea if I didn't have a compelling reason, combined with sound (no pun intended) evidence to justify it. As I keep pointing out, I'm metaphorically from Missouri. For me, scientific ideas not only need to be logical, they have to be demonstrable as well. I must be able to see them with my own eyes—or hear them with my own ears, or sense them with my own hands, and so forth—if I'm going to take them seriously.

Science is always on the lookout for new ways to measure things. The results are sometimes totally unexpected. We would never have imagined that our bodies, as well as the bodies of other animals, are constantly generating 12-gigahertz microwave signals—signals that can be detected by contemporary TV satellite technology.

Being Open to Surprises: From the *New York Times* to the Web

On August 17, 1993, the *New York Times* carried an article headlined "5000-mile Radio Telescope Set to Probe Depths of Time and Space." The article described a very long array of ten dish antennas, each eighty-two feet in diameter, spread across North America to the Caribbean—from Mauna Kea in Hawaii to St. Croix in the Virgin Islands.

According to the reporter, these antennas were "exquisitely synchronized" such that the instruments' resolving power—the smallest distance between two objects that could still be seen as separate from each other—was a "fraction of a milliarc-second," which in geometric terms (degrees of an angle) is extraordinarily tiny. The article explained that "with that kind of resolving power, an observer in New York City would be able to read a newspaper in San Francisco" and that the array was so sensitive that "any of the antennas could easily detect the faint radio waves emitted by the warm tissues of a human being." What? Human tissues emit "faint radio waves" that can be detected by a monster telescope?

I was intrigued by the mention that nearby animals caused major issues with the data from these telescopes. A bird flying past, for example, generated a significantly more powerful radio signal than the superfaint signals from deep space that the scientists were attempting to detect. To combat the problem, the signal-processing engineers had developed procedures for carefully removing this extraneous information.

To someone like me who is interested in measuring dynamic energies from living beings, the idea that telescopes developed for astrophysics were recording these signals was intriguing, to say the least. Moreover, the radio telescopes could measure the signals from a distance and track the momentary movements of a living system without attaching any electrodes.

It's sometimes said that one person's noise is another person's signal. Using the word "artifact" in the sense of a feature not naturally present but that is a product of an external agent, I like to say that one person's artifact is another person's fact. Having begun my undergraduate education as an electrical engineer, I could see potential applications of this radio-satellite-telescope technology to conventional biomedicine as well as frontier energy healing. However, being a seasoned professor at three universities, I recognized the virtual impossibility of getting permission to use a monster radio telescope designed for studying the heavens for my own more earthly purposes, which might well seem trivial to an astrophysicist.

These telescopes are huge, immobile, superexpensive, and fully dedicated to their research purposes. Being a realist, I concluded that I would never be able to raise the millions of dollars needed to purchase one for my own research. I would never have the opportunity to explore the possible power of using such technology for human-energy measurement and, by extension, distant human/machine electromagnetic communication.

My assumption, like many assumptions—sometimes called "ass-" umptions—turned out to be delightfully wrong. Five years after the

New York Times article was published, an item was placed on the Web by someone using the name "Jim Sky." The posting carried the title "12,000 Mhz Radio Telescope for $200." Now, 12,000 Mhz means 12,000 "mega" (million) hertz, which is simply another way of expressing 12 gigahertz—exactly the same frequency as the monster radio telescope that had stirred my imagination. I tracked down the author of the Web listing, who turned out to be Chuck Forster of the Society of Amateur Radio Astronomers (www.radiosky/12ghz.html). Showing a sense of humor, Forster's name for the system he had designed was "LBT"—for "Little Bitty Telescope."

In response to my e-mail, he wrote that he had been experimenting with an eighteen-inch TV dish antenna for a year; the complete system included the dish itself plus the device that detects the 12-gigahertz signals, called an LND. Forster mentioned that "the dish and LND have no problem detecting the difference between cold sky, the sun, warm bricks, or a person's body."

I could not believe what I was reading. If Forster was correct—and at that time it was a serious "if"—then his LBT with its little dish and signal processor could measure, from a distance, ultra-high-frequency signals emitted by the human body. Forster explained that his unit was not measuring infrared heat but rather ultra-high-frequency heat—in other words, energy—generated to varying degrees by all physical systems. That's the key phrase: "all physical systems." We're not simply talking here about human beings, or birds, or plants, or planets—we're speaking about ultra-high-frequency radio signals generated by all molecules, all atoms: everything that exists.

Can you imagine my excitement when I found this article on the Web? Whereas I could never raise the millions of dollars needed to purchase an MT (my own abbreviation for "Monster Telescope"), I could go to RadioShack, or the Web, and out of pocket purchase the parts needed to build an LBT based on Forster's design!

I wasted no time. One could even say I got slightly carried away, and instead of spending the reported two hundred dollars to build the LBT, I went a bit more elaborate, kicking in an extra hundred dollars. I purchased:

- An eighteen-inch digital satellite dish
- A portable and movable tripod-like stand to mount the dish
- An LND detector operating at 12 gigahertz, and
- A Channel Master signal-strength meter that measures the total signal coming out of the LND detector. This particular signal-strength meter had its own internal power supply—meaning it was battery operated, which made it more expensive than the model used by Forster.

The unit also included a speaker, which comes in very handy, in the same way as for the installer of a home digital satellite antenna when he's trying to aim the dish so as to maximize the strength of the signal picked up by the antenna. Instead of looking at the meter display to read the signal—which could be dangerous when he's standing on a roof and simultaneously manipulating the dish—he listens to the pitch of the audio signal. The speaker makes a sound from a "woo" to a "wee" as the signal strength increases from low to high, like a kind of biofeedback device, but in this case using a 12-gigahertz feedback device.

The equipment I ordered arrived in a week; I impatiently dropped everything else to connect the parts and try it out. My first task was to see if I could replicate what Forster claimed he saw—or more precisely, saw and heard.

Since he had been using his LBT for astrophysical demonstrations, he used the dish outside. He would point the dish at the sun, for example, and hear that the low-frequency "woo" rapidly jumped to a very-high-frequency "wee" as the needle on the meter of the Channel Master displayed the actual signal strength.

I lugged the LBT outside—on its stand, the dish was about six feet above the ground, taller than me. I first tried pointing toward and away from the sun. Sure enough, 100 percent of the time, the more directly I pointed the dish toward the sun, the higher the "wee" sound coming from the speaker. I tried pointing the dish at mountaintops, and clouds, and houses, and so forth, and observed and heard the relative changes in signal strength.

Every now and again, a bird would fly past the dish. Even if it was fifty or more feet away, sure enough, the signal I was hearing would increase in frequency.

However, for me the most memorable result came when I rotated the dish so that it pointed parallel to the ground, in a cold direction—*cold* meaning quiet in terms of background 12-gigahertz activity. Aimed like this, the background signal strength/sound was a "woo." I then walked fifty or so feet away. When I raised my hands about six feet in the air, hitting the hot spot of the dish, I could clearly hear Channel Master's speaker go from "woo" to "wee."

With the dish properly aimed, this effect happened 100 percent of the time. When I put one hand up instead of two, the "wee" decreased accordingly. When I began to walk closer to the dish, I heard the "wee" increase; when I walked farther away, I heard the "wee" decrease.

My invisible ultra-high-frequency radio waves were extending out into space—at least fifty or one hundred feet into space. My 12-gigahertz waves were somehow making contact with the dish, which collected my signals and focused on the LND. The dish and I were connected by waves that I never knew I had.

For a while I was frankly euphoric. A technology that had become relatively inexpensive because of its mass-market success had the potential to reveal something fundamental about our dynamical energetic nature. Moreover, I imagined that, in principle, the technology might be developed into a sensitive tool for measuring changing patterns of 12-gigahertz frequencies associated with our bodies.

I will never forget the moment that I carried the unwieldy dish on its stand back inside to replicate what I had observed outside and discovered instead, to my amazement and disappointment, that it stopped working!

More Surprises: The Challenge of Bringing the LBT into the Laboratory

No matter where I pointed the dish inside a building—in my lab or in my house—I could not detect the presence of my hands. Outside it worked, inside it did not. I could sort of get the LBT to work if I pointed the dish out a window toward a cold spot, with nothing that gives off 12-gigahertz waves in the antenna's line of sight, and then put my hand in front of the dish. That worked sometimes, but it was clearly not reliable.

My dreams for a practical application of the LBT seemed dashed. Yes, I could use the LBT for demonstration purposes—out of doors—but not for practical research purposes inside my home or lab.

Then one morning, as I was getting ready for my day (in the shower, to be precise), a thought popped into my head, a simple thought: "Get rid of the dish." I said out loud to myself, "Get rid of the dish?" And then it hit me. *Of course.* What was the dish doing? It was collecting faint signals and concentrating them. The inside of a building was generating too many signals, drowning out the ability of the dish to sense just my hand.

I was reminded that on a cloudless night when the moon isn't visible, if we're away from city lights, we can see thousands of stars with the naked eye, but once the sun comes up, the stars seem to disappear. The light of the closest star, the sun, is so bright that it blocks our ability to see the thousands of dim stars that are actually still there.

This was the reason why in order to best sense the presence of my hands outside, it was necessary for me to find a cold spot to point the dish. Indoors, the dish was collecting all sorts of 12-gigahertz signals generated by the walls, ceiling, floors, furniture, and so forth (recall that all physical objects generate ultra-high-frequency signals). However, if I got rid of the dish and simply used the LND by itself, the background 12-gigahertz activity would be dramatically reduced relative to what the LND was receiving.

The LBT was in my study. As you can probably guess, I hurried there. I unscrewed the LND detector from the dish and then tested its ability to register my hands.

Eureka. I could not believe what I was seeing and hearing. With the LND sitting on my desk, pointing toward the ceiling, when I moved my hands approximately twelve inches over the LND, the sound went from "woo" to "wee." This happened every time I tried. The closer I moved my hands to the LND, the higher the frequency of the "wee."

I explored the area around the LND, discovering where it was most and least sensitive. Without the dish, it showed the greatest signal strength when my hands were approximately six inches from the LND. If I moved my hands too close, it saturated the LND or the meter.

Finally it was possible to investigate what the LND was detecting.

For example, a fundamental question was whether the LND was detecting electrostatic charges. It was possible, though not probable, that although the device was designed to record 12-gigahertz activity, it was being influenced by electrostatic charges on my hands (recall the discussion of electrostatic body motion effects in chapter 3).

How could I test this? One way was to use something that was not my hand, something that had a larger electrostatic charge than my hand. It turns out that fur dusters can carry a sizable electrostatic charge. I purchased a fur duster—a ball of fur on a stick—and tried it with the LND. There was virtually no change in the "woo" as I moved it toward and away from the LND. But when I moved my hand in the vicinity of the LND, the "woo" changed to "wee," and as I moved my hand toward the LND, the "wee" increased further.

Meanwhile, when I used the fur duster with my portable EEG amplifier and electrodes, the electrostatic-motion effects were huge. This verified that the fur duster was creating large electrostatic-field effects and that these effects were not detected by the LND.

Another fundamental question was whether the LND was detecting infrared heat. Forster had claimed it was not, but I needed to examine this myself.

To test the effect, I placed a half-inch-thick notebook between my hand and the LND. If the device was detecting infrared heat, the notebook would serve as an effective insulator, greatly reducing the impact of this heat on the instrument. However, if the LND was detecting ultra-high-electromagnetic signals that readily pass through walls, ceilings, and, yes, notebooks, there should be no attenuation in the strength of the signal generated by my hand as sensed by the LND. I observed that the shifting from "woo" to "wee" was virtually the same whether or not the notebook was placed between my hand and the LND.

When I picked up the LND and moved it along my body, it received signals from my head, chest, abdomen—every part of my body.

Though the promise seemed significant, there were still questions needing to be answered. To what extent, for example, was I serving as an antenna for 12-gigahertz signals being generated by the walls, ceiling, floor, furniture, and so forth? To what extent was I serving as an antenna for radio and TV signals in the environment? How much of what the

LND was measuring from my hands was being generated by my physical being versus being amplified by my physical being? While physics clearly tells us that every material object, including our bodies, generates high-frequency electromagnetic waves, physics also tells us that any material object can serve as an antenna/receiver/generator of external electromagnetic waves as well. And that complicates trying to draw firm conclusions from this experiment.

The truth is that to perform this kind of research properly, it would be necessary to conduct the research in an electrically shielded environment, in order to determine how much of the signal is self-generated versus detected and amplified from the environment. I did not have access to a suitably shielded laboratory. Given that the LBT project was something I was doing as a sideline, with my own funds, I had to put it aside.

The Message for All of Us

There is no substitute for being outdoors—with the vista of the Tucson mountains as a backdrop—placing your hand in a special spot above your head, and hearing a meter device attached to a TV dish one hundred feet away metaphorically singing "I sense you."

There is no substitute for being indoors—in a laboratory at a university or in your home—placing a notebook between your hand and a detector that has been removed from the TV dish, and hearing the device connected to the detector a foot away metaphorically singing "I can still sense you."

In the near future, the meaning of this experience may be made less metaphorical. The device can be designed so that instead of generating the sound "wee," it generates patterns of sounds that sing "I sense you" and even "I still sense you."

Imagine what it would be like to experience being with a device whose original purpose was to detect 12-gigahertz signals coming from satellites in space but was now detecting 12-gigahertz signals coming from you, and the device was singing "I sense you." How do you think your experience of technology and your sense of connection with technology might change?

The meaning of energy detection would immediately be conveyed to your mind and heart.

The truth is, when you experience yourself as a generator of 12-gigahertz activity, your experience of yourself changes. What do our hearts, brains, bodies, and satellite dishes have in common? They are all interconnected to one another by invisible electromagnetic fields.

> *Hope sees the invisible, feels the intangible, and*
> *achieves the impossible.*
>
> —ANONYMOUS

Chapter 11

How Healers' Hands Affect
Magnetic-Field Meters

Since we all have energy, and hands, we all have the inherent natural power to be energy healers. We all have the possibility of learning how to harness this power for our own healing, the healing of our loved ones and friends, and even the healing of the planet. I hope you will keep this thought with you as you continue reading these pages.

Generally speaking, if anything powers the possibility of health, it is hope. Patients hope to be healthy. Health-care practitioners hope to help patients become healthy. Scientists hope to understand how healing works, and also how healers work.

In the process of writing this chapter, I came to realize that it's possible to be filling the three roles of patient, provider, and scientist all at the same time.

An old back injury has flared up, and I am currently experiencing pain. I am at this moment being a patient. Yet I am on a deadline, so I must continue writing.

However, as someone who was trained to be a clinical health psychologist and later learned energy healing, and whose values include practicing what I preach, I am being mindful of my back. I am trying to practice what I have learned as a provider. I am reminding myself not to

103

sit still for too long in any one position and to relax my back at frequent intervals. I am also sending relaxing, loving energy to my back, not only with my mind, but every now and again, with my hands as well. Hence, I am being a health-care practitioner—to myself—as well as a patient.

Finally, I am writing a chapter about how the hands of healers can affect magnetic-field meters. Not only am I writing about research, I am remembering my particular history of being a scientist who participated in the discovery you are going to read about.

It's my conscious hope that as a patient, I will become pain free again; that as a health-care practitioner, in this case to myself, I will help heal my back; and that as a scientist, I will be able to convey to you the details, and delights, of discovering how a healer's hands can affect a magnetic-sensing device that in turn helps us understand how healing hands work.

Part of transforming how we understand and experience the world, including ourselves, is to remind ourselves at regular intervals what Einstein knew in his mind and heart. Everything that is, is *energy*—or more precisely, is fields of energy. What we experience with our limited senses as matter is actually *organized fields of energy.* Therefore what is "real" is not matter but fields. As Einstein put it, "The field is the only reality." Though the concept of a field is abstract and can only be described as variables in physical equations, we can visualize aspects of fields with the aid of contemporary technology.

Extra-Low-Frequency Vibrating Fields and the Process of Healing

Living systems generate a vast variety of energy-field frequencies, most of which are invisible to the naked eye. Some of these frequencies are very high, such as the 12-gigahertz frequencies detected by TV satellite dishes. Other frequencies are very low, such as alpha brain waves, which vibrate in the range of 8 to 12 hertz—8 to 12 cycles per second. In the electronic terminology these are called "ELFs," for "extra-low frequencies."

Dr. James Oschman, the author of *Energy Medicine* and *Energy Medicine in Therapeutics and Human Performance,* is a world leader in both the science and art of energy healing. He is a leading light in this area and is an inspiration to scientists and practitioners alike. Trained in biophysics, biochemistry, and biology, he knows his bioelectromagnetics. For twenty years his specialty was electron microscopy. Then, as he describes it, "I developed a back problem, probably from bending over microscopes for long periods." Eventually he found his way to a combined body-manipulation and energy-healer technique called Structural Integration, which in Oschman's words "changed my life."

In an interview in 2002 titled "Science and the Human Energy Field" for the *Reiki News Magazine,* Jim explained:

> In addition to helping my back, the practitioner [Peter Melchior] told me about a whole field of research into human energy that I had not encountered during my years in academics. I was curious about what happened to the various fascinating and important discoveries he told me about, and why they never came up in courses or seminars or conversations in academic circles. It seemed that for some reason nobody wanted to talk about energy. This was strange to me. Following this curiosity led me into the field of energy medicine. I met many therapists who seemed to know a lot about energy, and I was curious about what science, if any, there was to explain their observations.

This particular interview is one of the friendliest, finest, most informative introductions to the use of bioelectromagnetic devices for healing, as well as the measurement of bioelectromagnetic fields. You can read the complete interview at http://www.reiki.org/Download/OschmanReprint2.pdf.

Oschman presents a table in his books that is particularly informative:

HEALING EFFECTS OF SPECIFIC FREQUENCIES
(FREQUENCY WINDOWS OF SPECIFICITY)

Frequency	Effects
2 Hz	Nerve regeneration, neurite outgrowth from cultured ganglia
7 Hz	Bone growth
10 Hz	Ligament healing
15, 20, and 72 Hz	Decreased skin necrosis, stimulation of capillary formation and fibroblast proliferation
25 and 50 Hz	Synergistic effects with nerve growth factor

The table refers to specific frequencies of electromagnetic fields and their healing effects, generated by specially designed devices used by energy-oriented complementary and alternative (CAM) practitioners, as well as by some conventional physicians. Note that 2 hertz, which is the frequency of the brain delta waves of deep sleep, is especially good for nerve regeneration and growth (raising a question about whether this is why we need to sleep). A frequency of 10 hertz, which is the frequency of the alpha brain waves of relaxation, is good for ligament healing. And 15, 20, and 72 hertz, frequencies of the brain waves connected with heightened alertness (beta waves), are good for blood flow (for example, capillary formation) and immune function (fibroblast immune-cell proliferation).

That leaves us with a question: If external magnetic fields generated by electronic devices vibrating at these frequencies can produce the specific healing effects listed in the table, is it possible that these same frequencies are generated by a healer's hands when he is "sending" energy?

Figure 11.1, also provided by Dr. Oschman, was recorded by a Dr. John Zimmerman from the hand of a practitioner of therapeutic touch, a healing method developed by nursing professor Dr. Dolores Krieger. Zimmerman used a SQUID, mentioned earlier, which is a supersensitive device for measuring magnetic fields.

You can see that the frequency was not steady, but varied from less than 1 hertz to approximately 30 hertz, with most of the activity in the range of 7 to 8 hertz. Each bracket represents a one-second window of time. You can see how the different windows reflect various frequencies—15 hertz, 10 hertz, 7 hertz, and 2 hertz—and how they correspond to physiological healing.

Because SQUIDs are very expensive and require large magnetically shielded rooms in order to take measurements, there has been very little research to date attempting to replicate and extend Zimmerman's observations with healers.

Scientists seek to record signals with as little noise as possible. Laboratory scientists tend to be purists—they like to do things "right." I put "right" in quotes because scientists, in their efforts to collect clean data, sometimes forget the real world. The truth is that healers practice their

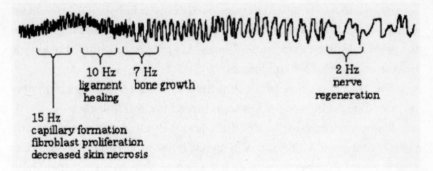

10 Hz   7 Hz
ligament bone growth
healing

2 Hz
nerve
regeneration

15 Hz
capillary formation
fibroblast proliferation
decreased skin necrosis

Figure 11.1 Changes in Extra-Low-Frequency Magnetic Fields Coming from a Healer's Hand during Healing

art in all kinds of environments—in homes, occasionally in places as unlikely as subways, and in hospitals—which are, unfortunately, often electromagnetically polluted from the wealth of electronic equipment present in patients' rooms. Energy-healing effects can therefore be observed under conditions that are less than optimal.

One conclusion might be that if SQUIDs require environments that are free of magnetic-field noise to reveal Zimmerman-like signals, and healers do not work in magnetically shielded environments, then whatever effects healers have can't be explained in terms of biomagnetic phenomena. Maybe healing-energy effects are just placebo or mind-body effects fostered by the combined hopes and expectations of the healers and the people they treat.

How could we bring biomagnetic measurement into the real world? Would it be possible to determine whether healers' hands operated magnetically in everyday environments?

Being forever hopeful, I am constantly looking for new devices to measure electromagnetic fields. I search for devices that are typically designed for a purpose other than energy-healing research but that might be applied to this work. With the advent of digital technology and enhanced materials science, spurred by the need to measure possible magnetic-field pollution in buildings (caused by wiring, computers, and so forth), portable magnetic-field signal-strength meters have been developed that turn out to be very sensitive.

One of these handheld devices is a three-axis ELF digital gaussmeter (figure 11.2). It has a digital display that presents numbers ranging from 0.1 milligauss (that's one ten-thousandth of a gauss, a unit of magnetic field strength) to 1,999 milligauss.

For use in our research, we purchased one of these gaussmeters from www.lessemf.com for less than three hundred dollars.

It's not as sensitive as a SQUID, and it doesn't produce an analog output that would provide a dynamic frequency curve like the data observed by Zimmerman. Also it's not possible to use a hand-held gaussmeter for capturing small changes in amplitudes and frequencies of the tiny biomagnetic fields. What the meter displays are moment-to-moment changes in total magnetic-field signal strength over a wide range of amplitudes and frequencies—the *sums* of the magnetic-field signal strength. In this sense it's like the Channel Master signal-strength meter described in the previous chapter—both meters provide sums of signal strengths occurring in a specific frequency range.

If the magnetic-field-strength meter is brought to an area in a lab or home that has low background magnetic activity, so the meter is reading less than 1.0 milligauss (recall that it goes as low as 0.1 milligauss), it's possible to track tiny changes in magnetic-field strength over time.

To detect whether changes are occurring in the magnetic fields coming from a healer's hands, a simple, quantitative procedure would be just to count the number of times the reading on the digital meter changes in a fixed period of time. If we count the number of numeric changes each minute over a period of time, for example, and we witness that this number has increased or decreased, this would mean that the dynamics of the healer's magnetic fields are indeed changing.

Figure 11.2 A Portable Meter That Measures Extra-Low-Frequency Magnetic Fields in the Environment

Is this an ideal procedure for measuring changes in magnetic-field frequencies? Of course not. However, does this mean that we should lose hope in employing such a device for investigating magnetic fields coming from the hands of healers? Absolutely not.

Meanwhile, did I have enough hope to prod me to conduct such an experiment? Truthfully, no. I was saved from that. Fate conspired to bring a new colleague to my laboratory who was filled with hope for such technology, and she had the time and energy to give it a fair test.

Putting a Portable Digital Magnetic-Field-Strength Meter to the Test

In 2003, Dr. Melinda Connor, a skilled PhD clinical psychologist who also happened to be a gifted energy healer, was admitted as a postdoctoral fellow to the Arizona Complementary and Alternative Medicine Research Training Program at the University of Arizona, a program headed by Dr. Iris Bell and funded by the NCCAM (National Center for Complementary and Alternative Medicine) of the NIH (National Institutes of Health).

During her work under this program, Melinda was given the opportunity to pursue her research dream: to explore different ways of measuring energy healing in master healers. I was her faculty mentor. In the process of our early discussions, I shared with her the possibility of using state-of-the-art digital magnetic-field-strength meters to detect purported changes in magnetic fields coming from a healer's hands.

Melinda was like a young kid—and we brought out childlike excitement in each other. She requested that we order such a meter, on the promise that she would play with it. The meter was ordered, and Melinda played. She tried it on herself as well as on some of her healer colleagues. She observed that in settings of low magnetic noise—especially when the meter registered less than 1.0 milligauss—during one-minute periods of time when she was consciously intending to "run" (or "send" or "channel") energy, the meter registered an increase in the number of changes in magnetic-field strength. Presuming that this was not the result of some unrecognized artifact, like moving or touching the meter, the results implied that Melinda and her colleagues were producing alterations in the magnetic fields coming from their hands sufficient to show up on the magnetic-field meter.

We designed a formal experiment to test this hypothesis, recruiting seventeen practitioners skilled in Reiki—which, again, is a form of energy healing that originated in Japan and has become widely used internationally. For a given trial, the meter was put in front of a Reiki healer, who placed one hand on the table a few inches from it. Each trial consisted of a one-minute baseline period, during which the healer simply relaxed, and a one-minute "running energy" condition, during which she attempted to channel Reiki energy and send it through her hand. Meanwhile Melinda or one of her two assistants would sit with the subject, giving instructions and silently counting each time the number on the digital display changed during the one-minute baseline trials and the running energy trials.

We ran a total of four trials per healer—two with the left hand and two with the right. The number of magnetic-field changes per minute were entered into a spreadsheet and analyzed.

The results were clear and dramatic. Figure 11.3 presents the findings for each hand separately. You can see that the baseline trials averaged around thirty to thirty-five magnetic-field changes per minute. This increased to forty-five to fifty-five magnetic-field changes per minute when the healers were running energy, a highly significant change.

It's one thing to imagine the possibility that a relatively inexpensive portable device can be affected by a healer's hands and might be sensitive enough to detect changes. It's quite another actually to conduct an experiment with a relatively low probability of success like this one, and discover that the experiment actually worked.

Experiments That Do Not Work

The life of a scientist includes experiments that work as planned as well as experiments that can't be replicated or do not work at all. My colleagues and I have conducted a series of experiments to determine if the absorption of gamma rays—cosmic rays measured with a sensitive gamma-ray detector—could be used to measure the effects of energy healings. It had been reported in the literature that not only do human

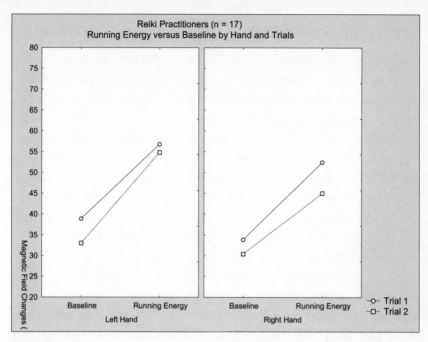

Figure 11.3 Results of 17 Reiki Practitioners, Baseline vs. Running Energy

beings absorb gamma rays, but healers who practice polarity therapy actually increase their rate of gamma-ray absorption.

We discovered, quite by accident, that human beings as well as other living systems, including plants, generate or emit high-frequency X-rays in addition to absorbing gamma rays. X-rays, including high-frequency X-rays, vibrate at a lower frequency than gamma rays. It is possible that the emission of the X-rays is caused in part by what physicists call "fluorescence"—in this case, a slowing down of the frequency of gamma waves as they interact with matter.

We have replicated the general pattern of gamma-ray absorption and high-frequency X-ray emission effects many times—in nonhealers and healers alike. Yet we have been unable to discover a reliable increase in gamma-ray absorption or an increase in high-frequency X-ray emission as a function of healing. Simply stated, the healing portion of this experiment has not worked.

Replication and Extension of the ELF Observations

The heart of science is replication. For me, it is a bottom line. Would the association between Reiki healers' "running energy" and increased ELF changes in micromagnetic fields replicate and extend to healers practicing other healing techniques?

Melinda and I were both eager to see if the ELF findings could be replicated. With the gracious support of a grant from the BSW (Body Spirit Wisdom) Foundation, we were able to conduct a comprehensive psychological and energetic evaluation of practitioners whom I like to refer to as "master healers." The funds covered the cost of the research assistants, equipment, and supplies necessary to collect the data.

Healers flew to Tucson from around the country, and each was tested for five days. Every practitioner gave up a full week of clinical income (as well as covering his or her own expenses) because they believed in this pioneering research. We collected a battery of self-report, biophysical, and psychophysiological measures—some conventional and well established, others exploratory, frontier, and controversial. Included in the battery of data was the recording of magnetic-field changes from healers' hands, following the experimental protocol we had developed.

The results for fifteen master healers are displayed in figure 11.4. You can see that the baseline trials on average ranged from thirty to thirty-five magnetic-field changes per minute, as in the original trial. But the number of magnetic-field changes when running energy, which were found to be forty-five to fifty-five per minute in the original trial, registered approximately sixty to seventy-five per minute for these master healers.

Though these measurements are not as precise or pure as what's possible to obtain with a SQUID in a magnetically shielded laboratory, they are clearly significant in terms of magnitude and reliability. Moreover, these measurements are clinically meaningful because they point out how a healer's magnetic fields can operate out in the real world of healing.

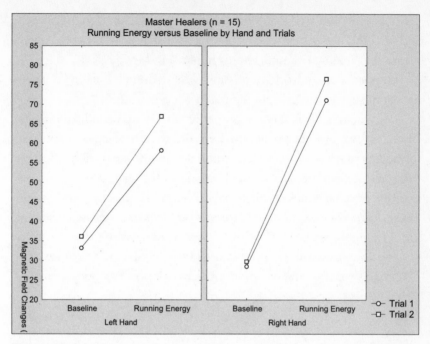

Figure 11.4 Results of 15 Master Healers, Baseline vs. Running Energy

Are Magnetic Fields Healing?

These magnetic-field-change experiments were not designed to address the question of whether magnetic fields heal. Our experiments were implemented to determine whether the kinds of magnetic fields already documented to promote healing in biophysics and bioelectromagnetics, and published in scientific journals like *Bioelectromagnetics* and the *Journal of Alternative and Complementary Medicine,* were emitted by the hands of healers.

We realized that if a relatively simple and cost-effective measurement device existed that could quantify the magnetic fields of healers, then a world of research and healing possibilities would be opened. As the technology improves and the prices of the devices continue to fall, all of us will eventually be able, if we so choose, to use portable energy-measuring meters to help us monitor and develop our abilities to become effective energy healers. Playing with such meters offers the possibility not only of fostering self-discovery but of accomplishment and fun. And like the process of playing an instrument, it can become a means for creating beautiful energy music.

It appears that a world of possibility may soon be opening not only for scientists and healers, but ultimately for everyone.

Because this book focuses primarily on research conducted in our laboratory, we are not presenting here the wealth of experiments performed by numerous investigators that document the healing effects of external oscillating magnetic fields on neurons, ligaments, fibroblasts, and cancer cells. James Oschman's books *Energy Medicine* and *Energy Medicine in Therapeutics and Human Performance* review these findings in a highly readable, clear, and inspiring manner. If the present discussion intrigues you, be prepared to be enlightened as you explore Oschman's writings and experience the wonders of magnetic healing.

> *Human beings, vegetables, or comic dust—we all*
> *dance to a mysterious tune, intoned in the distance*
> *by an invisible piper.*

> —ALBERT EINSTEIN

Chapter 12

How Healers Affect the Invisible Light from Plants

You may find this hard to believe, but it is accepted scientific fact: Most light is invisible to our eyes. We are blind to more than 99.999 percent of the light that actually exists in the universe.

Our retinal cells only resonate with a tiny slice of the band of energy frequencies that make up the total electromagnetic pie. If you imagine that the total band of electromagnetic frequencies is represented by the height of the Empire State Building, how tall would the slice of the band of frequencies be that you can see? Would it be ten stories high, five stories high, one story high, or one foot high? None of those: something much smaller. The band you can see is much less than the height of a grain of sand. Were it not for advances in science and the evolution of technology, most of the universe would be unknown to us.

And yet, what we do see is beyond magnificent. When we pause and take in our surroundings, the sight can be overwhelmingly beautiful, completely filling our consciousness. As I write these words, I can look out at the lush desert vegetation in my backyard. Even though the view through my study window shows me a span of space only some fifty feet wide, one hundred feet deep, and maybe fifty feet high (my window looks out on a small hill), within this relatively small spread, I see a landscape almost too detailed to recount. Hundreds of thousands of leaves—most of them smaller than an inch long. Tens of thousands of shades of green and brown, comprising the basic colors of desert trees, cacti, and grasses. Tens of thousands of pebbles, rocks, and boulders, some smaller than an ant, others larger than an antelope. I can see that no two pebbles, rocks, or boulders have the identical shape. I can see the water flowing across the four tiers of my natural rock waterfalls— the colors and patterns complex and constantly changing.

If my eyes were not restricted to the tiny slice of frequencies that constitute this vast conscious experience, my awareness would be overwhelmed. As it is, my mind would be readily overwhelmed by the complexity of just this small landscape if I thought too hard about it.

Ponder this: At night, we can have an experience of pitch darkness. Imagine being out camping in a lush forest of aspens and pines; the sun has set and there's no moon. You're deep in the woods away from street lights, cars, and fires. You know that there's grass underfoot, but when you look down, all you experience is a deep blackness. Your perception of darkness is not an accurate representation of reality.

Physics tells us that all objects that have temperature emit a spectrum of light in the range called infrared, meaning that the frequency of these electromagnetic fields is below (infra) what we consciously experience as the color red. If the human retinal cells and nervous system were designed to resonate with the infrared spectrum, you would see not only the grass glowing brightly, but you would see everything on the ground glowing as well—including the dirt, pebbles, rocks, bugs, your shoes, leaves, pinecones fallen from the trees, and so forth.

Physics tells us, in no uncertain terms, that everything that has temperature—everything that "is"—is constantly and dynamically emitting frequencies of electromagnetic signals (light) in the infrared spectrum: in the universe, there is actually no darkness. That infinite network or matrix of electromagnetic fields crossing one another in all directions in the so-called vacuum of space carries information of frequencies within the entire electromagnetic pie—including 12 gigahertz discussed in the previous chapter—not just the tiny slice we can consciously experience. The vacuum is literally filled with light.

Under special circumstances, people may sense the reality of this light. People whose hearts have stopped beating and who have effectively "died," but who have then been successfully revived, sometimes report having had a near-death experience. One of the common characteristics of the experience is an extraordinarily bright light—typically beautiful, peaceful, and loving.

Some neuroscientists have attempted to explain this experience as being caused by a misfiring of the visual portion of the brain—the occipital cortex—due the cessation of blood flow, thereby generating the illusion of light. However, this speculation is inconsistent with what actually happens following the cessation of blood flow to the brain. Dr. Pim van Lommel explains in his 2001 article in the journal *Lancet* that within ten seconds of the time that the heart stops beating, the EEG of the brain goes completely flat—meaning that the brain is actually showing no evidence of neural firing. Van Lommel argues therefore that neural misfiring cannot be the explanation of the near-death experiences.

The fact is, our eyes actually limit our perception of light. They focus our consciousness not only on a small slice of frequencies but in a specific direction as well. In my case, right now my eyes are focused on the screen in front of me rather than on the Native American artwork to my left or right or the books behind my back. So the near-death experience might actually be a more accurate perception of how physical reality, which is electromagnetic reality, actually exists. This is further evidence that there is more to the universe than meets the eye.

Our perception of light is not only limited to a tiny subset of frequencies. Our consciousness is further limited to a tiny subset of intensities of energies that make up the dynamics of the electromagnetic frequencies that our eyes can detect. Just as we can't see the vast ranges of infrared frequencies and below on the low end, and ultraviolet frequencies and above on the high end, we can't see the vast ranges of weak intensities of light that are below our luminal threshold on the low end and the strong intensities of light that are many levels above our saturation threshold.

Returning to our example of being in the woods in the "dark," not only do you fail to see the infrared light of everything literally glowing in the dark, but you also fail to see the light in the visible spectrum of frequencies that is too weak in intensity to be perceived normally. As you are about to learn, all matter, especially biological matter—what is conventionally called "living" matter—emits dynamic patterns of biophoton light that is sufficiently weak to be invisible to the naked eye but can be made visible with the aid of contemporary supersensitive cameras.

As long as I can remember, I have been fascinated with the invisible—with things I could not see with the naked eye. My personal rabbit-ears antenna experience as a young boy recounted in chapter 3 may have been an early turning point for my realizing that just because something was invisible did not make it unreal. As an undergraduate, I became fascinated with subliminal perception and unconsciousness awareness as well as perceptual illusions. I came to appreciate that science was partly in the business of making the invisible visible.

Optical Sciences and Astrophysics Meet Botany and Biology

It's not well known or accepted in the United States that all biological systems generate coherent patterns of light called biophotons. This research was originally developed in Russia, notably by Dr. Alexander Gurwitsch in the 1920s. His research apparently created a high level of excitement: within twelve years, more than six hundred experiments had been published documenting the effects of invisible light on the growth and functioning of cells. In Gurwitsch's era, light-sensing detectors were not sufficiently sensitive to register the light; rather, the light was inferred by the behavior of cells that were experimentally allowed or prevented from communicating with one another via optical means.

If any single person has brought the biophoton phenomenon to light, it is Dr. Fritz Popp in Germany. For more than three decades, he and his colleagues have recorded biophoton emission in plants, bacteria, and animals using supersensitive photo-multiplier tubes that can record single photons of light. (It's now established that the origin of these biophotons is subatomic: When electrons move between energy states during chemical reactions as part of metabolic processes, photons may either be absorbed or emitted. A major source of photons is the breaking down of larger molecules into smaller ones, such as in the production of oxygen and free radicals in the body.)

The advantage of a photo-multiplier tube is that in a pitch black environment, it can record moment-to-moment changes in these chemically based, extraordinarily weak emissions of light.

Incidentally, there's a downside to using a photo-multiplier tube: it measures light received in only one location—the location of the detector. The image or picture of an entire object emitting light can't be captured with a single photo-multiplier tube. It would take many hundreds of photo-multiple tubes to create a two-dimensional image of an object "glowing in the dark."

I have had a long-standing fascination with astrophysics, and I try to keep up with advances in technology for visualizing the universe. We have already discussed the use of radio telescopes to visualize invisible properties of the universe, and Forster's development of the LBT—the Little Bitty Telescope—which not only registers things astrophysical but things biological, such as birds and people, as well. Following my research with the LBT for detecting biological systems, I began to wonder whether advances in supersensitive digital cameras used in astrophysics to visualize distant galaxies and stars might be applied to the imaging of biophotons emitted by plants or the hands of healers.

The best of these cameras can cost many hundreds of thousands of dollars. They are typically supercooled to minus one hundred degrees centigrade, which is one hundred degrees centigrade colder than the temperature needed to freeze water. I knew that I could never borrow a camera that was used in astronomy and attached to an expensive optical telescope, in order to use it for biophoton imaging. I also knew that I could never raise the funds to experiment with this possibility.

However, in reading newsstand astronomy magazines, I discovered that a few companies sold supersensitive cameras for a few thousand dollars, and one of these companies was located in Tucson. I visited the company and tried to convince them to loan me a camera so that I could attempt to capture images of, say, geranium leaves placed in a light-tight box. From the calculations they made, they concluded that their cameras would not be sensitive enough to detect the levels of bio-photon release described by Popp and colleagues. It turned out that their calculations were correct.

Though I was not optimistic that I could ever test this possibility, I nonetheless never gave up hope. As it turned out, fate intervened in a most curious way. I had the privilege to meet, and then mentor, Dr. Kathy Creath, a distinguished research professor from what was then called the Optical Sciences Center (now the College of Optical Sciences) at the University of Arizona, where I'm also a faculty member. Dr. Creath is an authority on dynamical interferometry—a technique for measuring the surfaces of objects at very high resolutions.

My mentoring of Kathy did not involve optics; it involved psychology and energy healing. Kathy had decided to get a second PhD in music, and she wanted to do an experiment-based dissertation. Her dream was to integrate three of her interests—science, music, and healing—and she wanted to do something usually considered undoable: she wanted to complete her dissertation in less than a year.

It occurred to me that maybe she should consider the possibility of exploring the effects of music on the germination of seeds. Not only did Kathy like this idea, her dissertation committee accepted it as well. I was able to raise the funds for Kathy to complete five experiments on the effects of music—and healing intention—on the germination of seeds. Kathy and I discovered that gentle flute music provided for okra and zucchini seeds actually resulted in their germinating more quickly. We published a paper on her findings in 2004 in the *Journal of Alternative and Complementary Medicine.*

One day I happened to share with her my interest in the possibility of obtaining biophoton images of plants and people, and I asked her if she knew anyone in the Optical Sciences Center who had access to a supercooled low-light digital camera. It turned out that an optical-sciences colleague and former fellow graduate student of hers, Dr. Arthur Gmitro, had just received an NSF grant that included the purchase of a $100,000 super-low-light digital camera system for the purpose of exploring its potential applications to biology and radiology. His studies involved the use of fluorescent dyes that made specific areas and processes of biological systems glow in the dark. I wanted to see whether we could use this equipment to measure spontaneous light naturally generated and emitted by living biological systems.

As you might imagine, I was thrilled to learn about the camera and set out to convince Kathy that she should ask Arthur if we could borrow some time with his camera for our biophoton imaging, perhaps using the camera during off hours. Arthur was persuaded by the research possibility, he appreciated the science behind the study, and he trusted Kathy—who had the expertise to run the equipment and to mentor me in how to use it.

What transpired was an adventure of discovery that forever changed my consciousness of invisible living energy in a living energy universe.

Plants and Hands Glow in the Dark

Though I never had a green thumb, I quickly came to love plants—partly because they had certain research advantages. First, the university didn't expect me to ask for approval from its Human Subjects Committee or its Animal Subjects Committee before conducting plant research. Plants don't need to sign subject consent forms, they almost never sue, and I've never heard of a professor being plagued by a plants' rights group for abuse of our friends the flowers. (For the record, despite poking a little gentle fun in the preceding, I'm a strong advocate of protecting the rights of humans, animals—and, yes, even plants—and I completely agree with the spirit and requirements of human and animal subjects committees.)

For another thing, plants are readily available. Kathy might call me about doing an experiment. We would decide which subjects we wanted to work with—geraniums and ferns, say, or string beans and cucumbers, or whatever—and then a quick trip to a local nursery or supermarket, and we'd be ready.

On top of that, plants are apparently quite happy to sit still for long periods of time in the dark. They're normally sedentary, and they are used to nightly periods of low light. We quickly discovered that biophoton imaging required taking pictures in the pitch black using exposure lengths that could range from minutes to hours in duration, which demanded complete immobility—something that our plant subjects provided, seemingly without objection.

What we discovered was unabashedly amazing and enthralling. Plants and people really glow in the dark. There is a fundamental generation of light from all living things, normally invisible to the human eye, that expresses the essence of their being. (A technical report summarizing the research is available at www.drgaryschwartz.com.)

The four photos in figure 12.1 are of a single geranium leaf that was cut down the middle. The leaf was already dying when we cut it off the plant.

Photo A was taken in the light, technically called a "white-light photo." It shows the leaf lying on a metal plate that was adjusted in height to bring the leaf in focus with the digital camera (you can see the nut holding the plate in place in the upper middle portion of the

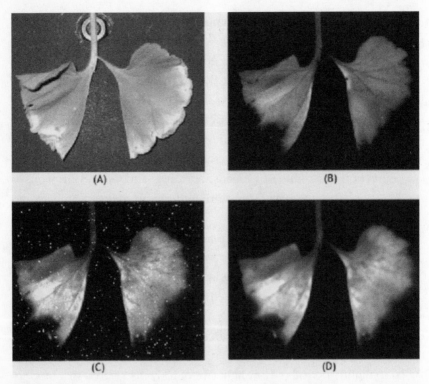

(A)   (B)

(C)   (D)

Figure 12.1 Four Views of a Single Leaf; Views B and C are Time Exposures in Complete Darkness

photo). The camera, mounted on top of the light-tight metal box that contained the movable plate, was cooled to minus one hundred centigrade with a Cryotiger refrigeration system.

Photo B was taken after we had closed the door of the light-tight box, turned off the lights in the room housing the camera and refrigeration unit, and closed and sealed the door to the room—leaving a dark box in a dark room. The exposure was set for one minute, during which the camera recorded all the photons reaching it from the leaf; the camera then sent the digital information to the computer in our control room for processing and display. This is technically called a "chlorophyll-fluorescence image": the chlorophyll of a plant placed in darkness fluoresces for about thirty minutes, and that's what has been captured in this picture. We were not primarily interested in chlorophyll fluorescence, but it's an example of how plants glow in the dark, emitting photons that the human eye can't register. Though the image is somewhat dim, the detail is quite striking.

Photo C was remarkable to us. After the leaf had been in the light-tight box for five hours, we began a two-hour time-exposure photo; the long exposure makes it possible to see extensive detail in the biophoton image of the leaf. You can clearly see the structure of its veins (dark lines in the leaves) as well as areas of increased and decreased biophoton release (shown by the lighter and darker colors in the leaves).

The individual bright spots in this image are actually high-energy cosmic rays that passed through the roof of the building and the ceiling of the laboratory and were then detected by the supercooled camera. They are thousands of times brighter than the photon release from the leaf. I like them esthetically because they remind me of what happens to every leaf exposed to the night sky.

Photo D was created by starting with a copy of photo C and subjecting it to a statistical technique that, in effect, removes the artifacts caused by cosmic rays. (In the process of subtracting the rays from the image, the "median filter," as it is called, unfortunately blurs some of the detail.)

One of the first things we discovered was that we could distinguish between healthy and unhealthy leaves by their biophoton emission. The pattern we saw was the opposite of what was observed for chlorophyll fluorescence. (See figure 12.2, following page.)

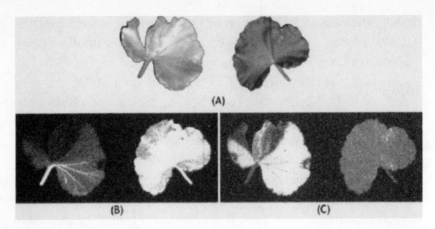

Figure 12.2 Three Images of Unhealthy (Left) and Healthy (Right) Leaves in the Light (A) and Darkness (B and C)

In figure 12.2, photo A shows white-light images of two leaves. The left leaf, dying, is relatively dry; the dark area is already dead. By comparison, the right leaf is healthy and appears green to the naked eye. (The color versions of figures 12.1 and 12.2 can be seen at www.drgary schwartz.com.)

Photo B shows a chlorophyll-fluorescence photo of the same two leaves, taken with a one-minute exposure after the door to the light-tight box was closed and the leaves were left in darkness. The leaf on the right—the healthy leaf—is emitting substantial photons compared to the unhealthy leaf on the left.

Contrast this with photo C, produced with a ten-minute exposure taken after the two leaves had been in the light-tight box for twenty-seven minutes. Because biophoton images have much lower intensities of light than chlorophyll-fluorescence images, we have made the scale more sensitive so that you clearly see the images.

Notice that in this photo, the unhealthy leaf on the left is glowing more brightly than the healthy leaf on the right. You might wonder why a dying leaf would emit more biophotons than a healthy leaf. Various researchers have hypothesized that in instances of injury or illness, an organism's energy is focused on the afflicted areas to support the metabolic process of attempting to heal itself. Healing requires energy.

Biophoton release is an indication of the underlying biochemical healing attempt.

Imaging a Human Hand

It stands to reason that if we can capture images of the emission of biophotons from plants, we should be able to capture images of the release of biophotons from animals, including humans. In principle this is possible. The difficulty is that plants generally emit more biophotons per unit of area than animals, and plants are better at sitting still than animals—at least those animals in a waking state. Kathy and I wanted to see if we could capture biophoton images of human hands. She agreed to be our first subject, while I would operate the computer to take the pictures.

We created a special light-tight cloth cover that made it possible for Kathy to place her hands in the box. I took sets of pictures of her hands, one with her thumbs near each other, the other with her thumbs apart.

In figure 12.3, the bottom two pictures are white-light pictures, the

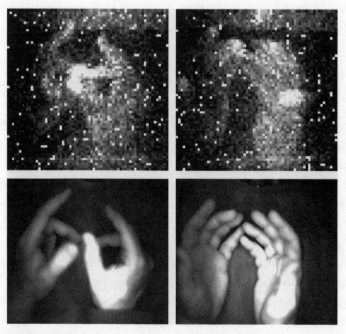

Figure 12.3 Light-Box Photos of Human Hands

left with her thumbs and palms in a semi-closed position, the right with her thumbs and palms in a more open position.

The top two pictures are ten-minute exposures in total darkness. To boost the camera's sensitivity, we had to use a procedure called "binning," which increases the size of the area of each pixel and makes the images more blurry. Because Kathy did not sit nearly as still as a leaf, the image became even blurrier. You will see that we did not remove the cosmic rays from these images; the cosmic bursts appear as bright squares.

The resulting images look more like X-rays than photos. However, if you look closely, you can see the outline of Kathy's hands. There is no question that like plants, we too glow in the dark. In a deep sense, our bodies give off light that extends into space.

Can Healers Influence the Biophoton Emissions of Plants?

Is it possible that plants can serve as sensitive energy detectors—what we might call "biofield sensors"—of the healing process, changing their biophoton emission as a function of energy healing? After seeing the striking results of our leaf photos, Kathy and I began to wonder: Could we use biophoton imaging of plants not only as a demonstration of the process of energy healing, but also as a quantitative measure of a given healer's skill or power in healing?

We decided to examine what would happen when healers sent healing energy to geranium leaves. For each trial, we cut two leaves into quarters. Four of the pieces received fifteen minutes of healing from an energy healer, the other four pieces served as untreated controls. We made sure that the treated and untreated leaves were exposed to comparable amounts of light. We initially thought that the plants would show an increase in biophoton release following healing. Our prediction was wrong.

After fifteen minutes of being exposed to energy healing, we observed that the plants responded to energy healing with a *decrease* in biophoton emission when compared to the untreated controls. At first, that doesn't sound reasonable, and it's certainly not what we had expected. But on further reflection, we realized that if healthy leaves had lower biophoton emission than sick leaves, the leaves were actually looking, biophotonically speaking, more like healthy leaves.

The questions then arose, What if healers were to attempt to make the leaves glow? Would they be able to excite the leaves into generating an increase in biophoton emission—even though this wasn't necessarily related to healing? Again we used two leaves cut into quarters. This time four of the pieces received fifteen minutes under the focus of a healer who was intent on trying to make the leaves glow. Compared to the untreated control leaves, the treated ones did actually show a relative increase in biophoton emission.

By that point, Kathy and I had spent well over a hundred evening and weekend sessions using Arthur's camera, taking more than five thousand pictures of glowing plants—as well as glowing hands, and even glowing crystals.

We couldn't quit there. No scientist would want to get results like these, and not follow up. The experiments proved an incentive for my decision to purchase a small super-cooled low-light camera for my laboratory, which Melinda, Kathy, and I then used for further testing with some of our "master healers." The results were dramatic. The best of these healers were able to increase or decrease the photon emission in plants as much as fivefold, and in a few cases even as much as *tenfold*.

These results raise a fascinating possibility: that biophoton release in plants might in the future serve as a biofield marker of extraordinary healers.

Can you imagine what happens to your mind after you have witnessed, over and over, the invisible glow of matter? You become forever aware of the invisible energy of everything. You cannot see a rose or walk past a tree without remembering that it is glowing and pulsing with life and vitality. You envision its invisible field of light and remember that light is an electromagnetic wave.

On the one hand, you celebrate the masterpiece of the human eye that allows us to see 16 million different shades of colors. On the other hand, you simultaneously stand in awe and humility as you recognize that there are potentially billions or trillions of invisible and unimagined colors that make up the complete rainbow of our living universe.

Are we all interconnected by invisible light? Do we all have auras of invisible light? Can plants teach us about the foundational nature of invisible-light communication? The journey continues.

The greatest problem in communication is the illusion that it has been accomplished.

—GEORGE BERNARD SHAW

Chapter 13

Plant Communication and Botanical Cell Phones

All communication is a process of exchanging energy and exchanging information. Each of those two functions is essential to the process. Let's be clear about what these terms really mean and how the processes relate to each other. Energy provides the power that enables the information to be generated, transmitted, and received. Information, the purpose of the exchange, provides the form, substance, text, and instructions.

Information without energy is powerless; energy without information is purposeless. Together, they are a remarkable team.

Though communication can be thought of as a one-way process, it's actually two-way—especially when viewed from an energy systems perspective. Physics tells us, quite emphatically, that all material objects engage in the dynamic process of emitting energy and information on the one hand and absorbing energy and information on the other. The emission and absorption of energy and information isn't random—it's highly selective, and it's limited. Objects cannot come into existence and continue to survive—that is, sustain themselves—and they can't evolve unless they can modulate the precise frequencies and intensities of the energies they receive as well as those they release.

If we have two objects, each of which is engaged in the process of receiving and releasing energy and information, they have the potential to affect each other. The energy released by one of them can potentially be received by the other, and vice versa. To the extent that each responds to the energy and information of the other, they are implicitly engaged in a process of communication, whether conscious or not.

Let's turn to that cell-phone example again and attempt to understand better the truly remarkable fact that cell phones actually work. This gadget that we take so much for granted today functions as a communication device because it's designed to be both a receiver and transmitter of invisible radio frequencies. For your cell phone to work successfully, it must be in dynamic and accurate communication with a complex network of transmitters and receivers located on the ground as well as in space.

Ponder the fact that many millions of cell-phone calls are occurring simultaneously, right now, their signals all mixing in the vacuum of space and the air around us. Yet the cell-phone signals rarely interfere with one another!

If you're in Boston and you call me on my cell phone in Tucson, your phone and mine must share fields of energy and information that we ultimately experience as sound. Each of them are in constant, dynamic two-way communication with a local land-based receiver and transmitter, connected to a chain of receivers and transmitters.

Much of this dynamic, simultaneous two-way communication process is wireless. We're connected to each other, at least in part, through invisible fields of energy and information between our respective cell phones and their closest land-based receivers and transmitters. Other aspects of our communication linkage may be over telephone wires, fiberoptic cables, and satellite links. A complex, dynamic two-way network of sounds, radio waves, electricity, magnetism, and light enable me to experience your voice in my ear, and vice versa.

Unless we happen to hit what I think of metaphorically as a "black hole," a pocket of poor cell-phone reception, we typically take all this for granted. We simply assume that the energies will be transmitted successfully and the information will be conveyed perfectly. However, if we take a moment to reflect about how all of this occurs, we have the potential to experience a profound sense of wonder, awe, and reverence for a universe that makes all of this possible. The truth is, though we have harnessed a collection of fundamental properties of the universe so we can communicate effortlessly over great distances, the process is ultimately mysterious and might be thought of as magical.

Consider this. In a city the size of Boston and its suburbs, there are probably hundreds of thousands of cell-phone conversations going on simultaneously, to cities all over the United States and abroad. The same applies to a city the size of Tucson and its suburbs. We are talking about many hundreds of thousands of people making sounds, cell phones generating and receiving radio waves, electrical and magnetic signals traveling over wires, and light traveling through fiberoptic cables. And it all works; indeed, it works more or less perfectly.

Is this amazing, or what? Cell phones interconnecting us with people around the world, and all of this occurs accurately enough to enable us to share very precise details of our personal and professional lives. Worldwide, this represents millions and millions of radio waves mixing simultaneously at every moment of the day and night.

From Man-Made Cell Phones to Little Bitty Cell Phones—Wireless Anatomy

As if cell-phone communication wasn't amazing enough, think of the following: Every one of the 60 or more trillion cells in your body can be thought of as a little bitty cell phone (an LBCP). Contemporary bioelectromagnetics tells us that each and every one of your cells operates as a little wireless transmitter and receiver of electromagnetic energies, including visible light.

Some of your LBCPs are precisely fixed in physical space, such as the hundreds of billions of neurons in your brain or the hundreds of millions of retinal cells in your eyes. Other LBCPs travel from place to place throughout your circulatory system, such as the trillions of white and red blood cells that flow through your arteries and veins.

Of course, each of your cells communicates locally and distally via chemical messengers. In the nervous system, these chemical messengers are called "neurotransmitters." Our hormones enable two-way chemical communications to occur between distant organs in the body. However, in addition to these chemical means of communication, our cells are engaged in wireless communication as well.

The idea of "wireless anatomy" was described in the mid-twentieth century by Dr. Randolph Stone, the creator of an energy healing technique called "polarity therapy." Dr. Stone envisioned that the body functions as a dynamically intricate and outstandingly complex wireless energy field. Contemporary biophysics supports Stone's conceptual framework, which describes the body's communication network in ways that are surprisingly similar to today's digital cell-phone communication system. It appears that human technology has recreated at a global level the way communication occurs at an individual biophysical level.

Dr. Popp and colleagues, mentioned in the previous chapter, as well as the Russian embryologist Dr. Alexander Gurwitsch (who is sometimes referred to as the founding father of biophoton research), propose that light is one of the ways that cells communicate—in animals, plants, and even single-celled organisms. Each cell is like a little bitty light-communicating cell phone, generating and receiving invisible beams of light as its method of sending and receiving information.

When I think of my body as a collection of 60 trillion or more cell phones that communicate not only by radio waves but also by light, I feel inspired, even a bit overwhelmed. It's somewhat easier for me to grasp the idea that our hearts and brains, for example, function as large, integrated wireless and neurologically hard-wired systems. Besides communicating chemically, our 60 trillion or so cells communicate wirelessly as well.

One reason, I suspect, that even conventionally trained physicians have a hard time accepting the idea that matter is ultimately organized energy—and that our bodies therefore function as dynamic energy systems—is because the implications of this model of reality are so mind-boggling, almost to the point of producing a mental meltdown.

The idea that we humans are composed of more than 60 trillion little bitty wireless cell phones communicating with one another, simultaneously, may seem virtually impossible for us to comprehend. Yet just because we have a hard time imagining this possibility doesn't mean that it's wrong. If such a vision leads us to feel more amazed and humbled by the seemingly miraculous nature of energy fields—if this is the way the universe actually works—then we have a responsibility to heed Einstein's phrase quoted earlier, that "the field is the only reality." (Later on, in part III, I'll offer some thoughts on how our lives would change if we accepted this conclusion.)

It's in this context that I share with you new research suggesting the possibility that science can demonstrate, at least in plants, connections from one plant to another via invisible light. These plants function, in effect, like botanical cell phones. Demonstrating this observation is the first step in determining whether plants, and ultimately all living things, communicate with one another like complex cell phones and Bluetooth devices.

Searching for Auras and Light Communication in Plants

In the process of viewing thousands of biophoton plant images, I began to wonder if the light extended out beyond the individual leaves. It occurred to me that Dr. Gmitro's camera used a black metal plate, somewhat scratched up, to hold the samples being imaged. Black absorbs light. I remembered that healers who claim that they can see auras around the body typically say they see the auras most clearly when their patients or clients are standing in front of a white wall. White surfaces reflect light.

I posed three questions to Professor Kathy Creath, my optical-sciences colleague. First, if we dramatically increased the gain on the software, which would completely saturate the image of the leaf itself—causing the leaf to appear all white—might we discover that light extends out beyond the leaves? Kathy said, "In principle, yes."

The second question grew out of my basic premise that all living systems, including leaves, communicate not only chemically but also electromagnetically—and this includes the sliver of the spectrum of frequencies that we experience as light. If that premise is true, might we be able to image structures between adjacent leaves that could reveal beams of possible connection and a matrix of communication? Kathy was somewhat skeptical about this, but she agreed it was worth examining.

The third question involves the background against which the leaves were tested. If we placed them on a white background instead of black, might we be able to better image light extending beyond the leaves—which would appear as auras—as well as the normally invisible beams of biophotonic light connection and communication? Kathy was quite enthusiastic about this. Not only did it make sense to her as an optical scientist, but it was also in step with her personal experience as a healer in training.

In order to see the details clearly, we had the camera collect biophoton light in the light-tight box for a total of two hours, using the procedures described previously. The two-hour exposure made it possible to see subtle replicable patterns that would otherwise have been missed.

I had no idea whether this experiment would work or not, and I didn't even know precisely what I was looking for. What I did know was that I had to keep an open mind and look at the resulting images with fresh eyes.

I will never forget the excitement I experienced as we began to explore these three questions. At first I couldn't believe the results we were getting. The data seemed to show that our camera was actually capturing the auras around the plants. And more than that, it was apparently capturing the light connection between them.

As in the earlier experiments, we used a supercooled, low-light digital camera. The black-and-white images of the geranium leaves shown in figure 13.1 (processed to remove the cosmic rays) offer a faint suggestion of the results; the original color images are dramatic, striking, and quite beautiful. (Again, the color versions of the images in this chapter can be seen at www.energyhealingexperiments.com.)

In image A, the four leaves on the left were placed on a white piece of paper; the leaves on the right were placed on a black piece of paper, and the software was set to focus on the leaves themselves, not on the light between the leaves, so that the details of the individual leaves are visible. This part replicated what we had done before. You can see that the leaves on both the left and the right vary in their average brightness as well as in the local areas of brightness within each leaf.

When we greatly increased the amplification or sensitivity of the

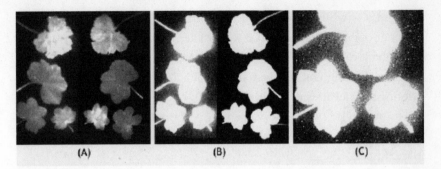

Figure 13.1 Images Revealing Presumed Communication between Adjacent Geranium Leaves

software, producing the result in image B, the leaves appear completely saturated, making them seem to be all white. Note that the leaves on the left appear bigger and fuzzier around the edges than the leaves on the right. Against the white background, we can detect light that extends beyond the physical edges of the leaves. When we added color to these images—a standard procedure used in astrophysical as well as medical imaging to make the significant elements stand out more clearly—what appear to be auras surrounding the leaves are even more starkly visible.

Image C is a magnification of the bottom left half of image B. Note the areas of brightness between the leaves. You can see that the areas between the leaves are generally brighter than those areas just beyond the edge of each leaf that are not near an adjacent leaf. You can also see evidence of apparent connection between the leaves, little spheres of light, and a stringiness that appears to link the leaves.

We were seeing not only an actual invisible aura around the leaves but something potentially much more startling.

Is this apparent structure between the leaves evidence of energetic connection between them? That's a serious probability. The logic scientists use to draw conclusions about the existence of connection *within* physical objects in visual images is the same logic I have used to draw conclusions about connection *between* physical objects in these images and dozens of others we have taken.

Since these particular images were taken with relatively long exposure times—two hours—they do not directly speak to the moment-to-moment communication process predicted to occur between the plant parts. Exploring that will require using several photo-multiplier tubes to measure the ongoing two-way stream of light between the plants. Considering the decades of positive research by Popp and colleagues using photo-multiplier tubes, there is a very real possibility, if not probability, that evidence for light communication will be documented successfully in the future.

If it should turn out that plants can indeed communicate with one another via invisible light, is it possible that plants and animals can communicate with one another via invisible light as well? It's worth remembering that physicists tell us all electromagnetic signals, not just those in the visible light spectrum, are made up of photons.

In quantum physics, photons can be described as being both particles and waves. Simply stated, all electromagnetic waves are ultimately light waves. If we limit our ideas about light simply to what we can see with our eyes, we are actually blind to the fact that the universe is a light universe, a dynamic light universe, what we can even call a living light universe.

Is this what we mean by "enlightenment"?

> *Be careful about reading health books. You may*
> *die of a misprint.*
>
> —MARK TWAIN

Chapter 14

Testing Energy Healing in the Laboratory

Studies by medical epidemiologists reveal that tens of millions of people worldwide have received various forms of energy healing and that energy-healing techniques are being provided by millions of trained practitioners. Think about this. As you are reading these words, literally thousands of people in various places of the world are receiving energy treatments.

These treatments are being provided by many different kinds of practitioners, applying arts that include Reiki, Johrei, Qigong, healing touch, therapeutic touch, quantum touch, and vortex healing. Healing is also performed by practitioners such as Sufi healers, ayurvedic physicians, spiritualist mediums, Christian Scientist practitioners, shamans, and Native American medicine men and women.

Are their patients improving? Studies indicate that many patients experience significant benefits, and the literature is replete with case studies of cures beyond all reasonable expectation, which tend to be labeled "miraculous"—excruciating pain that vanishes in minutes, as recounted in the opening story of this book; chronic pain that disappears after a few treatments or sometimes after only a few minutes; injuries that heal exceptionally fast; malignant tumors that vanish.

Numerous authors have summarized the clinical research, including those mentioned in the recommended readings list at the end of this book.

Of course, energy-healing techniques do not benefit everyone. Not every patient heals. But enough people experience significant relief to motivate millions of sick and injured individuals to seek out these healing practitioners. As you've read, I have personally witnessed a number of healings that Western medicine would call impossible.

Of the patients who do heal, how does their healing come about? Might they have healed anyway, in the process referred to as "spontaneous recovery"?

Could the results primarily arise from the expectancies and hopes of patients and healers—the so-called placebo effects?

Or is energy and consciousness somehow involved in this healing?

I began to wonder if there were ways to test whether the successful cures might be examples of true energy healing.

Designing Energy-Healing Experiments

Simply documenting that some patients heal doesn't tell us why they heal. Scientists want to know, what are the mechanisms?

To study the topic, we need to know if energy healing truly involves energy. Science insists on finding out if the healer's intentions, consciousness, and skills actually modulate the energy healing in specific ways that contribute to recovery and health.

Finding these answers is not easy. It requires bringing open-minded energy healers into the laboratory and designing controlled experiments that carefully test their claims.

If energy healing is real, then we would expect to find that what works on humans also works with rats and even with cells in a test tube. Studying the effects on traditional laboratory animals and materials offers many advantages. A major one is that it removes the effects of beliefs and expectations that human patients bring to the experiment, therefore eliminating placebo effects. Fortunately most rats don't understand English, and as far as we know, most cells in test tubes have little or no understanding of anything at all, English included. The research does not require that we explain to them what we are doing, or why.

In addition, researchers and university administrators don't have to concern themselves with the rats or cells suing for medical complications or malpractice. This doesn't mean investigators are unconcerned with animal welfare—quite the contrary. We're exceptionally sensitive to the needs of laboratory animals and their comfort. However, the university lawyers are relieved when we work with lower animals and cells because the legal consequences are minimized. Scientists can also explore questions with rats and cells that they can't explore with healthy human subjects or patients.

My colleagues and I designed an experiment in which we would subject *E. coli* bacteria in test tubes to heat stress. We would then bring Reiki healers into the lab, allow them to use their healing techniques, and observe whether the effects of the heat stress were reduced.

In a related experiment, we planned to subject laboratory rats to noise stress sufficient to cause vascular inflammation. (We would not be causing severe damage, but the effects would be readily observable at the microscopic level.) Once again Reiki healers would exercise their healing techniques. We would then determine whether the blood-vessel damage had been reduced.

I wasn't certain what I expected the results to show. However, so many people offer personal testimony to the positive results of energy healing that I admit to being highly curious about whether the experiments would provide any confirmation.

The *E. coli* Experiment

Beverly Rubik is a biophysicist by training—she holds a PhD in the subject from the University of California, Berkeley—and she is recognized as a pioneer in biofield science. More than that, she was part of the NIH consensus panel that coined the term "biofield." Beverly has received training in numerous healing techniques, including therapeutic touch and Qigong, a type of Chinese healing.

As part of the work at my NIH-funded center, Beverly and I, along with statistics expert Dr. Audrey Brooks, worked out the details of the *E.*

coli heat-stress experiment. *E. coli* is of particular interest because it's a bacteria found in both rats and humans. Our ability to digest food effectively depends upon the well-being of the *E. coli* that live within our digestive tract.

Based on well-established research, if we subject *E. coli* bacteria to heat of a certain temperature for a given period of time, we can determine the extent to which colony growth is slowed due to cells damaged or killed. For this experiment, we set parameters so that growth rate would slow to approximately 50 percent of the normal level.

After preparing the cells in test tubes, we placed each test tube in a rack and set the racks into a cardboard box. Hence the cells could not "see" whether a practitioner was present or not. (Was that a silly precaution to take? Even if it was, it ruled out the possibility of anyone complaining later that a failure to do this invalidated the results.) Our first experiment was simple in design but complex in analysis.

We arranged for fourteen Reiki practitioners to come into the laboratory. Each would come on three separate days and would work with a unique set of *E. coli*–filled test tubes each time. When they first entered the laboratory, we had the practitioners fill out a standardized well-being form. They were then told that inside the box were cells that had been heat-stressed, and they were asked to perform Reiki directed to the box of test tubes.

Unbeknownst to the practitioners, there was a box of matched test tubes in a separate part of the laboratory that served as the control group. Hence, the total of forty-two treated boxes of test tubes (fourteen practitioners times three days) had a matched set of forty-two control boxes of test tubes.

If a particular Reiki healer was effective, the results would show that the number of surviving cells, on average, would be greater in the test tubes exposed to the healing than in the controls.

The results turned out to lean toward the predicted direction, but in fact the findings were not statistically significant. Indeed, almost half of the samples went in the wrong direction—the *E. coli* in the *untreated* test tubes survived better than the *E. coli* subjected to the Reiki healing.

That didn't seem to make sense. Clear data showing that the healers had achieved some success would have opened an intriguing path for further research; data showing they had no effect would have made me think I needed to close the door on that path and to turn to some other avenue of exploration. But something like half the samples responding *negatively* to the healing efforts? That seemed bewildering. What could account for this result? Could we dream of another experiment to make sense of it?

I pondered the challenge for several days. And then it struck me. What if the cells had been responding not just to the energy and conscious intentions of a particular Reiki practitioner but also to that healer's emotional state?

Beverly's biochemistry laboratory is in the greater San Francisco area. She noted that some healers, on some days, came into the laboratory stressed, which could have been caused by traffic, personal problems, health issues, patient crises, or other problems. If a healer was feeling stressed during the experiment, would his emotional stress affect the *E. coli* bacteria?

To examine this possibility, we separated the data for *E. coli* pairs (treated versus control) into those where the treated increased in number (the healthy response) and those where the treated decreased (the unhealthy response). We correlated this with the well-being scores of the healers when they came into the laboratory.

The results were clear and statistically significant. We found that when the cell growth increased following Reiki treatment—the healthy response—the healers had entered the lab reporting that they were feeling physically and emotional healthy. If the cell growth decreased following treatment—the unhealthy response—the healers had entered the lab reporting they were more stressed and feeling less well.

Equally interesting was that after fifteen minutes of doing Reiki on the *E. coli* in the test tubes, all the healers reported feeling better. If their subjective reports can be relied on—and we have replicated this finding many times—doing Reiki on cells in test tubes makes the practitioner feel better than when she began. The process of doing Reiki appears to be positive for healers, regardless of whom or what they are treating.

We then wondered what would happen if we repeated the experiment, this time having the practitioners perform Reiki on a person first, and having them treat the test tubes afterward. Since we had already learned that doing Reiki increases one's state of well-being, the practitioners' emotional state should improve, which in turn should increase their ability to have a positive effect on the *E. coli* bacteria.

In the interim, before we began the second series of experiments, Beverly Rubik badly sprained her ankle. This gave us an available patient.

The fourteen practitioners all agreed to come back for two more sessions. As before, they began by filling out the well-being form. This time we had each start by doing fifteen minutes of Reiki on Beverly. They then filled out the well-being form a second time before going on to repeat the *E. coli* experiment for another fifteen minutes. When finished, we had the healers fill out a third well-being form.

I found the results revealing, convincing, and satisfying. As expected from the earlier findings, after doing Reiki on Beverly, the practitioners' average well-being scores increased substantially—they felt more "in the flow."

When they subsequently worked on the *E. coli* bacteria, the overall increase in cell growth for the twenty-eight test-tube pairs (fourteen practitioners times two sessions) reached statistical significance. Almost three-quarters of the test-tube pairs showed positive growth.

But what about the one-quarter that did not? If we examined this group, would we find that the practitioners who had worked with those test-tube sets had entered the laboratory in a particularly stressful state? Indeed, when we examined their entry well-being scales, we discovered that they had in fact reported being more stressed than the others. In other words, the bacteria still responded negatively to practitioners who were most stressed.

Remember, the *E. coli* cells had been placed in test tubes inside a sealed box. If the Reiki practitioners were stressed, their own *E. coli*—the billions inside their guts—were also probably stressed (influenced by the stress hormones circulating throughout the practitioners' bodies). One possible explanation is that the *E. coli* cells in the test tubes were resonating with the *E. coli* inside the practitioners. Is it possible that there really was "little bitty cell phone" *E. coli* communication between the practitioners and the subjects? As far-fetched as this might seem, I think you'll agree that it's a question worth further scientific research.

The Rats and Reiki Experiment

Ann Baldwin, a Brit with a delightful English lilt to her voice, received her PhD from the University of London and is a renowned professor of physiology at the University of Arizona School of Medicine. She accidentally discovered that rats housed in noisy areas showed increased damage to their tiniest blood vessels (the microvascular capillary beds), as evidenced by increased leakage of blood molecules. The rats also exhibited behaviors that are associated with stress, such as excessive fighting. Simply stated, the rats were showing stress responses to the noisy environment.

The pattern of symptoms that arise in rats exposed to noise stress is identical to humans suffering from inflammatory bowel disease. Research has shown that psychological stress in humans aggravates intestinal diseases such as Crohn's disease and colitis. The stress findings in rats therefore have direct implications for stress findings in humans.

Ann loves people and animals. She is happily married, and her life includes two children, two cats, and a horse that she rides most days. A few years ago, introduced to Reiki by one of her research assistants, she took to it like a fish to water, in time becoming a Reiki practitioner. When my NIH research center was funded, Ann came to ask me if I thought it might be possible to use her animal-testing procedure to determine whether Reiki could reduce the physiological effects of stress in rats.

Ann and I resonated both on the intellectual level and in our love for animals. When I was a professor at Yale, I lived in Guilford with my wife and five Welsh corgis (the queen of England at one point had eleven of these dogs). For a while I had three pet French Alpine goats—which many people are surprised to learn are very smart and affectionate, like dogs.

Ann and I designed an experiment to test whether Reiki could reduce the microvascular inflammation she had discovered in noise-stressed rats. Since the rats could see the Reiki practitioner, it was important to have a comparison condition where a person not trained in Reiki spent the same amount of time with the rats and made the same kinds of hand gestures modeled after Reiki practitioners.

We studied four groups of rats:

Group 1: A normal, nonstressed group—to obtain baseline rates of microvascular inflammation

Group 2: A noise-stressed group—to verify Ann's finding that noise produces increased microvascular inflammation

Group 3: A Reiki-treated group of noise-stressed rats—to see if Reiki healing produces a decrease in microvascular inflammation

Group 4: A "sham-treated" group of noise-stressed rats—the control condition to determine if the presence of a person with no Reiki training would be sufficient to produce a corresponding change in microvascular inflammation. This controlled for a possible placebo effect in the rats.

The rats in groups 3 and 4—treated with Reiki or sham—received their respective fifteen-minute treatments every day for three weeks from two Reiki practitioners or from two sham practitioners. The experiment was repeated three times. A summary of the experiment is shown in figure 14.1.

In analyzing the results, we first observed the expected dramatic increase in microvascular inflammation in the noise-stressed rats (for example, 3.0 leaks) compared to the nonstressed rats (0.5 leaks). The percent increase in number of leaks in the noise-stressed group was 600 percent (3.0 divided by 0.5), confirming Ann's earlier results.

The findings for the real Reiki (1.2 leaks) were consistent and important, especially compared with the sham-treated group. Sham alone (2.1 leaks) resulted in a 420 percent increase in the number of blood-vessel leaks in response to the noise stress, as compared to 600 percent with noise alone. Apparently the presence of a person, even a person with no training in healing techniques, helps reduce the effects of stress.

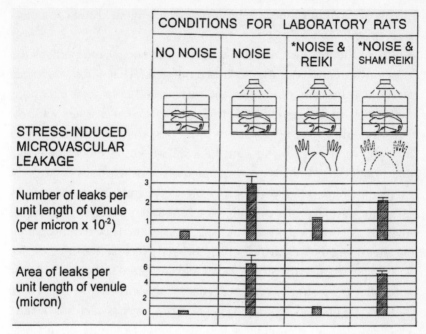

Figure 14.1 Number and Total Area of Microvascular Leakage in Rats Subjected to Noise Stress and the Improvement after the Stressed Rats Were Treated with Reiki or Sham Reiki

However, the Reiki-treated rats showed only 1.2 leaks. This represented a 240 percent increase in the number of leaks as compared to 420 percent increase in sham and 600 percent increase in noise-alone rats.

As a way of providing confirmation for the findings, the rats were examined not just for the number of leaks but also for the total area of damaged vessels where the leaks occurred. As can be seen in figure 14.1, the results in terms of area of leaks is even more dramatic.

Sham helped reduce both the total number of leaks and area of leaks, but Reiki was significantly more effective than sham. The Reiki treatment did not eliminate all the effects of the stress, but it clearly reduced them substantially.

One could say that the sham treatment reveals the "psychological" effects of the intervention—the rats could clearly see the people doing the fake treatment. However, the increased effectiveness of the Reiki compared to the sham suggests that above and beyond these psychological effects, there appear to be demonstrable biofield and conscious-ness effects.

Could the rats have somehow sensed the energy and perhaps the conscious intentions of the Reiki practitioners? That's not a frivolous question. If humans can detect the energy and conscious intentions from people (as suggested by the research detailed in chapters 4 and 5), even when they have no conscious awareness that they are able to do this, why can't rats do the same? For all we know, rats, cats, goats, horses, and other animals may be even more sensitive than we are.

In the third experiment, I had the Reiki and sham practitioners record their feelings of well-being on a zero-to-ten scale in categories of physical, psychological, social, and spiritual health. They did this before and after doing the treatments, which they did every day for three weeks. On average, whereas the sham practitioners reported feeling very slightly better after the treatments (average increase in well-being scores of 0.5), the Reiki practitioners reported large increases (average increase of 3.0).

Doing a sham treatment is at best boring. Doing Reiki with rats, however, apparently feels at least as good, perhaps even better than doing Reiki with *E. coli.*

What can be stated, quite definitively, is that the energy and con-scious intentions of healers can modulate cellular functioning in rats and even *E. coli* cells in test tubes. The findings support the claims of healers that their energy and intentions make a difference in the suc-cess of their efforts.

Probably my favorite finding from our Reiki *E. coli* experiments was that among the fourteen practitioners, one practitioner had a perfect five out of five record: for her, the treated test tubes always had greater cell growth than the untreated control test tubes. What was unique about this healer?

It turned out that her specialty was using Reiki to treat animals. Indeed, she is a professional, full-time animal healer. This practitioner deeply identified with the bacteria. In fact, she felt compassion for the bacteria that had to be sacrificed after each run in order to make the measurements. Her love of animals, great and small, including cells, and her connection to life and its energies is profound. Did this allow her to consistently provide healing for the *E. coli*?

The axiom called Occam's razor says that the simplest explanation is usually the correct one. If we follow the accepted canons of science, we are led, slowly but surely, to the simple explanation that caring energy and loving intentions are the key to healing and health.

Can Healing Affect Water?

Living systems—people, animals, and single-celled organisms—are made mostly of water. Human infants are more than 90 percent water; as we age, the percentage of water in our bodies decreases to approximately 70 percent. Doctors have long advised that drinking regular amounts of fresh water is good for one's health.

Water, especially if it contains salt and other conductive minerals, is an excellent carrier of electricity, so it should come as no surprise that our bodily fluids are also excellent conductors. This is what allows your doctor to record your electrocardiogram to chart the electrical activity of your heart by attaching electrodes to your skin. In fact, the EKG can be obtained by placing the electrodes anywhere on your body, from the top of your head to the bottom of the feet. The electrical currents swim, so to speak, within our bodily fluids.

In the laboratory, we measure the structural dynamics of water using a device called the "gas discharge visualization" system, or GDV. Developed by Konstantine Korotkov, a PhD physicist in Russia, the instrument detects coronal discharges created by passing a high-voltage, high-frequency, very-low-current signal through water. The passing of the voltage creates tiny sparklike patterns, or auras, that can be detected in the dark using a sensitive digital camera. The image data are fed into a computer and then quantified using high-powered statistical algorithms.

Using a GDV camera in our laboratory, we took the following pictures of drops of three kinds of water—a superpure water (called HPLC), a regular purified water, and tap water.

You can see in figure 14.2 that the tap water (on the right), with its greater concentration of minerals, is more electrically conductive, creating a larger and more complex GDV image.

When a health practitioner works with a client or patient, both

Figure 14.2 Water Drops (GDV images)

generate complex bioelectromagnetic signals—biofields—that extend beyond the body, just as a radio transmitter creates signals that extend beyond its antenna. Could these biofields be involved in the process of healing, a mechanism that could help explain the healers' success?

In *The Living Energy Universe,* I described how all physical systems, including atoms and molecules, have the potential to store information and energy. William Tiller, PhD, during his years as a professor of material sciences at Stanford, documented that the human mind can alter the pH of water—its alkalinity/acidity balance—because water is able to store information and energy. That's a startling idea, but Professor Tiller established it scientifically.

My researchers and I began to wonder if a practitioner's healing energy could affect the water in their client's body. Could the water's structure be altered by the healer's bioenergetic state?

Curious, we designed and conducted research to find out. In one experiment, we asked a healer to work with samples of the same three kinds of water—HPLC, purified, and tap—and attempt to alter the water's structural dynamics. His task was to "energize" some water samples and "relax" other samples. The water was kept in syringes, which were attached to the GDV camera for analysis.

The chart in figure 14.3 shows one of the statistical measures (termed the Be coefficient) of the GDV images.

When we compare this measure for water samples that have been given "energizing" energy healing to those that have been given "relaxing" energy, we discover differences in the Be coefficient (figure 14.3). On average, the coefficient increases with relaxation intention, and decreases with energizing intention. These effects are observed in all three kinds of water.

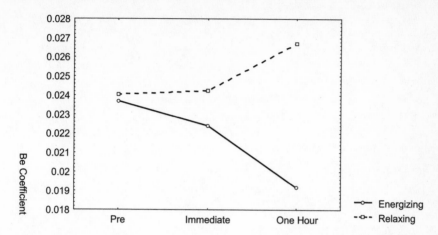

Figure 14.3 Effects of Energizing and Relaxation Intention on Water

The experiment needs to be conducted and the results confirmed by other experimenters. If similar results are achieved by others, the results would be undeniable: healers *can* affect the structural dynamics of water as measured by the GDV.

If energy healing can reliably affect microvascular cellular functioning in a rodent's intestines, the growth of *E. coli* bacterial cells in test tubes, and even the structural dynamics of water itself, then we have every reason to believe that the so-called healing miracles being observed to various degrees every day, worldwide, may be part of the fundamental energetic fabric of the universe itself. Dr. James Oschman, author of the book *Energy Medicine,* calls this the "energy matrix."

This evidence supports the notion that everyone, healers in particular, appear to have the ability to influence the energy state of animate and even inanimate systems. Once again, the implications for us all are profound.

Is it possible we might be looking at a first step toward universal healing?

The only real valuable thing is intuition.

—ALBERT EINSTEIN

Chapter 15

Testing Medical Intuition in the Laboratory

At a conference on integrative medicine where Dr. Andrew Weil and I were both lecturing in the late 1990s, at the Canyon Ranch Resort and Spa in Tucson, I asked him a seemingly simple question: how much of his treatment recommendations—which combined conventional, alternative, and complementary medicines—involved actual scientific evidence versus intuition.

The reason I asked this question was because conventional science tends to be reductionistic. That is, science typically reduces complex processes to a collection of simpler elements and studies the elements in isolation. This makes the task of science easier to conduct and the results easier to analyze and more precise, as well as experimentally controlled. And less expensive. Unfortunately, the procedure makes the findings less applicable to the real world, where elements don't conveniently operate in isolation. In the area called "whole person systems research," there's little scientific evidence that can help guide Dr. Weil, or any integrative physician, in how best to combine diverse medicines and techniques.

What Dr. Weil said was honest and telling. He said that he makes more than 50 percent of his recommendations intuitively. By this he did not mean that he makes guesses in a vacuum. Rather, he combines his

151

knowledge of medicine and his years of research and experience treating patients with his intuitive hunches and gut sensations—with ideas and feelings that "pop into his head." Dr. Weil has learned to discern these often spontaneous images and feelings, and in the process, to trust them.

Where do these intuitions come from? Do they emerge from Dr. Weil's unconscious? Do they involve him sensing the invisible energies and intentions of his patients before he can properly make diagnoses and recommendations? When Dr. Weil functions as a highly focused listener and observer, does he tune in to his patients, come to resonate energetically with them, and therefore communicate with them not only through sound and light, but more broadly electromagnetically, and even psychically? Does Dr. Weil sometimes connect tele-energetically with his patients? Is it possible that he sometimes receives invisible guidance from other sources—even spiritual sources?

No one knows where anyone's intuitions come from. Shamans and medicine women and men believe that their intuitions come partly from the energy and consciousness of the beings they're serving—whether humans, animals, or even plants—as well as from the spirits of their ancestors, which may not only be deceased humans, but animals and, again, even plants.

As a Western-trained scientist, I was taught to view the ideas of shamans and medicine women and men as reflecting ancient superstitions combined with vivid imaginations that were accentuated by trance states and drugs. I was taught that such thinking was pathological and even a symptom of schizophrenia. However, the history of science reminds us that we used to believe the earth is flat, that the sun revolves around the earth, and that material objects are solid (while modern physics tells us objects are actually collections of vibrating quantum particles and waves and that more than 99.999 percent of any object is empty space—that is, empty of particles with mass).

The question arises, whose ideas are correct? Is conventional Western science correct that the shaman's ideas are the conclusions of uneducated, primitive, hallucinating human beings? Or are the shamans correct in their beliefs? If so, it follows that Western science is limited by its emphasis on reductionistic methods. Perhaps Western science often also ignores valid evidence that challenges our overly simplistic, materialistic models. What if we were to consider more systemic and "energyistic" models?

If science as an institution is to remain true to its calling, it must seek the truth: scientists must acknowledge opposing evidence and be willing to change their models and theories according to what the evidence reveals. If any profession has the responsibility to both seek and follow the truth, it is science. The edifice of science is built upon its capacity and commitment to grow and evolve as a function of what it discovers.

I never expected to bring specific claims of shamans into the laboratory and put them to experimental testing. Frankly, I try to avoid people who claim to be shamans. The fact is, like a classically conditioned dog that has been trained to salivate when it hears a bell, I have been classically conditioned by my Western science training to sometimes experience disgust (or to giggle) when I hear a shaman tell me about how his raven or frog totem animal provides him with diagnostic information about the people who come to him for healing.

However, just because I have been classically conditioned by my professional education to experience negative or dismissive reactions in response to the claims of shamans doesn't mean that the basis of my conditioning is valid. Not long ago, a young psychology graduate student who had been receiving training in contemporary shamanism led me to reexamine my beliefs.

A Shaman Scientist's Journey

Sheryl Attig is a tall, attractive woman with a calling. Now in her early thirties, she has been on a quest to integrate shamanism with contemporary health psychology. Her credentials and commitment, coupled with her family history, make for an impressive future researcher.

Sheryl's mother is a practicing cardiologist, her father a professor of philosophy, and her grandfather was a distinguished professor of the philosophy of religion. As an undergraduate, Sheryl majored in philosophy, then went on to earn a master of theology degree. Meanwhile, she began exploring and taking workshops with purportedly gifted shamans in the United States and South America.

When she learned of how my research bridged health psychology, psychophysiology, energy psychology, and spiritual medicine, she decided that I might be open enough to foster her dream to bring shamanism into the laboratory. This required that Sheryl get the equivalent of a second undergraduate degree in psychology and then set out to convince the psychology department to allow her to create a specialized interdisciplinary PhD program for herself in a field we labeled "integrative health psychology." Sheryl prevailed and ultimately became a graduate student in the Department of Psychology at the University of Arizona.

For her first year as a graduate student with me, we met weekly to discuss her burgeoning experiences in shamanism. I heard stories and claims that went beyond anything I was prepared to find credible. Not only are the claims of shamans difficult to fathom but even more challenging is the fact that gifted shamans tend to be eccentric and follow voices that others don't hear. Consequently, they tend not to be good research subjects because they are uninterested in and unwilling—perhaps even unable—to follow precise protocols.

After she had worked somewhat unsuccessfully with a few local shamans as potential research subjects, I proposed that instead of working with shamans themselves, we test some of their purported abilities in people who claim to have the same abilities but who do not practice shamanism. This suggestion grew out of something Sheryl had mentioned earlier: shamans commonly claim the ability to receive information intuitively about a person's physical and emotional health. It occurred to me that medical intuition was a similar phenomenon that could be brought into the laboratory and tested rigorously.

The claim of being able to receive information intuitively about a person's physical and emotional health is made not only by shamans but by medicine women and men as well as psychics and healers. They claim to do this not only when the patient is with them, but even distally—when the patient is tens, hundreds, even thousands of miles away. Medical intuitives claim that they can read a patient's energy—locally or distally—and see the patient's aura, typically as an image in their own mind. The information conveyed by the aura, as well as any feelings they might experience as they tune in to the patient, are said to represent information about the patient's physical and emotional health. These intuitive images and sensations are not logical, as in "reasoned"—they are experienced spontaneously when the medical intuitive is in the appropriate state of consciousness.

Unlike shamanism, with which I had no personal experience, I had received some advanced personal training in a consciousness-development program that happened to employ medical intuition as a way of testing its students' progress in developing their consciousness skills. The circumstances under which I received this personal training are ironic to say the least and are worth reporting for historic purposes.

Exploring and Experiencing the Silva Method

In 2002 I was invited to speak about *The Afterlife Experiments* book at a conference hosted by the Silva Method (www.silvamethod.com). Developed by José Silva, the method is described as a "focused-thinking program designed to help you reach your desired goals in health, education, relationships, business, and sports." The organization claims that "Silva sets your thinking right." On their Web site they write:

> The Silva Method program is a scientifically-proven conditioning process that has stood the test of time. Sixteen progressive exercises help you obtain the mental edge necessary to accomplish your desired goals. They steadily help you increase your ability to remain focused and direct your thinking. With your expanded creative and innovative thoughts, you learn to develop essential elements required to achieve any success in life.

I was impressed with the kindness, goals, and seeming genuineness of the leaders of their organization. However, having conducted no research on their methods, I was agnostic if not skeptical about their claims. I told them that if the opportunity arose in the future, I would be happy to receive a two-day training course in the Silva Method given by one of their advanced teachers and would then consider the possibility of conducting some research to investigate their claims.

An unexpected opportunity arose the next year when I was invited to speak at the twenty-fifth anniversary conference of what was then called CSICOP—the Committee to Scientifically Investigate Claims of the Paranormal (www.csicop.org). CSICOP is a watchdog organization that publishes *Skeptical Inquirer,* a magazine devoted to debunking claims broadly related to the paranormal. The CSICOP meeting was held in Atlanta, where one of Silva's advanced teachers lives.

I was able to spend two extra days in Atlanta and received a crash course in the Silva Method. At the end of the training, the instructor explained that the way they evaluated their students was by examining their medical-intuition skills. The students were asked to relax following the Silva Method procedures and set up their "mental screen"—an imaginary laboratory that you create in your mind. After being requested to set up my mental screen, I was asked to imagine what a certain person looked like. I was given only the person's name, age, and address; Silva has a list of people with their addresses and physical maladies from around the country. I was instructed to scan the person's body on my mental screen and indicate what symptoms or problem areas I saw.

Normally students do ten such cases. I only had time to do five. Each case had two or more areas of symptoms. To my great disbelief, when they showed me their written records, my accuracy in intuiting areas of the body that had maladies and identifying the nature of the maladies—for example, cancer of the throat, heart failure, or arthritis in the knee—was more than 90 percent. To this day, I have no idea how that was possible. For example, was I reading the mind of the examiner, who held the cards containing the symptoms? Was I simply extraordinarily lucky in making correct guesses at that moment? Or was I actually connecting with the energies of the people I was trying to diagnose?

The Silva Method does not typically pretest their students' ability in medical intuition before they receive the training. Therefore, if I do indeed have some special ability to make medical intuitive diagnoses, I have no idea whether the training program improved that ability.

What I do know is that I was not cheating, they were not cheating, and the results were statistically far beyond what one would expect by chance. And most importantly, the Silva teachers I was dealing with were research oriented and interested in having their medical intuitive skills documented.

A Double-Blind Medical Intuition Experiment

I suggested to Sheryl that we consider conducting a double-blind experiment examining medical intuition. Not only would the medical intuitives be kept "blind" in the experiment, but the people judging the accuracy of the medical intuitives would be kept "blind" as well. What this means is that the medical intuitives would neither be told the medical histories of the patients they would read nor which subjects were the patients and which were the matched controls.

In addition, we designed the experiment so that the people who scored the data provided by the medical intuitives—including cardiologists as well as undergraduate students—were not told which data provided by the medical intuitives belonged to patients and which belonged to the matched controls.

I had access to medical intuitives—four teachers of the Silva Method (three completed the study) and two psychics who claimed to have medical intuitive skills. Sheryl was able to round up the patients and control subjects, thanks to the interest and support of her mother, Dr. Elizabeth Attig. Sheryl also tapped one person who was in training to be a shaman who had a deep interest in research.

We decided to have the medical intuitives attempt to diagnose the health status of twenty of Dr. Attig's patients, all diagnosed with congestive heart failure (CHF), and a group of matched control patients (we were able to get complete data on nineteen patient-control pairs). The patients had all been seeing Dr. Attig for at least a year. In terms of gender, the patients were equally divided between male and female, and we selected only patients who were married and whose spouses did not have congestive heart failure. For the matched controls, we simply used the spouses of the CHF patients.

Dr. Attig confirmed the presence of CHF in the patients and the absence of CHF in the spouses. She also recorded the presence of up to five additional diagnoses, from both patients and their spouses. Patients with CHF typically have other health problems. Since the age of the patients and spouses ranged from advanced middle age to elderly, it was expected that all thirty-eight would have a diverse range of medical conditions, although on average the patients would be expected to have a greater number of diseases and symptoms than their spouses.

According to the diagnoses made by Dr. Attig, the patients had an average of 3.5 diagnoses compared to an average of 2.6 diagnoses in their spouses. This difference was statistically significant. The pattern of diagnoses was similar for the nine female patients and ten male patients (3.4 and 3.6) versus their respective spouses (2.8 and 2.4).

Twelve of the patients had a higher number of diagnoses (average of 3.8) than their spouses (average of 2.3); seven of the patients had a comparable number of diagnoses (average of 3.0) to their spouses (average of 3.1). This difference is important because if the medical intuitives were accurate, they would distinguish between the twelve patient-control pairs who differed in the number of diagnoses compared with the seven patient-control pairs who did not.

For all thirty-eight subjects, the intuitives were given the subject's name, date of birth, and gender, as well as the city and state where they lived. This information was sent, four subjects at a time, to the intuitives every month. Again, they were not told which subjects were the patients and which were the controls. They were asked to record as many diagnoses as they could determine for each subject. Of course, they received no feedback about their accuracy during the period of the study.

We conducted the study for nearly two years, obtaining complete data from six of the seven intuitives (three Silva Method teachers and three other purported medical intuitives) on the nineteen patient-spouse pairs.

In order to score the data, a coding system had to be developed for counting the number of diagnoses and symptoms provided by the medical intuitives. Under my direction, Sheryl worked out a formal and teachable coding system.

She tested the system initially by scoring all of the data herself. When we were sure the method was useful and reliable, we trained a team of undergraduate students to score the data independently, and it was this set of scores that we relied on for the final results. Again, the student scorers were kept blind to which subjects were the patients and which the controls.

The scoring showed that the medical intuitives found the patients to have an average of 3.8 diagnoses and symptoms, compared to an average of 3.2 diagnoses and symptoms in their spouses. This difference was statistically significant.

Moreover, when we examined the twelve patient-spouse pairs Dr. Attig had originally diagnosed as having more diseases in the patient than the spouse, we found that the medical intuitives generated a higher number of diagnoses and symptoms (average of 4.4) in these patients than in their spouses (average of 3.4). And when we examined the seven patient-spouse pairs whom Dr. Attig had originally diagnosed as having a comparable number of diseases to their spouses, we found that the medical intuitives generated a comparable number of diagnoses and symptoms (average of 3.3) in these patients and their spouses (average of 3.2). In other words, the medical intuitives, as a group, generated a pattern of diagnoses and symptoms that was similar to the original medical diagnoses made by Dr. Attig.

Analysis of the individual medical intuitives revealed that they varied in their overall accuracy scores. We split them into two groups: three who were very accurate (successful medical intuitives) and three who were moderately to mildly accurate (to be conservative, we can label them as unsuccessful medical intuitives).

We then had Dr. Attig and a second cardiologist, Dr. Katherine Burleson, independently use a medical scoring system that specifically addressed the diagnosis of congestive heart failure. For each subject, the cardiologist was asked to assess whether the diagnosis provided by each intuitive fit the diagnosis of congestive heart failure, scoring on a scale from one to four. One was "no evidence of congestive heart failure"; two was "meets one or more minor criteria for congestive heart failure"; three was "meets one or more major criteria for congestive heart failure"; and four was "consistent with congestive heart failure by major criteria with no contradictory information."

Drs. Attig and Burleson were kept blind to who the patients and controls were. We predicted that only the successful subset of the medical intuitives, as determined by their ability to accurately describe the overall number of diagnoses and symptoms in the patients and spouses, would be sufficiently accurate to provide a precise description of CHF.

The main question here was whether the successful medical intuitives did a better job of providing data that showed which person in each couple was the one with congestive heart failure. For the successful intuitives, the patients had an average CHF score of 2.0, versus 1.7 for the spouses (a statistically significant difference); for the unsuccessful intuitives, the patients had an average CHF score of 2.1 compared to 2.2 in the spouses (a nonsignificant difference). So the successful medical intuitives did indeed accurately describe the symptoms of CHF for the patient as distinguished from the spouse, while the unsuccessful intuitives did not. Though these differences were small in magnitude, they were in the predicted direction and statistically significant, and therefore are worth considering.

The Michael Jordans of Medical Intuition

It's one thing to hear stories about shamans from South America, medicine women and men from North America, avatars from India, and Qigong masters from China making remarkably accurate diagnoses simply by tuning in to a patient's energy fields and intuiting their health status. Or to read carefully recorded accounts of Edgar Cayce, the famed American of a hundred years ago who many believed had distance medical-intuitive and healing powers.

But it's quite another to experience personally your own 90 percent accuracy after only two days of training. And it's quite another, as well, to formally test this purported ability in the laboratory under conditions of a highly controlled experiment and to uncover evidence that is consistent with the stories and written accounts.

In the past few years I've had the privilege of coming to know and work closely with a handful of individuals who are, so to speak, Michael Jordans of medical intuition. Like Michael Jordan, they do not make all their shots. They are not perfect. However, like Michael Jordan, they often make "dazzle shots"—amazing three-pointers—that take your breath away.

Are at least some medical intuitives real? My conclusion is yes: *some* appear to be real. I have come to this conclusion first and foremost as a scientist who has examined the claims in the laboratory, second as a health-care provider who has witnessed the phenomenon practiced in numerous situations, and third as a human being who has directly experienced the ability himself on a number of occasions.

Do we know how these individuals do what they do? My answer is a definite no. Different healing traditions have theories about it that include the intuitives being able to receive information from deceased doctors and animal spirits. Or being able to obtain guidance from angelic beings and even the universal source itself (given many names, from Great Spirit and God to the Infinite). Not even the people who appear to possess these abilities really know.

However, is it possible for science, in principle, to discover how medical intuition works? My answer is yes. As I have illustrated in *The Afterlife Experiments* and *The G.O.D. Experiments* books, for example, it appears that science has great potential to address seemingly anomalous and controversial questions in a systematic and successful manner. Our challenge is to be creative and courageous enough to be willing to ask the questions in a humble yet open-minded fashion.

When one of the Michael Jordans of medical intuition tells me that she sees energies around and inside the body with precise colors and structures, for example, it's my responsibility to listen with an open mind to what she's saying, to give her the benefit of the doubt, and to bring her claims into the laboratory. And when another Michael Jordan tells me that Edgar Cayce, whom she calls "Eddie," regularly helps her with medical diagnoses, treatment recommendations, and healings, it's my responsibility to stifle my giggle reflex, to honor what she is saying, to give her—and potentially Mr. Cayce—the benefit of the doubt and bring her claims into the laboratory.

If we remain open to these possibilities, we have the opportunity to discover the hidden nature of energy and the invisible powers of the mind.

Part III

All Healing Involves Energy and Conscious Intention

> *The real voyage of discovery consists not in seek-*
> *ing new landscapes, but in having new eyes.*
>
> —MARCEL PROUST

Chapter 16

Energy Healing and the Placebo Effect—A New Vision

People have strongly diverse reactions to the possibility of energy heal-ing, generally falling into one of three major groups. The first is made up of adamant disbelievers, those who "know" that energy healing is impossible. The individuals in group 2 are what I choose to call "con-fused agnostics"; they are fence-sitters on the issue, not knowing what to believe. The believers constitute group 3; they're convinced that not only is energy healing real, but that an energy approach to healing has profound implications for our understanding of health, life, and even evolution. As with most issues in life, the people in each of these three groups vary a great deal in the depth of their convictions.

Though I was originally educated to believe that energy healing was impossible (group 1), my personal philosophy is one of fervent agnosti-cism (group 2) until proven otherwise. My writing partner, Bill Simon, likes to say that I was raised to be an orthodox agnostic. What this means is that regardless of the question—for example, Is there gravity? or Is there a god?—my first response is always the same: "I don't know; could be yes, could be no; I'm open. Show me the data."

However, my research experience in energy healing over the past eleven years, coupled with my clinical observations plus direct personal experiences, have led me to become enthusiastic about the concept of energy and its applications to healing, well-being, and evolution. In other words, I've shifted to group 3 as a function of the totality of the evidence.

Which group do you fall into? If you began reading this book as a skeptic (group 1) but you're comfortably accepting the experimental evidence presented so far and you're open to new concepts and ideas, you may be in the process of shifting your views toward accepting energy healing as possibly, if not probably, true. On the other hand, you might still be skeptical. Perhaps you think the apparent evidence of energy healing is actually the result of something else—spontaneous remission, or some sort of placebo effect.

Whether accepting or skeptical, you're entitled to wonder about other possible explanations, just as a scientist does—examining and evaluating the claims critically, with integrity as the goal. It turns out that if we accept the experimental findings of the earlier pages, our vision of the placebo effect itself is expanded and even transformed in surprising and exciting ways.

I have organized the different theories of apparent energy-healing effects according to a ladder of possible explanations. This system first came to me when I participated in the "Think Tank Working Group Meeting on Biofield Energy Medicine" held at the National Center for Complementary and Alternative Medicine (NCCAM) in May 2006, at the National Institutes of Health (NIH) campus in Bethesda, Maryland. The session brought together people representing the disciplines of biophysics, biochemistry, cellular biology, electrical engineering, psychology, epidemiology, internal medicine, oncology, and radiology. Earlier in these pages, I described some of the research I presented at this gathering.

Following the presentations, the group attempted to make sense of the diverse set of findings and the possible explanations. As you can probably guess, different disciplines favored certain explanations and deemphasized or dismissed others.

It occurred to me that the total set of alternative explanations could be effectively organized as seven steps of a ladder. In the formal document that summarized the findings of our committee, the chairman chose to use only four of my seven; here, I'll present the complete list. In the process, you'll have the opportunity to understand why all seven are necessary to address the totality of the scientific evidence as well as the experiences of advanced energy healers. I include all the steps not because they represent the current debate, but more importantly because I've come to the conclusion that the nature of healing involves, to various degrees, all seven steps of understanding. I have also included what I playfully call "step 0," which is the argument that there is no effect and therefore no need for a ladder in the first place.

The ladder of possible energy-healing explanations is summarized below. The steps are arranged from the highest to the lowest, as on a real ladder.

Step 7   The observed effects involve spiritual mechanisms

Step 6   The observed effects require new physics

Step 5   The observed effects are the result of advanced physical phenomena

Step 4   The observed effects are the result of quantum fields

Step 3   The observed effects are the result of electromagnetic fields

Step 2   The observed effects represent belief or expectancy (placebo)

Step 1   The observed effects are the result of spontaneous remission

Step 0   There are no observed effects and therefore no need for a ladder

For the record, a more conceptually accurate representation of the logical process I'm employing would be a set of seven concentric circles, organized hierarchically, or even better, a set of bowls within bowls, or Russian dolls within dolls. However, it's easier for most of us—scientists and health-care practitioners included—to imagine walking up a ladder than separating bowls in a kitchen. Though the ladder image is a metaphor, here it's a very useful one.

As you take each step, the view gets higher and wider, the air gets thinner, and the implications become increasingly challenging and controversial. You could describe this ladder as a set of necessary steps, informed by experimental evidence, for climbing from the conventional and mainstream to the frontier and beyond.

But as you climb the ladder, I fully expect you'll find the emerging views breathtaking, inspiring, and inherently optimistic for humanity and the planet as a whole. So here we go.

Step 0: There are no observed effects and therefore no need for a ladder

Some people believe that patients who receive energy healing typically show no improvements—in physical, psychological, or spiritual measures—compared to patients receiving standard care. The only way to reach the no-effects conclusion is to presume that all the findings published in the literature to date on energy healing are completely false. It also requires that one dismiss all the findings published in the field of mind-body medicine on spontaneous healing as well as placebo effects. Taking such a stand, which means joining forces with the superskeptics, requires that one completely avoid or reject the entire literature in the area. Superskeptics refuse to climb the ladder at all.

Step 1: The observed effects are the result of spontaneous remission

This is the argument that a subset of patients will get better spontaneously or naturally. Even from the worst, most deadly illnesses, some people do recover. Therefore, a person who accepts step 1 but refuses to climb higher has concluded that those who improve after energy healing would have gotten better anyway.

In some cases this is undoubtedly true. However, there are hundreds of published experiments documenting that patients in the placebo group in a test of a novel treatment often respond favorably when compared to people receiving no treatment. The literature is also filled with experiments demonstrating that more patients show improvement following novel treatments—be they drugs, psychotherapy, energy healing, or whatever—when compared to rates of spontaneous healing in patients not included in the study.

A person unwilling to go beyond step 1 is ignoring the wealth of evidence that is the foundation of psychophysiology and mind-body medicine.

Step 2: The observed effects represent belief or expectancy (placebo)

Similar to the preceding step, this one addresses people who recover not spontaneously but because of a placebo—a sugar pill instead of real medicine, or fake treatment instead of real—that leads them to improve because they *expect* to improve. This is the argument that changes in physical, psychological, and spiritual symptoms and measures can be explained through a combination of personality, environmental, cognitive, and social-psychological mechanisms.

Serious research usually demands double-blind studies, arranged so that neither the patient nor the provider knows which pill is the active treatment and which the placebo. Even if the active medication results in greater improvements in symptoms compared to the placebo, patients receiving placebos typically show greater improvement compared with patients who are given neither the placebo nor the active medication.

People familiar with the literature on placebos and the larger literatures in psychophysiology and mind-body medicine appreciate the power of belief and expectancy on healing. The question then arises, can placebo effects explain *all* of the observations in energy-healing research? Some people would prefer to reach step 2 and go no further.

However, many studies using sham or fake healing in patients or animals have found that the real energy healing produces greater improvements than the sham healing. Moreover, energy-healing effects can be observed in single cells such as *E. coli* bacteria (chapter 14), or even in plants such as geranium leaves (chapter 12). Trying to blame these effects on the cells' and plants' belief or expectancy simply doesn't wash.

Findings like these require us to move up the ladder of possible energy-healing explanations.

Step 3: The observed effects are the result of electromagnetic fields

The electromagnetic-fields viewpoint holds that the observed physical and psychological changes (and, some believe, even spiritual changes) can be explained as caused by the patient resonating with bioelectromagnetic fields generated by the healer's body, or electromagnetic fields generated by energy-healing devices. This explanation draws on the application of well-accepted models in conventional physics and biophysics. A leader in these applications is the interdisciplinary specialty of bioelectromagnetics (one source of information on the subject can be found at www.bioelectromagnetics.org).

While there are hundreds of studies documenting bioelectromagnetic effects on molecules, cells, organs, and beyond, few physicians or scientists, much less members of the public, are familiar with this body of research. James Oschman's books *Energy Medicine* and *Energy Medicine in Therapeutics and Human Performance* provide a clear and compelling overview.

If electromagnetic fields are fundamental to the structure and function of all matter, and bioelectromagnetic fields are fundamental to the structure and function of biological systems, why do we need to have more than three steps? The reason is that healers claim, and experiments verify, that there are observed effects in healing that cannot be explained by bioelectromagnetic theory itself. One major factor to consider is that healing can occur over long distances above and beyond the effective reach of electromagnetic fields.

Step 4: The observed effects are the result of quantum fields

Step 4, the application of quantum physics, including concepts of quantum fields, nonlocality, and entanglement—what Einstein called "spooky action at a distance"—is becoming recognized as a necessary explanatory framework for understanding certain anomalous findings in energy healing and related areas of consciousness science and parapsychology. In some of the experiments described in parts I and II, the observed effects appear to occur independent of distance. These observations are inexplicable at step 3—which is why they are described as anomalous— but they can be predicted to occur when we include the quantum-fields explanation. If we accept these observations as genuine, then it becomes necessary for us to keep climbing higher on the ladder of energy-healing explanations.

Dr. Edgar Mitchell, a former astronaut who walked on the moon and had a profound transformative experience of consciousness while in space, has referred to a transcendental experience as the feeling of being "one with the universe." He founded the visionary Institute of Noetic Sciences (www.noetic.org). Dr. Mitchell is a strong proponent of applying what is called "quantum holography" to healing science, consciousness science, and parapsychology.

One of the senior scientists at the Institute of Noetic Sciences, Dr. Dean Radin, has written a seminal book on quantum physics and the mind. Called *Entangled Minds,* it's stirring in its reasoning and experiments and is a pleasure to read. The truth is that so-called spooky actions at a distance do occur in quantum physics and energy healing. Responsible science requires that we examine their potential integration into our consideration of the mechanisms at work in healing.

Step 5: *The observed effects are the result of advanced physical phenomena*

There are certain phenomena in energy healing and consciousness science that go beyond predictions of quantum physics—phenomena that even quantum physicists consider anomalous. Most scientists are willing to ignore these effects, dismissing them as the result of experimental error or sufficiently unreliable as to be of no importance. Magnetic monopoles, scalar waves, string theory, and other areas of advanced physics are explored as possible explanations for certain very spooky observations.

One of the oldest organizations dedicated to exploring such phenomena is the U.S. Psychotronics Association. Although considered a fringe group by some, their membership includes a number of mainstream scientists, and the organization does useful, valuable work. On their Web site (www.psychotronics.org), they state as a basic premise that ESP is a "natural occurrence." (Though ESP is usually an abbreviation for "extrasensory perception," I prefer using this abbreviation to mean *"energy-*sensory perception.") The organization states that its purpose is to "seek to understand how [ESP] occurs, and to use that understanding for the benefit of mankind."

The association was founded by the late J. G. Gallimore. Apparently a talented psychic and scientific researcher himself, Gallimore sought to "understand the rules governing the energy fields and currents he could see and feel around people, objects, and machines."

According to the association's Web site, "USPA is not an experiential group; our orientation is towards the technical and scientific aspects of psychotronics and its practical applications, merging the esoteric/spiritual and scientific worlds. . . . This is the physics of the year 2100."

The USPA appears to address steps 4, 5, and 6. I include the organization because it illustrates how a small community of scientists is exploring advanced physics to discover possible explanations of energy healing.

Step 6: The observed effects require new physics

As Dr. William Tiller, a distinguished professor emeritus of material sciences from Stanford University, reminds us on his Web site (http://tiller foundation.com), Sir Arthur C. Clarke once said, "Any sufficiently advanced technology is indistinguishable from magic." In Dr. Tiller's book *Some Science Adventures with Real Magic,* he writes:

> In this book, using almost no mathematical aids, we have summarized the key experimental findings of our two earlier books [*Science and Human Transformation* and *Conscious Acts of Creation: The Emergence of a New Physics*] and have outlined our more recent results on the successful replication experiments at several laboratories in the U.S. and Europe. Together, this large body of experimental data forms a firm foundation upon which we lay out a greatly expanded paradigm for future science wherein human consciousness can play a significant role in the manifested expressions of nature and in the technologies that might thereby be created.

Dr. Tiller continues:

> [B]oth the experimental research findings and the new concepts needed to be assimilated are at considerable variance with our day-to-day, present cognitive world so some stretch of self is required for easy assimilation.

Based upon more than twenty years of research related to mind-machine effects and psychotronics (which involves the connection between the human mind and some type of electronic device), Dr. Tiller proposed a "new energy in nature that produces very long range information entanglement and appears to be related to movement of magnetic charge in the vacuum level of reality." He goes on to say that "it uses the experimental data to formulate theoretically a new reference frame for viewing nature, one that encompasses both conventional space-time science and the psychoenergetic phenomena." To some, this may sound like gobbledygook. However, if you examine Dr. Tiller's writings, you discover that he comes to these conclusions based upon a series of carefully controlled experiments that require extensions in our understanding of physics and the nature of reality.

Dr. Tiller is a pioneer—a controversial genius whose work bridges the physical, the psychological, and the spiritual. He comes to the conclusion that his experiments into the effects of mind on electronic devices, the pH of water, and the healing of cells require that science envision a "new energy in nature." The only way to discover whether you agree with his conclusion is to read his work.

It should be noted that physics is in a constant state of evolution. Physicists are not afraid to invent ideas such as dark energy, dark matter, and superstrings if the data and equations warrant it.

Step 7: The observed effects involve spiritual mechanisms

My personal experience is that individuals who reach steps 5 and 6 are almost universally open to step 7 as well, even though these individuals are more often than not "closet" step-7 people.

So far we haven't considered the spiritual side of energy healing except in passing. You'll find a discussion of research addressing these controversial claims in a later chapter.

For now, what's important to mention is that historic and anecdotal reports, coupled with contemporary research integrating spirituality and science, such as in my books *The Afterlife Experiments* and *The G.O.D. Experiments,* provide an intriguing reason, even a compelling reason, to entertain seriously that beyond what we experience as matter, energy, and even information is the existence of a conscious intelligence that pervades everything, including us. And that in order to fully understand and advance energy healing, science will have to accept the currently taboo possibility that pervasive intelligence exists throughout the universe.

For a host of reasons—including credibility, acceptance, and funding—institutions like the National Institutes of Health and the National Science Foundation are unwilling to acknowledge and investigate the possibility of such a cosmic intelligence. A dear colleague and friend, who will remain anonymous, refers to this possibility as one of the "unmentionables."

However, just because a topic is taboo does not mean that it should be ignored, especially if scientific evidence supports it. If the intuitive side of energy healing involves, at least in part, spiritual energy, spiritual information, and even spiritual intelligence, and if these processes can be addressed experimentally, it is a scientist's solemn responsibility to bring them into the laboratory and honor their potential contributions.

Expanding Our Vision of the Placebo Effect

Imagine for the moment that each of the seven steps on the ladder of explanations occurs and is real:

Some people do get better "spontaneously" (step 1)

Belief and expectancy play a role in healing (step 2)

Electromagnetic fields play a role in healing (step 3)

Quantum fields play a role in healing (step 4)

Scalar waves and other advanced physical phenomena play a role in healing (step 5)

Yet-to-be-envisioned energies, fields, and phenomena play a role in healing (step 6)

And spiritual processes at various levels, from discarnate spirits to the Great Spirit, play a role in healing as well (step 7)

If science were to establish that each of these levels was true, then we could apply the higher levels or steps to understanding how the lower levels or steps operate.

For example, evidence that people get better "spontaneously" (step 1) doesn't tell us *how* they got better. Could they have healed in part because they were inspired by loved ones to believe they would get better (step 2)? In other words, could step 2 help explain how step 1 works? This is, in fact, what mind-body researchers typically propose.

Could they have healed "spontaneously" (step 1) in part because they received love and affection from people and pets (step 2), which involved electromagnetic fields of their loved ones resonating with them and helping them heal (step 3)? Could step 3 help explain not only step 1, but maybe step 2 as well? This is, in fact, what certain bio-electromagnetic researchers propose.

Or could they have healed "spontaneously" (step 1) in part because their loved ones, who were many hundreds or thousands of miles away, were sending them loving intentions and loving energies, and through their quantum connections, called "quantum entanglement," helped foster the healing (step 4)?

Once you see the logic of how higher levels or steps can be employed to examine lower-level processes, you can envision how an evolving science can become more comprehensive, integrative, and complete.

Scientists like Dr. Dean Radin and Dr. William Tiller in the United States, as well as Dr. Rupert Sheldrake and Dr. Harold Wallach in Europe, have been exploring the applications of steps 4 through 6 for expanding our understanding of consciousness, and therefore of what traditionally has been called the placebo effect. In the process, innovations in the design of experiments emerge as a result. This also involves including placebo controls in conventional physics experiments to determine if the mind of the physicist is influencing the outcome of his experiments with subatomic particles or light.

For example, as Dr. Sheldrake has documented, it is a fact that the majority of biologists, chemists, and physicists do not conduct their experiments according to double-blind protocols. But if consciousness, via energetic mechanisms, can influence the functioning of cells, water, and even electrons—as described in part II of this book—then some of their findings may have been inadvertently influenced by the consciousness and intentions of the researchers.

Also, my colleagues and I have conducted a double-blind experiment funded by NIH that investigated the possible effects of distant energy healing and prayer on patients in recovery following cardiac surgery; this study was done with practitioners of Johrei, a form of spiritual healing. Analyzed by Dr. Audrey Brooks, we discovered that it was the combination of belief and awareness plus actually receiving the distant energy-healing practice that resulted in the greatest decrease in stress and pain. It was not belief *versus* distant energy healing, it was belief *plus* distant energy healing that produced the best results. Using the ladder of explanations, it was a combination of at least steps 2, 3, and 4 that produced the results. If scientists like Tiller and also if the Johrei practitioners are correct, then it's very possible that steps 2 through 7 were involved in the findings we obtained in this clinical-outcomes study.

Where Do You Stand on the Ladder of Possible Explanations?

Each person must ultimately decide for herself or himself how far up the ladder of possible explanations she/he is willing to climb. When I first began this journey, I was comfortable with steps 1 and 2 and had some experience, through my training in electrical engineering and physics, in the possibilities of steps 3 and 4. However, over the past eleven years, my experience in the laboratory, my exposure to master healers, plus my direct personal experiences as a patient and a healer in training have pushed me to explore and acknowledge all seven steps.

Again, the ladder image is only a metaphor. But we're now ready to shift from metaphor to metamorphosis and metascience (the search for universal principles in nature) to see the emerging possibilities with new eyes.

You see, wire telegraph is a kind of a very, very long cat. You pull his tail in New York and his head is meowing in Los Angeles. Do you understand this? And radio operates exactly the same way: you send signals here, they receive them there. The only difference is that there is no cat.

—ALBERT EINSTEIN

Chapter 17

How Energy Healing Works— The Living Cell Phone

In light of all the experiments reported in this book, what can we conclude about how energy healing works? Does contemporary science provide us with not only a reason to believe in the reality of energy healing, but also a way to understand its nature, mechanisms, and potentials?

I have come to the conclusion that the answers are decidedly yes, and yes. Not only does science give us a solid reason to believe in energy healing, but it provides us with the means to understand the essence of how this healing, and all healing, operates.

Now I want to become explanatory in one sense and visionary in another. My purpose is not only to synthesize and integrate, but to extend and envision. The goal here is to look not only at the present, but more importantly at the future. Energy healing can be thought of in a narrow sense as a set of complementary methods used for healing and health. It can also be thought of, in a wider sense, as an emerging paradigm for understanding the nature of all healing and even of the nature of existence itself.

177

I want to use the evolution of cell-phone technology as an aid to envisioning the evolution of our understanding of energy healing and what some scientists and healers have referred to as our "wireless anatomy" or "energy anatomy."

This isn't meant to suggest that knowledge gleaned from the evolution of the cell phone is a metaphor for the way our anatomy functions and healing occurs. This point is worth repeating—I'm not suggesting that the cell phone is a metaphor for energy healing. Rather, I have come to the conclusion that *the evolution of the cell phone itself—and its associated network structures—reflects a novel implementation of how our anatomy evolved and how it actually functions as a wireless network of living cell-phone systems.*

I'm suggesting that the explicit model of emerging cell-phone technology actually comes from the implicit model underlying our anatomy, the anatomy of all biological systems, and ultimately the anatomy of what we call the "physical world" itself. Simply stated, our contemporary cell phones are derived from the very network or matrix nature of the universe, including our fundamental anatomy. Today's portable cell phones are an expression of the inherent living cell-phone nature of all physical entities.

In the following discussion, I will be using the prefix "meta-" in the sense of "a higher level of description." For example, when I write playfully of putting on my metaglasses, I mean that I am viewing the concept—whatever it is—at the highest, most comprehensive, most universal level I can conceive. (The interested reader will find a thorough discussion of the use of "meta-" in the appendix "Understanding Universal Energy" at the end of this book.)

Be prepared to have your mind stretched and your vision expanded as you view energy healing through conventional as well as "meta" glasses.

Basic Premises

With apologies in advance, the following material offers some insights that, though highly valuable, are not essential for understanding the main ideas of this book. If you find yourself bogging down in the material, I invite you to skip ahead to chapter 18.

Energy healing begins with the premise that energy exists and that it can produce healing. Since by definition energy is the capacity to do work and overcome resistance, energy therefore has the capacity to produce physical healing. Whereas matter is not defined as the capacity to do work and overcome resistance, energy is. If we are to use these terms carefully, accurately, and consistently, then we should conclude that the underlying mechanism of producing physical healing always involves energy. I repeat, from the perspective of physics, all physical healing, by definition, involves energy.

Yes, we can ingest atoms and chemicals—in the form of herbs, foods, or man-made drugs—and healing can occur. But in terms of physics, the molecules per se do not do the healing. It's the energy associated with the atoms and chemicals that actually heals.

The question then arises, if energy is involved in all healing, must the energy only come from chemicals that are ingested in the body, or can the energy come from chemical systems outside the body, regardless of their size and complexity—from atoms of oxygen in the air, from other human beings, from the sun? According to physics, size doesn't matter. What matters is that the energy is present and is expressed as quantum fields. As we've observed earlier, all material systems are in their essence dynamical energy systems that emit energy fields; therefore, in principle, they can all affect our health and healing.

As Sherlock Holmes might have said, "It's elementary, my dear Watson."

Lessons from the Extraordinary Evolution of Cell Phones

Energy healing involves more than healers—or bioelectromagnetic devices, sound and light generating machines, or even minerals and crystals—generating appropriate energy (or meta-energy) patterns to bring about resonance between the healing agents and their subjects. The energy-healing process is much more interesting, exciting, and challenging. This is where the emergence of cell-phone technology illustrates the underlying nature of how all dynamical systems interact to various degrees through the universal process of wireless energetic communication.

A meta (or universal) definition of cell phone could be:

A Note for the Technical Reader: Energy and Matter

Historically, physicists once thought that matter was primary, and that energy was produced by matter. Energy was, so to speak, a side effect of matter. This was the kind of thinking that characterized Newtonian physics prior to the twentieth century. This same thinking characterizes conventional medicine today—despite the fact that physics has long moved beyond this point.

In physics, following Einstein and then quantum theory, a radical transformation of thinking occurred. In fact, virtually everything was turned upside down and inside out. Instead of viewing matter as primary and energy as secondary, energy came to be viewed as primary and matter as secondary. Not only could energy be converted into matter and vice versa, but matter came to be considered a subset, or special state, of energy.

Implicitly wearing his metaglasses, Einstein expressed this when he said that "the field is the only reality." At one level, objects have apparent structure and mass; however, at a higher level, a level both more comprehensive and more fundamental, material objects are actually understood to be vibrating organizations of energies whose fields are extending infinitely into space in all directions as complex field spheres. Einstein not only knew this intellectually, he seemed to experience it in the core of his being.

Let us put our metaglasses on for the moment and expand our thinking about energy and energy healing. Energy healers use the word

a wireless device or system that (1) detects energy and information, (2) converts this energy and information into electromagnetic signals that can be transmitted over great distances, (3) receives energy and information in the form of electromagnetic signals, including signals that have traveled over great distances, (4) converts this energy and information into audible, visual, and even vibratory signals, for the purpose of (5) communication.

Now, what is curious about this straightforward metadefinition is that all material systems, to various degrees, can function like cell "energy" not simply in the lower-level, electromagnetic-field sense, or even only in the quantum-field sense, but in a metalinguistic sense to refer to the capacity to alter anything—be it physical, psychological, social, or spiritual. They speak about their consciousness "having energy." They speak of their intentions as having "energetic consequences"—meaning being able to do work—on any level of the functioning of a human, animal, or plant. They conclude that their consciousness and intentions involve some sort of energy because they can obtain measurable effects on people's chemical, biological, and psychological states. Since the concept of the capacity to do work can be thought of in the most comprehensive, general, and even universal manner, the physical term "energy" implicitly includes the concept of meta-energy."

It's important that we be logical and that we use logic consistently. In the same way that physics infers the existence of electromagnetic fields and quantum fields, scientists can infer the existence of other fields such as information fields, emotion fields, and intention fields—but they will make this inference if, and only if, the empirical evidence derived from controlled experiments supports it.

The totality of the experiments described in parts I and II indicate that not only do people, but also rats, *E. coli* bacteria, and even geranium leaves have the capacity to respond to the conscious intentions of healers, as well to the healers' emotional states. These empirical observations require that we view the emerging evidence through a lens that is wide enough truly to see it.

phones. Meaning that whether the material system is a molecule, a cell, an organ, a whole body, a planet, a star, a galaxy—the size or scale does not matter—the material system engages in the process of detecting, processing, transmitting, and receiving energy and information in a dynamical, interactive fashion.

When the core concepts of physics are integrated with the core concepts of what is sometimes called dynamical systems, network, or matrix theory, we come to the realization that everything that exists is engaged in a constant process of multi-way communication, to various degrees of complexity.

And when we remember that what we call a "material system," as viewed by contemporary physics, is a dynamically organized pattern of vibrating energies, fields, or even "strings," we can understand and appreciate that energy communication is a universal bridging process that connects everything.

Chapter 13 put forward the idea that plants could be viewed as botanical cell phones and explored a little of the stupendous complexity of how contemporary cells phones operate. We considered how hundreds of thousands of cell phones can be communicating simultaneously within the boundaries of a single compact city. And we pondered the mind-expanding idea that our 60-plus-trillion cells could be functioning simultaneously as LBCPs—little bitty cell phones.

What you are about to read is even more humbling. Which do you think is more complex—a Treo model 700 cell phone or a single heart cell?

Obviously, the cell phone is bigger, heavier, and has more atomic mass. But which is more complex in terms of its moment-to-moment functioning? Is the computer in the cell phone as complex as human DNA? Which has a greater number of simultaneous channels of energy and information processing and communication, the cell phone or a single heart cell?

The answer, as you anticipate, is that our current cell phones don't hold a candle to our heart cells. Nor to any other cells in the human body, for that matter.

I don't mean to belittle or minimize our evolving global wireless communication system. Far from it: I celebrate the collective genius that makes our technology possible. However, it's worth remembering that the extraordinary complexity of our unfolding planetary wireless communication system is relatively crude when we recognize that each human body functions as an even more extraordinarily complex wireless-communication network.

When we remember that biological systems have been around for millions of years, whereas cell phones emerged only in the past few decades, logic takes us to the conclusion that what we are witnessing with the evolution of multipurpose cell phones is a recapitulation of the multipurpose nature of LBCPs.

We can liken the cell phones' transmitting and receiving stations that integrate and coordinate the network of signals to organ systems within the body—huge collections of networks of components that function in a coordinated fashion.

It follows that in a deep sense, our bodies are like a whole network of individual cell phones plus coordinating stations. All of the components, at all levels, whether they are in direct contact or connected wirelessly, are all sharing energy and information. Simply stated, each of us individually is like an entire Verizon or Sprint network. And remember, as complex as Verizon and Sprint are, they do not come close to competing with the essence of your anatomy.

Like Verizon and Sprint, your body is an integrated "wired plus wireless" anatomical system of mind-numbing complexity and heart-inspiring beauty. All of it not only runs on energy, it *is* energy. Material anatomy is energy anatomy. Though you may experience yourself as a physical being, like everything else, you are fundamentally an energy being. When you put on your metaglasses, your ability to experience your energyness is dramatically enhanced.

How Cell-Phone Communications Provide a Model for Two-Person Healing

If all of this is not remarkable enough, consider the fact that if I use Verizon in Tucson and you use Sprint in Seattle, you and I can still communicate with each other. You can send me a picture that you took moments earlier from the Seattle Space Needle, and though I am more than a thousand miles away, I can tell you how beautiful the picture is while I'm sitting in my living room in Tucson. The technology and networks have been designed so that all the cell-phone networks can communicate with one another, and your Samsung phone and my Motorola can exchange information.

On a human scale, one person to another, you and I can connect in much the same way. Our 60-plus-trillion LBCPs not only communicate within each of us, they can communicate between you and me as well. Consider what happens when you hold someone you love. Or more explicitly, what happens when you are being physically intimate with someone. Can you imagine to what extent the bioenergetic signals from our cells and organs are interacting and communicating?

Recall what happens when a cardiologist records the EKG of the fetus in a mother's womb: the screen displays EKGs of both the fetus and the mother.

Also recall that we do not actually have to touch physically for our electromagnetic fields to interconnect us. When we consider the totality of the experiments described in parts I and II, the science tells us that the capacity for interconnection, and therefore communication, is not only extensive, it is fundamental to the nature of energetic reality.

Biologists are beginning to understand that cells, tissues, and organs not only engage in apparent physical communication, they engage in energetic and informational communication as well. A cutting-edge area in contemporary biological science is termed "informational biology." As you know, even DNA is referred to as an information "code."

Energy provides the source of power, information provides the patterns for structure—and it's the combination of energy and information that allows for the existence of stable and healthy as well as evolving physical entities.

The concept of wireless anatomy—using "cell phone" not only in a metaphorical sense but in a fundamental structural and functional sense—provides a framework for understanding how energy healing can occur. A whole book on energy healing could be written from a wireless network communications point of view.

What Is a Living Cell Phone?

I want to address one additional conceptual question before we move on: the nature of life itself. Are only biological systems alive? Or can a network be alive? Indeed, is it possible that everything, from an energetic perspective, is in a deep sense alive?

When we put on our metaglasses, even life itself can be seen in a new light—a living light.

One of the greatest mysteries in all of science is the nature of life, how it originated and how it is maintained. There are basically two fundamental ways of looking at this issue. The first one, which is accepted by the majority of scientists alive today, is that material systems are either nonliving or living. Atomic and chemical material systems are considered nonliving, whereas biological systems are considered living.

From a lower-level perspective, if our cells are functioning as little bitty cell phones, and by definition our cells are alive, then we can think of our cells as living cell phones. However, when we put on our meta-glasses, a bigger and grander picture comes into focus.

Biological systems have various properties, including metabolism and dynamics. Probably the most extensive description of living systems was provided by Dr. James G. Miller and a group of twenty-plus colleagues in his book *Living Systems.* Miller et al. presented a list of nineteen "functional subsystems" that they concluded characterized all living systems. The book points out that not only did cells, tissues, organs, and organisms manifest this complete list of functions, so did groups of people, institutions, and even large cultural communities of people—all evidencing the same set of functions. What the Miller team had done was to examine properties of life from a higher level; they were, to use the terminology suggested here, seeing life through a set of metaglasses.

A primary reason why many Western people, scientists included, view chemicals and atoms as nonliving is because atoms and chemicals do not appear to self-replicate. Though atoms may appear to "mate" with each other, even for life—for example, atoms of hydrogen and oxygen can bond together and create a "couple" as a molecule of water— we're not accustomed to thinking of atoms or molecules as being alive, a condition we only ascribe to those classes of objects capable of reproducing to continue their species. Since we've never spotted any newborn water molecules or new little baby atoms created by full-grown atoms, they don't qualify.

But there's another way to look at this that takes modern science and technology into account. A branch of computer science called "artificial life" deals with software that exhibits the properties of life—yes, even including self-replication, through subroutines that are designed to make copies of themselves. Moreover, we can design material systems that can repair themselves and even replicate themselves. Hence, so-called nonliving material systems can be designed to behave as if they are alive.

The other way of looking at life is that everything is alive to some degree. People who adopt this vision don't define life as requiring self-replication, but focus instead on the dynamical, interactive, and evolutionary nature of the life process. This view, while often considered more "primitive" because of its association with native peoples, holds that life exists in everything through the operation of what in China is called *qi;* in Hawaii and the Philippines, *mana;* in India, *prana;* and in the United States the *Great Spirit* of the Native Americans.

Meanwhile, as we have said, what contemporary physics tells us, in no uncertain terms, is that everything that exists vibrates—even at the theoretical temperature of absolute zero—and is in continuous interaction and communication with everything around it. As we've also observed, everything that exists is interconnected with everything else to various degrees. Moreover, everything that exists is a manifestation of energy and information. Energy and information are "no-things" in the sense that they do not have "mass" in the sense of matter.

Hence, physics claims that out of "no-things" come "things." These "no-things" are in a constant state of creative and complex change. In a deep sense, energy gives birth to what we experience as matter. When we integrate concepts of energy and information with network and systems models, we realize that energy and information are constantly circulating within and between material systems, and in the process of circulation—created by what are termed "feedback loops"—storage, memory, and evolution can occur. In the book *The Living Energy Universe,* this principle is playfully expressed as "What goes around, and stays around, evolves around."

This means that, in principle, everything that has circulating feedback loops also exhibits the properties of dynamically storing and evolving energy and information. It follows that everything that exists has a kind of memory and therefore engages in a remembering process that sustains its history, structure, and functioning.

Think about this. We do not need to be rocket scientists, or cellular phone engineers, to integrate the above information and come to the conclusion that if everything is alive in the sense of vibrating and interacting (though not necessarily in terms of reproducing), then this includes manmade cell phones as well as biological cell phones. When we put on our metaglasses, we can see that in a deep sense, not only are manmade cell phones "alive" because they too are composed of vibrating energy and information, but they actually contribute to memory and evolution on the planet with their two-way communication process, which creates circular feedback.

Do you remember how big and bulky the first cell phones were? Elvis Presley had one that filled a large carrying case, which a member of his entourage lugged around for him. It weighed a ton (figuratively), the reception was poor, it didn't have a musical ring (I wonder what song Elvis would have chosen), it didn't take and send pictures or keep his calendar. My current cell phone has a two-gigabyte memory stick and speaks in a gentle voice to remind me of my upcoming appointments. It synchronizes its information with my desktop and laptop computers. When my significant other calls me, her beautiful face appears in brilliant colors on the screen. Witnessing all this through the revealing lens of our metaglasses, we can envision the dynamic vibration of this seemingly unbelievable—but nonetheless real—infinitely complex matrix of apparently living energies and feel more alive and awake than we could ever have imagined.

Love cures people—both the ones who give it and the ones who receive it.

—KARL MENNINGER

Chapter 18

How Spirit and G.O.D. Play a Role in Energy Healing

Love can be thought of as both energy and a conscious intention. Though it's not widely appreciated—physicists don't advertise this fact—Sir Isaac Newton, one of the world's most distinguished and influential scientists of all time, was so deeply religious and spiritual a man that he believed his theory of gravity testified directly to the existence of God.

As noted earlier, Newton conceived that everything in the material world has mass and that all mass has a gravitational field that extends out in all directions, interconnecting with all other masses in the universe to various degrees. Contemporary physics presumes that although the gravitational-field strength decreases with distance, the field itself extends infinitely into space.

The earth, sun, and moon have relatively large masses and associated strong gravitational fields that pull on one another as they extend into space. Since our physical bodies have mass, we too have gravitational fields that extend in all directions. Our bodies therefore pull on the earth, sun, and moon, and they pull on us. Though our gravitational fields are a cat's whisker compared to a mountain relative to the planets and stars because we have such minuscule mass by comparison, to raise

189

that issue misses the main point. The fact is that all material objects manifest a universal gravitational field that literally holds the universe together.

Newton's concept of the gravitation field is special for a number of reasons. It is completely dependable and utterly trustworthy. It has no prejudice and is thoroughly unconditional—it is present in white stars and black holes, kittens and scorpions, saints and tyrants. It is mutually attractive and holds everything within its embrace. Newton envisioned this invisible force to be an expression of God's universal love for everything, including us.

For Newton, gravity expressed both energy and intention—it was a ubiquitous force whose physical and spiritual purpose was to create and sustain the universe as a whole.

All physical fields—gravity included—are inherently invisible. They can only be observed indirectly, through their effects on material objects. Even what we experience as vision, for example, is presumed to involve our retinal cells (tiny material objects) which have evolved the specialized ability to register the presence of invisible, virtually massless, purportedly infinitely small particles termed photons.

Consider stars once again: on a clear night, if we are deep in a forest or on a mountaintop far away from city lights, it's possible for us to see thousands of stars. The more sensitive our eyes, and the more acute our vision, the more stars we can see. With the aid of powerful telescopes and supersensitive low-light cameras, we can see millions or billions of stars, even millions or billions of galaxies. These distant stars and galaxies are invisible to the naked eye, yet they exist in the seeming blackness of space.

Neuroscientists have discovered that retinal cells can respond to single photons of light—and yet, no one has ever experienced a photon of light. Think about this. We don't experience photons; what we experience are birds and trees, computer screens and stars. Until relatively recently, we had no idea that there were photons of light. We also had no idea that information about billions of galaxies of stars was actually entering our eyes as we stared at the night sky. The take-home lesson from contemporary physics is that just because we can't typically see something does not mean it doesn't exist. Rather, we must be open to the existence of seemingly invisible processes and entities that are still to be discovered when the appropriate technology becomes available.

Envisioning How Energy Is the Bridge between Science, Spirituality, and Healing

When Einstein, as quoted earlier, said that "imagination is more important than knowledge," he didn't mean imagination in the sense of an inventive process used to create a make-believe reality, but imagination as used in the creative process of envisioning the yet-to-be-discovered truth about reality.

A familiar cliché tells us that truth is stranger than fiction. In the field of energy healing, that saying applies in particular to people known as spiritualist healers, of whom one of the most renowned is the Brazilian known as John of God.

Surprisingly, it turns out that research supports some of the most incredible claims made about this healer. John of God is more than controversial, he is an enigma. A farm boy who grew up in poverty in a small country town in Brazil, he is said to have had a set of anomalous experiences as an adolescent that transformed him into one of the most acclaimed healers of the twenty-first century. Tens of thousands if not hundreds of thousands of people have come from all parts of the world to his small clinic to be cured through him. I say "through him" because he claims that he himself does not do the healings. He believes that he channels more than thirty different saints as well as some deceased surgeons who purportedly take over his body and channel their healing through him.

John of God claims to do his healing work in a trance and reports having no memory afterward of what has transpired. A devoted group of mediums who assist him during the sessions believe that they help to generate and focus loving energy to support and enhance the healing. During a session, John makes recommendations involving both conventional and alternative treatments. The healing is not exclusively spiritual. On occasion he'll use a medical instrument—inserting forceps into a person's nose, using a scalpel to scrape the cornea of an

eye, or wielding a serrated knife to make incisions in breasts, stom-
achs, and backs.

The physical surgeries are performed completely without anesthesia or sterilization. Thousands of videotapes of his surgeries have been
made, some by Western physicians and scientists. The videos show that
patients almost universally exhibit minimal or no pain, they show
almost no evidence of distress, and the wounds evidence little bleeding
and show little or no evidence of infection afterward.

The claims about John of God seem preposterous. Even after having conducted the highly unconventional research reported in this
book, I find it exceedingly difficult to believe what I observe in the
videotapes of him. Nonetheless, ongoing experiments in my Laboratory
for Advances in Consciousness and Health provide some surprising evidence that is remarkably consistent with spiritual healers' most controversial claims involving John of God.

In fact, many of the most experienced energy healers report, to various degrees, having had the kinds of experiences attributed to John of
God. Scientific integrity requires that we discuss in this book some seminal experiments that justify our including step 7 as being a necessary
rung on the ladder of possible explanations for energy healing. The
challenge for all of us is to examine this evidence with the kind of imagination Einstein recommended so that we may discover its provocative
meaning and significance.

Energy, Intention Detection, and After-Death Communication Experiments

If I were to select the most unanticipated findings that have emerged in
the research I have conducted during my thirty years of investigations at
Harvard, Yale, and the University of Arizona, I would have to include the
discoveries reported in this chapter. Moreover, I would never have
guessed—in fact I could not have imagined—that they would prove to
be as propitious and profound as they turned out to be.

You will recall our early experiments investigating whether college
students could detect hand energy (chapter 4) and the conscious intentions of others (chapter 5). It turns out that people's openness to spiri-

tual beliefs, as well as people's actual spiritual experiences, predict who will be accurate in both an energy-detection task and a conscious-intention task. In fact, one of the strongest spiritual-experience predictors turns out to be communication with a deceased loved one.

Here's the experiment that demonstrated this; it's a minor though significant variation of the experiment described in chapter 5. We were interested in determining whether college students, acting as receivers, could detect whether someone sitting behind them, in the role of an experimenter, was staring at their head or at their back. We selected forty student experimenters and asked each to bring a receiver with whom they had a close relationship.

Each experiment consisted of thirty-six trials. The receivers were told that half were to be "stare at the head" trials, the other half were to be "stare at the back" trials. The receiving student was asked each time to guess "head" or "back."

In fact, the procedure was actually different than what the receivers were told: the experimenters performed only half of the trials with their eyes open. On the other half of the trials, the experimenters were instructed to keep their eyes closed and simply *imagine* staring at the head or the back. So we were looking for answers to two questions. On the trials with eyes open, could the receivers tell whether the experimenter was staring at their head or back? And could they tell the experimenter's *intention* when their eyes were closed?

Figure 18.1 shows the percent of correct and incorrect detections for the forty receivers, for both the "look" (actual stare) and "intend" (imagined stare) conditions. You can see that the percent correct detections was 56 percent for the look (stares) trials, which increased to almost 60 percent for the intend trials. These percent accuracies were highly statistically significant (probability less than one in a thousand by chance).

As part of this experiment, subjects were asked to fill out a straightforward questionnaire (the Openness to Spiritual Beliefs and Experiences Scale) that asked about their beliefs in certain spiritual and psychic phenomena as well as whether they had had any personal experiences with these phenomena.

You can scale yourself to see how you score on these items. For the following questions, answer each using this seven-level scale:

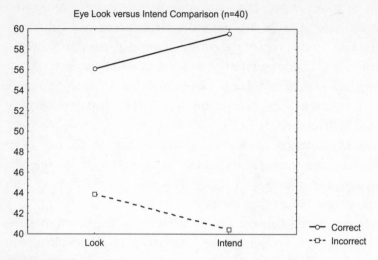

Figure 18.1 Eye Look (Stare) vs. Intend (Eyes Closed)

1 = definitely no	5 = possibly yes
2 = probably no	6 = probably yes
3 = possibly no	7 = definitely yes
4 = maybe	

Here are the questions:

1. Do you believe in the existence of God or a Higher Power? ____

2. Do you believe in the survival of consciousness after death? ____

3. Do you believe in the existence of "angels" or "guides"? ____

4. Do you believe that extrasensory perception (ESP) or para-psychology can allow the passing of signals or messages between people? ____

5. Do you believe that prayer can have an effect on health and well-being? ____

6. Have you ever experienced the presence of God or a Higher Power? ____

7. Have you ever experienced the presence of someone who had passed away? ____

8. Have you ever experienced the presence of an "angel" or "guide"? ____

9. Have you ever experienced ESP between people such as connecting with a loved one from a distance or having a predictive dream about someone? ____

10. Have you ever experienced prayer actually helping to promote health and well-being? ____

To analyze the data, we created a summary score for the first five items, the belief items, and a separate summary score for the second five items, the experience items.

The results were beyond surprising. We found that the higher the receiver's scores were in terms of believing in these spiritual phenomena, the greater was his or her accuracy in detecting the actual stares. But the accuracy of detecting the imagined stares also correlated with the level of belief. What's more, those who had the higher scores in actually experiencing these phenomena achieved a higher accuracy than those with lower experiencing scores. The probability values in all categories were typically less than one in a hundred by chance.

Interestingly, the strongest predictors were "experience of someone who has passed away" (probability less than one in a hundred) and "ESP between people" (probability less than two in a thousand). The God and prayer items did not reach statistical significance.

When we split subjects into three subgroups of "experience of someone who has passed away" (no, maybe, or yes subgroups regarding experience of survival of consciousness after death), we recognized a potentially important discovery. As you can see in figure 18.2, students who answered maybe or yes to the survival of consciousness question did significantly better than those who said no. In other words, people who did not believe they had experienced communication with a deceased loved one showed little evidence of being able to detect stares or intentions.

Why is this important? The research indicates that one person's mind can sometimes detect the intentions from another person's mind, especially if the people are emotionally close and love each other. In addition, accuracy of detecting energy, detecting intention, and experiencing after-death communications are related.

The experiments also show that people who believe they have had

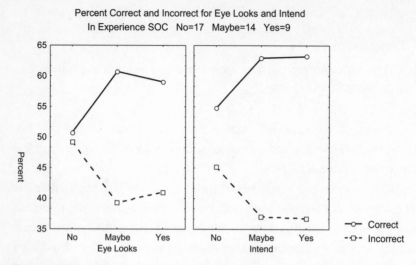

Figure 18.2 Percent Correct and Incorrect for Eye Looks and Intend, as Related to No Experience with Survival of Consciousness

experiences of communications with deceased loved ones are able to detect human energy and to detect conscious intention. It follows then that logic requires us to be at least open to the possibility that healers like John of God could also be having experiences of communications with deceased individuals.

In our books *The Afterlife Experiments* and *The Truth About "Medium,"* Bill Simon and I presented a series of controlled experiments documenting how certain mediums—such as John Edward of the TV show *Crossing Over,* and Allison DuBois, whose life is dramatized in the NBC television series *Medium*—can obtain highly accurate information about deceased individuals. The experiments rule out fraud and trickery as credible explanations of the findings. When these experiments are combined with the energy and conscious-intention experiments described in this book, the scientific possibility of spirit-assist healing becomes plausible and deserving of our serious consideration.

A Connection between After-Death Communications and Cardiac Surgery

At the University of Arizona, we have conducted a large-scale clinical-outcomes study involving patients recovering from open-heart surgery as one of the studies under my grant from the National Institutes of Health for research in the area of biofield science. We set out to examine whether distant energy healing and prayer, provided by lay healers practicing Johrei, could impact recovery of patients following cardiac surgery.

Prospective patients were recruited from the University of Arizona Health Sciences Center and also the Tucson Medical Center. They were told that they would be randomly assigned to receive the energy healing and prayers provided by practitioners located at the Johrei Center in Tucson—the practitioners were not physically present in the surgery room, recovery room, or bedside. Neither the surgeons, nurses, nor patients knew whether a given patient was receiving distant Johrei or not.

The patients filled out an extensive battery of presurgery questionnaires that included the ten-item Openness to Spiritual Belief and Experiences questionnaire. For three days following surgery, patients filled out standardized questionnaires assessing their degree of anxiety, depression, and pain.

We completed our analysis of the pretest questionnaires on eighty-two of the patients. We first looked to see whether the sum of the five belief items or the sum of the five experience items, or both together, correlated with the outcome following surgery. What we found was that the level of belief did not predict outcome—but the level of experience *did* predict outcome. People who reported higher spiritual experiences indicated having significantly less anxiety, depression, and pain following surgery. The probability of this occurring by chance was less than one in a hundred.

We then analyzed each of the experience items separately to see which of them, if any, reached statistical significance by themselves. What we found was striking. The item concerning the experience of God or a Higher Power correlated significantly with decreased depression and pain (though not decreased anxiety).

However, the best predictor once again turned out to be the item concerning the experience of the presence of someone who had passed away; people who scored high on this item reported significantly less anxiety, depression, and pain.

Though I had not predicted this finding, once I saw it, it made complete sense. Imagine that you are facing serious surgery for a life-threatening condition. You understand that you could die. Now imagine that you have at some earlier time in your life had the experience of the presence of someone who has passed away. What does this experience mean to you?

First, if you believe through direct experience that your consciousness will continue after you die, then you know that if your heart fails and you pass, you will still be able to meet your loved ones after they in turn pass. Moreover, if you know that you can experience the presence of someone who has died, you will know that it is possible that your loved ones will be able to experience *your* presence if you should die as a result of your surgery.

Even if survival of consciousness after death is not true, you would still think you had experienced it and believe it to be true. Hence you would be less stressed entering surgery, your immune system would be less compromised, and you would be better able to heal after the surgery. You would feel less anxiety, depression, and pain.

Now consider how the findings from the stare-and-intention-detection study mesh with the findings from the cardiac-surgery study. The first tells us that if you think you have experienced the presence of someone who has died, you are better able to detect stares and even the intention to stare. The second implies that if loving practitioners are intending that you survive surgery and heal, you will be more open to receiving their intentions.

This logic would apply not only to your loved ones who are physically alive, but also to your loved ones who have died. It follows that if your deceased loved ones also care about your continued physical survival, they and others might send you loving intentions.

The question is whether you would be open to receiving their energies and intentions. If you scored high on the experience subscale, the data suggest that you would be more open.

Energy and spiritual healers often profess that they receive guidance from above—that deceased loved ones, healers, saints, angels, light beings, and even the Source play a role in the healing work they do. The most humble healers believe that they have very little to do with the actual healing that occurs. They believe they serve a Higher Being and a Higher Intelligence.

What is quite remarkable is that basic research as well as clinical research can speak to the plausibility of these beliefs, as we have seen.

Jesus Christ and Mother Teresa, Sir Isaac Newton and Albert Einstein all seem to have held a common belief that integrates spirituality and science. Spirit and God may play a role in our lives beyond anything we have yet imagined. The challenge is to be open to what the universe shows us, in our hearts and in the laboratory—and celebrate the evidence that is revealed.

Energy as the Universal Bridge Connecting Science, Spirituality, and Healing

The concept of energy is one of the most remarkable and far-reaching ideas conceived in the history of humanity. When we really think about what energy is—the capacity to do work and overcome resistance—and we fully digest that energy is a capacity, something that has virtually no mass yet has the power to create everything, including what we experience as matter, the connection between it and more ancient ideas of spirits and the Great Spirit becomes self-evident.

Energy, as a scientific premise, has the power to be the universal bridge connecting science, spirituality, and healing. To understand how energy is the universal bridge connecting these three things, it's again helpful to look skyward.

Imagine you are outside on a clear night, away from the city lights, and the moon is not visible. You are lying in a hammock and you are gazing up at the sky. What you will see are hundreds or thousands of stars.

Now imagine that you fall asleep in the hammock and you awake after daybreak. What science tells us is that you can't see the stars during the day because the intensity of the light coming from the closest star to us, our sun, makes it impossible for us to see the stars that are still there.

Like the stars in the night sky that disappear when the sun comes up, experience tells us that it is sometimes necessary to be in the dark in order to see the light.

If our energies are like the dynamic light from distant stars—extending into space and continuing their journey long after the atoms composing our physical bodies have returned to the earth—then perhaps what the ancients called our "spirits" and what contemporary physics calls "energy" are, in a deep sense, one and the same. Moreover, if we consider Dr. James Levin's metaphor that "energy is the voice of spirit," we have the potential to appreciate the conclusion reached by one of the founding fathers of quantum physics, Dr. Max Planck, who said, "All matter originates and exists only by virtue of a force. . . . We must assume that behind this force a conscious and intelligent mind exists. This mind is the matrix of all matter."

Are we ready to wake up to the fundamental reality of energy? Are we ready to discover that energy is the means by which a conscious and intelligent mind manifests matter? Time will tell.

> *The important thing is not to stop questioning.*
> —ALBERT EINSTEIN

Chapter 19

Envisioning the Future of Energy Healing—Awakening to Energy Living

Let's review the conclusions that emerge from this book and explore some of the wide-ranging implications for the future of medicine, healing, and humanity.

If we are prepared to accept the fact that energy is the capacity to do work and overcome resistance—a core premise of classical physics—and that what we call "matter" not only emits and absorbs energy, but is, in its essence, organized energy—a core premise of quantum physics—then logic takes us to a controversial but inevitable conclusion: everything that exists is alive because it interacts with, and it communicates by, dynamically vibrating energy.

It follows that you, me, and everything at every level—from subatomic particles to supergalaxies—are in a deep and ultimate sense "energy beings." The reasoning is straightforward: contemporary physics shows us that to be anything is to be energy. And because energy is constantly vibrating and changing, we can see that energy is constantly *being*. As Einstein tried to teach us, there is no matter, at least not as we normally experience it. Einstein knew that we—and everything else—were not, in our essence, material beings, but rather we were, and are, energy beings.

What this requires is that we transform our consciousness and the way we view the world, and instead of being materialists, we become "energy-ists."

When we remember to put on our "energy glasses," we can see that the phenomenon of energy healing is not only an essential property of energy reality but is a subset of what might be called "energy living." We can view energy living at lower levels—electromagnetic fields and quantum fields (our ladder steps 3 and 4 from chapter 16)—or higher levels of physics (steps 5 and 6). If we extend our energy glasses by adding a set of clip-on metalenses, we can envision energy living as including higher spiritual levels (step 7) as well.

Building on that, we can consider a number of questions about the possible evolution and manifestation of energy healing in all aspects of human life—from conception to transition (death), and everything in between. Over time, this will include pregnancy and child rearing, the education of children and health-care professionals, the methods and practice of health care by physicians, nurses, psychologists, and healers of all sorts, the payment of fees for service, the design and construction of homes, hospitals, and businesses, the advancement of human interpersonal and intimate relationships, the playing of sports and music, the caring for animals, the environment, and the planet as a whole, the maturation of our spiritual understanding and living, and, finally, our personal self-healing.

The truth is that—save for the phenomenon of consciousness itself, particularly the idea of universal consciousness, which may be the ultimate mystery—nothing is more fundamental and far reaching than energy. To honor the concept of energy healing, and do it justice, requires that we open our minds and hearts to the infinite vastness of its reach, and celebrate both its scientific understandability and its implicit spirituality.

How Will Techniques of Energy Healing Evolve?

Using the long history of energy healing as a guide—extending back thousands of years to a time when it was practiced worldwide by native peoples—we can envision a rapid extension of techniques in modern times. Ancient as well as new applications of energy are being explored and will continue to evolve. (Examples of contemporary applications— some of them quite astounding—are included in the recommended readings section at the end of this book.)

I especially look forward to seeing the growth of one ancient healing approach that today is in only limited use: the use of sound. Sound energies have been employed for thousands of years: singing and chanting, the speaking of mantras such as spiritual Sanskrit words or phrases, and the playing of bells, bowls, and drums. Today, practitioners use CDs of natural sounds and beautifully composed music combined with tuning forks that are placed on acupuncture points to achieve "needleless" acupuncture effects. Music plus nature sounds—ocean, winds, birds, and rain—are being used before, during, and after surgery to reduce stress, decrease pain medication, and speed healing time.

There is also a long tradition of using light for healing. Today new applications of light therapies have evolved, including full-spectrum lighting for the treatment of seasonal affective disorder and, lately, light-emitting diodes and "cold lasers" for the relief of pain and the promotion of healing.

Some proponents of these treatments are installing chambers where a combination of sound and light create optimal healing environments. It seems reasonable to guess that integrative energy-healing systems combining two or more energy modalities may have greater healing effects than any single modality by itself.

Electromagnetic devices are being invented that appear to have strong effects on the repair of bones, the reduction of pain, the promotion of blood flow, and the absorption of chemicals. Some of these devices use pulsating magnetic fields that vibrate at biological frequencies, such as the brain theta-wave frequency of 4 to 8 cycles per second. A UCLA medical school report has announced a finding that electrical stimulation at 4 cycles per second, applied to specific acupuncture points in sessions lasting thirty to forty-five minutes, effectively reduced the craving for cigarettes. I have witnessed diabetic patients with severe peripheral circulation problems, potentially requiring amputations, who have regained circulation in their limbs following the use of magnetic-field resonating devices.

It's also possible that the bioelectromagnetic field patterns of master healers may contain information that could be recorded digitally and then played back through magnetic-generating coils, allowing patients to be treated at distant locations. This would also potentially allow the curative powers of a master healer to continue being used even after the healer's death.

Once the power of energy healing becomes widely recognized and appreciated, we might see home bioelectromagnetic devices that use sound vibration and light stimulation, as well as electrical and magnetic fields, become as commonplace as electric toothbrushes and electronic thermometers.

How Will Techniques of Energy Diagnosis Evolve?

Experienced healers report that they can see energies around and within the body. Using this information, and employing other intuitive processes as well, healers have demonstrated their ability to go beyond making medical diagnoses and offering recommendations for treatment, to being able to foresee the occurrence of physical problems before they have manifested.

Healers claim that disorders in the flow and structure of energy around and within the body not only play a fundamental role in disease, but they occur before physical changes and symptoms occur. Just as it took thousands of years before humans figured out how to make machines that would fly—and we ultimately succeeded—it's my sense that we are on the brink of having a Wright brothers of energy diagnostics. While Wilbur and Orville needed to master an understanding of aerodynamics, what we need is credible evidence that preclinical energy assessment is real. The good news is that the prototype devices are now being built and tested.

Instrument manufacturers are currently exploring a variety of bioelectromagnetic measurement devices that hold the promise of making these preclinical energy assessments in order to provide early warnings of major disorders like heart disease and cancer. Though health care will always be concerned with treatments of emergencies and acute conditions, there is a growing movement to foster disease prevention and health promotion to improve quality of life as well as reduce cost.

Also, what if energy flow can be enhanced through physical manipulation or the "untwisting" of our physical and energy structures? (See the Web site www.healthabounds2.com). Could it be that this is part of the mechanism by which massage and body-manipulation therapies work?

Wouldn't it be a wonderful world if we were to reach the place where we each paid our medical caregiver a monthly fee to keep us healthy, and owed him nothing for the medical attention he provided when we fell ill!

How Will Applications of Energy Healing Evolve?

Since everything is energy, it's only a matter of time before energy theory will be part of everything and energy techniques will be applied to everything.

Beyond applying energy-healing techniques to the diagnosis, treatment, and prevention of disease and the promotion of health, energy healing will be applied to increasing longevity, quality of life, and even producing "super" or "ultra" health, as some practitioners describe it.

One of my favorite future potential applications of energy healing involves enhancing the process of conception, pregnancy, and early childhood development. What if a loving couple were to employ their energy-health promotion during the woman's pregnancy, practicing various energy-intention techniques such as meditation, healing touch, Reiki, and sound techniques (including talking to the fetus)? What if the process of birth included energy-healing techniques? What if the couple continued this approach to what might be called "energy healing living," through the child's infancy and youth?

Would such babies be healthier, stronger, and happier? Would they grow into better adjusted, healthier adolescents and adults? Would they become "superbabies" and eventually "superadults"?

Even if the process of living by the principles of energy healing primarily reduced medical complications only during pregnancy and birth, this would more than justify the practice. It's prudent that we remain open to the possibility that there is more to human potential than we currently recognize. The truth is, no one knows what might transpire if babies were conceived, born, and raised under optimal energy-healing conditions. If we are not willing to entertain the question, we will never receive an answer.

My other favorite example concerns potential applications to hospices. Energy-healing techniques are currently being incorporated into hospice environments, primarily for pain relief. However, the energy perspective has deep implications for our ability to understand the dying process and the nature of what we experience as physical death. *If* our energy and consciousness is like the light from distant stars, continuing long after the star has died—and I underscore *if*—then logic leads to the conclusion that what we currently call "death" should be reframed as "transition."

Many patients in hospice report experiencing so-called deathbed visions and near-death, out-of-body experiences. Conventional medicine interprets these experiences as hallucinations created by a dying brain—some combination of steps 1 and 2. However, the new energy medicine would reinterpret these experiences as potentially valid perceptions of the next stage in the patient's life journey—not a firing from the job of life but a promotion to a new stage. Energy healing could help patients make this a positive transition to be made with grace, dignity, and hope.

It has been estimated that 30 percent of U.S. medical costs and as much as 50 percent of Canadian medical costs are incurred in the last six months of a patient's life, especially when time is required in an intensive care unit. How much money could be saved, how much family pain and suffering, if people knew that death was not the end of their energy and they could choose to let go of biomedical life support for the purpose of saving their loved ones, themselves, and society the task of postponing their life promotion? Yes, questions such as these fly in the face of the historic beliefs of certain religions. However, so too did questions about whether the earth revolves around the sun.

One of the reasons why energy healing implies a vast and challenging paradigm change is precisely because it raises questions such as these.

Will Energy Healing Ever Be Covered by Medical Insurance ?

Various energy-healing techniques have reached the point of being authenticated by substantive research and are being accepted to some degree by the medical establishment, so that insurance companies are beginning to cover services like acupuncture and massage. This foretells what will be emerging for energy healing.

Though some scientists, physicians, and laymen prefer to explain the findings only in terms of steps 1 and 2 on the ladder of energy explanations (spontaneous remission and placebo effects), this requires that they ignore a sizable body of literature clearly establishing that additional explanations are required—from bioelectromagnetics and quantum-field effects (steps 3 and 4) to more innovative and challenging explanations (steps 5, 6, and 7).

Insurance companies will increase their coverage of energy-healing techniques only with further research findings, increased public pressure, and changes in public understanding of the fundamental role of energy in health, nature, and life. Only then will patients and insurers be able to slash expenditures for medical care by turning to energy-healing treatments.

How Will Training in Energy Healing Unfold?

At the present time, medical students receive very little classroom training in energy-healing techniques. Most medical schools do not have formal courses in the subject. Physicians interested in these techniques typically learn them on their own. The one exception I'm aware of is in comprehensive efforts like Andrew Weil's Program in Integrative Medicine, but these are aimed at medical professionals already in practice.

However, young people today, certainly as undergraduates, and increasingly in high school and grade school, are being exposed to meditation, yoga, tai chi, Qigong, massage, and so on—techniques that are sometimes classified as mind-body activities but that actually involve energy as well. By the time college graduates enter medical school, many have already had personal training in yoga or the martial arts.

They are starting their premed training with minds already awakened to the healing power of energy and consciousness. These young people will some day transform medical education.

More students are becoming chiropractors, osteopaths, naturopaths, and homeopaths—healing arts that include energy to various degrees. Also, nurses are learning therapeutic touch, healing touch, Reiki, Johrei, and other energy-healing modalities. And some laymen as well are embracing Reiki, Johrei, Christian Science, and other energy- and spiritual-healing approaches that are being used not only for their personal health but for the health of their families and friends.

Energy-healing training is spreading; I am tempted to say spreading like wildfire, though I confess this might today be an exaggeration. Yet I do anticipate that soon the growing flames will be apparent to all. I expect that the growth of energy-healing training will be balanced and controlled—like flames in fireplaces throughout the world—providing warmth, comfort, beauty, and hope in addition to healing.

How Will Energy Healing Be Monitored and Controlled?

Various groups are developing their own codes of ethics for healers, as well as licensing and certification procedures. Because different energy-healing practices come from different traditions and are fostered by various groups and also practiced by unaffiliated individuals, there is currently little coordination or integration of techniques. Master healers have their own schools and followers. Even among specific healing groups, such as Reiki or Johrei, there are factions that follow somewhat different philosophies and practices.

Certain groups, like Healing Touch, have their own professional meetings. Professional organizations such as the International Association for the Study of Subtle Energies and Energy Medicine and the U.S. Psychotronics Association hold annual meetings about the broad area of energy-healing clinical practice, theory, and research. We can expect both opportunities and challenges for not only fostering the responsible practice of energy healing by all health-care professionals, but also in distinguishing the wheat from the chaff in terms of which techniques are the most effective.

In my laboratory, Dr. Melinda Connor is actively working on developing bioelectromagnetic measures and laboratory protocols for assessing a practitioner's ability to heal. One goal is to develop standards for determining the efficacy of healers and to implement methods for quantifying their abilities.

What about Energy Healing in Animals and Plants?

Dr. Ann Baldwin and I have examined the effectiveness of genuine versus sham Reiki on stress-induced microvascular damage in rats, and Dr. Baldwin personally uses Reiki treatments on her horse and her cat.

The experiments discussed in this book complement real-life applications of energy healing not only with humans, but with animals and plants as well. For example, Cecily Knepprath, a successful fundraiser and budding Reiki student who has worked in my laboratory, shared the following experience with me. She wrote:

In the fall of 2004, my friend Debbie called to tell me that her dog Buddy had not responded well in surgery and she had taken him to Angell Memorial Animal Hospital in Boston. She learned he had serious problems with his liver and kidneys and was in critical condition. I wanted to help in some way so offered to come give him Reiki at the hospital. He was listless on the floor of his kennel when I first arrived. I cautiously climbed into his kennel and gave him a treatment. A couple of days later I went and gave him another treatment, and after this one he perked up. The vets were very pleased and surprised he was doing so well as they didn't think he was going to survive this condition. He hadn't responded to their traditional treatment. After Buddy came home, I gave him a couple more Reiki sessions and now, over two years later, Buddy is happy and well.

Just as energy healing will potentially become part of the mainstream, if not a foundational stream, of all human healing and the practice of medicine, energy healing will potentially do the same for animal healing as well. The logic extends further to farming and plant health.

Johrei healers practice a form of natural farming in which healing is applied to the soil and seeds and then to the emerging plants as they grow. As mentioned in chapter 12, Dr. Kathy Creath and I have published a double-blind study documenting that music as well as energy healing can increase the germination of seeds.

Shamans and medicine women and men have long claimed that they can not only heal plants, but communicate with them. As discussed in chapters 12 and 13, Dr. Creath and I have also published a series of papers on apparent energetic communication between plants, and healers' ability to alter the plants' biophoton release.

Famous cooks and loving grandmothers claim that cooking with loving intention increases the tastiness and health of food. A great many grandmothers and dedicated cooks would, I'm certain, applaud future research to test these claims.

Let's also consider the possibility that energy and intention affect all material systems, not just humans and animals, but plants and herbs, and even drugs as well. Perhaps we will discover the energy-healing context of growing and harvesting plants. Perhaps we'll also discover that this energy-healing context can improve the digestibility and nutritional value of food and medicine. Perhaps we'll even discover, too, that projecting healing energy during the manufacturing process of pharmaceuticals can enhance their healing potency.

If the conclusions of this book are correct, the potential effects of energy healing extend in all directions, just as does energy itself.

What Implications Does Energy Healing Have for the Evolution of Human Relationships and Healing Environments?

Whole books could be written that address the profound and far-reaching questions of what benefits a better understanding of healing energy might bring to human relationships and healing environments. Whether we're aware of this effect or not, if your energy and intentions can affect me and my energy and intentions can affect you—which is the fundamental conclusion of the research and theory presented in this book—then the very definition of human interaction needs to be evolved, if not radically transformed.

Recall my personal discovery described earlier of how a TV satellite dish could detect 12-gigahertz frequencies emitted by my hands and body when I was fifty to one hundred feet away from the dish. What this implies is that our 12-gigahertz frequencies extend out at least fifty to one hundred feet, and therefore we are all "touching the dish" with our energy.

From an energy perspective, touch is ultimately not merely physical, it is also *energetic*. What we call "physical touch" is a special case, or subset, of the energetic touch associated with our electromagnetic and quantum fields—fields that, as we've seen, in principle extend out infinitely in all directions.

When we become aware that the energy and intentions of those around us—as well as of the larger community of humans and animals around the globe—can potentially affect each of us in various ways and to various degrees, our sense of personal responsibility is shifted. The implications of energy consciousness for global peace and health are so vast, and so important, that they should neither be underestimated nor undervalued.

Let's consider a concrete situation. Imagine you've had an injury from an automobile accident that requires surgery. You are recovering in a hospital filled with health-care providers who vary in their degree of stress, fatigue, frustration, and even anger. You understand that the doctors and nurses are trying to do the best they can under conditions that force them to race from patient to patient. The health-care providers are overworked, underpaid, and underappreciated, and this affects their emotions and state of well-being.

In chapter 14, I described an experiment that indicated that the emotional well-being of a group of Reiki practitioners predicted whether *E. coli* bacteria that had been heat stressed would have an increased or lessened chance for survival; if a particular healer entered the laboratory feeling stressed, his or her energy had a negative impact on the cells that were struggling to recover from the heat stress.

Is it possible that patients who are surrounded by stressed health-care professionals will heal less rapidly and effectively than patients who are surrounded by unstressed health-care providers? Do you believe that you would heal more effortlessly and effectively if you were recovering in an energy- and intention-nurturing environment?

Also, consider the fact that hospitals historically have not been built with an awareness of electromagnetic pollution in mind. Though medical devices are designed to be safe in terms of electrical shocks, they have not been optimally designed in terms of their electromagnetic emissions.

Where would you prefer to heal—in a building filled with sound, light, and electromagnetic noise, or a quiet, gentle, energy-friendly environment? And where do you think health-care providers would prefer to work?

What are termed "negative" and "positive" energies can be interpersonal or environmental, or even both simultaneously. The energies of a place, whether health damaging or health promoting, include the people and the structures. By extension, the energies include animals and plants as well as electronic devices and furnishings. It is the total mixture of negative and positive energies that ultimately determines the health and wellness consequences of any environment.

Human rage and pain, especially generated by terrorism and war, create a global energetic climate whose negative effects can extend from the physical and environmental—potentially including climate—to the psychological and ultimately spiritual. We are all metaphorically staying in the same "hospital" in this sense: hospital Earth. If the thesis of this book is correct, then pollution is not simply chemical, it is ultimately energy based and therefore conscious as well. When we put on our metaglasses, the vision of this possibility becomes crystal clear.

Loving relationships are loving energy relationships—at all levels. The question is, will humankind become able to perceive this?

How Will the Evolution of Energy Consciousness Unfold in the Future?

If the emerging theory and research in physics and psychology continue—with a corresponding awakening to the fundamental role of energy and consciousness in nature and the universe—then we can hope that in time people everywhere will accept the fundamental nature of reality-as-energy in the same way that people currently assume that the fundamental nature of reality is matter. We will shift from a materialistic world view to what I am calling an "energy-istic" (or "energistic") world view (in the meantime, hoping someone will devise a less awkward term).

People today assume that energy exists but that energy is somehow caused by or created by matter—meaning solid mass. However, when the predicted metamorphosis of mind takes hold and the new vision becomes widely accepted, people of the future will adopt the new assumption: that matter is caused by or created by energy. And they will live their lives accordingly.

Over the past eleven years, and especially over the past nine months, I have been experiencing this shift in my own consciousness. Though I can still put on my "material-first" glasses, I find it now more natural to wear my "energy-first" glasses. And when I remember to put on my metaglasses, I see it all even more clearly.

As I have come to know a diverse group of gifted energy healers, I have learned that they tend to be sensitive, caring, loving, compassionate, adventurous, health focused, and spiritual. They tend to use the word "energy" in diverse contexts, and they behave as if they are connected to people, animals, plants, the earth as a whole, and higher levels of spirituality, including guides and the Divine. They are sensitive to the weather and the phases of the moon.

The truth is, once we open our minds to the reality of energy, we recognize that the fields created by the planets and stars affect our energies in the same way that they affect the weather on the earth. Our personal atoms are no different than those of the earth—in fact, they are of the earth. In a deep sense, our bodies are no different than the earth, they are just smaller.

Though the gifted energy healers I have known typically hold controversial views—especially when compared to the views of mainstream, matter-focused people—and some of their individual views may be completely false, most of them have not been flakes. They have children, pay their taxes, hold down responsible jobs, vote, take care of their automobiles, and watch television. Some play sports, others drive fancy cars. Some read mysteries. Some, a few, are scientists. Yes, there are some healers who are weird, and, sadly, some who are unethical. However, on the whole well-trained energy healers appear to be sane and the real deal, and they should be taken seriously.

What Effect Will the Emerging Energy Consciousness Have on the Structure of Businesses and Institutions?

Historically, businesses and institutions—from hospitals and medical schools to state and national governments—have not recognized the need for a centralized organization dedicated to interconnecting and distributing energy (and information) to every component of the system to sustain the organization as a whole.

There is a deep lesson to be learned from the evolution of biological organisms and the emergence of the heart. The heart has no agenda other than to serve the whole by insuring that every component in the body is interconnected and invigorated—biochemically and bioelectromagnetically—so that the organism can survive and thrive. Its unique purpose is to help sustain all the components of the body in a dependable, gentle yet firm, supportive, and loving fashion.

Given the essential energetic role of the heart in a biological organism, perhaps it will eventually be seen to make sense for business organizations that metaphorically have brains (managers and executives) to also have *hearts*. Of course, many organizations already have some individuals who provide the heart function, but these people usually have other roles that may interfere with the essential heart role.

Is it possible that in addition to CEOs, COOs, and CIOs (chief executive, operating, and information officers), corporations might someday create a position that for fun I will call a CHO—a chief heart officer? If we would consciously attend to the energetic needs of every component at every level in an organization—by making energetic connections and flow a priority—would our capacity to heal, sustain our health, and evolve be fostered?

Will this ever happen? I'd like to think so.

What Will Happen When People Experience Reality as Energy?

When people experience reality as energy with the same matter-of-factness that people currently experience reality as matter, they will have the awareness and opportunity to make choices that foster energy living with an emphasis on caring, cooperation, compassion, and creativity. In the process, not only will everyone engage in personal self-energy healing, but they will naturally find themselves experiencing energy as an expression of an Infinite Source of Potential and live more spiritually mature and inspiring lives. We may even transform our consciousness from being *Homo sapiens* to becoming *"Energy* sapiens" in the fundamental way we conceive of our species, nature, and universe.

I offer these wide-ranging speculations and future possibilities in the spirit of balancing creativity with humility. One of my academic heroes, the late Professor Neal Miller of Yale University and Rockefeller University, was fond of saying, "We must be bold in what we try, but cautious in what we claim." His words complement the wisdom of one of the twentieth century's most gifted manglers of the language, Yogi Berra, who reminded us that "it is tough to make predictions, especially about the future."

Using the history of science as our guide, it's prudent that we heed Einstein's recommendation "not to stop questioning" and remain vigilant for inevitable surprises in the future.

> *Our separation from each other is an optical*
> *illusion of consciousness.*
>
> —ALBERT EINSTEIN

Chapter 20

We Are All Energy Healers

One morning in 2002 I was having a research meeting with Reverend Gerry Nangle. The director of the Tucson Johrei Center, she was discussing with me an experiment that was being conducted in my NIH-funded center; the experiment involved measuring the brain waves, heart waves, and respirations of two people simultaneously—one person giving Johrei, the other person receiving. Our conversation explored not only the physiological and energetic effects of the energy-healer/subject relationship, but the subjective experiences of both people. As I listened to Gerry's personal experiences of giving Johrei, it struck me that her subjective experience seemed to be at least as positive, if not more positive, than the experiences of the people she was serving as a healer.

As described earlier in these pages, certain kinds of energy healing (such as Johrei, Reiki, and healing touch), as well as certain spiritual healing techniques (Christian Science and Sufi healing, for example), are typically reported as being energizing and invigorating for the healers themselves—relaxing, peaceful, loving, energizing, and vitalizing. All these benefits taken together sound as if they might well add up to provide *self-healing.*

If so, perhaps what we're witnessing is two healings for the price of one. Especially in the case of Johrei, this is truly a bargain, because Johrei practitioners do not charge for their healing sessions.

Certain techniques, ranging from Johrei and bio-magnetic touch healing to Sufi healing and Christian Science, were not specifically designed for health-care professionals; they were created for everyone. In fact, they were conceived of by laypeople to be used by laypeople. They are general healing methods and philosophies that can be learned and practiced by anyone. Though we may seriously question aspects of their philosophies and practices, emerging science provides strong support for at least a subset of their claims. What you are about to read applies in principle to any person who wishes to be of service to others as well as to themselves. Though the experiment was conducted with Johrei practitioners, the findings are consistent with the claims of most energy-healing practices.

It turned out that Gerry's daughter, Katie Reece, then an undergraduate student at the University of Arizona, was interested in doing an honors thesis on the practice of Johrei. She decided to examine in systematic fashion the subjective experiences of people giving and receiving Johrei.

Katie, Gerry, Dr. Audrey Brooks, and I designed a twenty-one-item rating scale that addressed common experiences claimed to be associated with Johrei. There were seven negative items including anxiety, physical pain, stress, and depression, and fourteen positive items, including alertness, feeling energized, feeling relaxed, experiencing compassion toward others and compassion toward self, sensing hope, empowerment, and gratitude. Givers and receivers of Johrei filled out the rating scale before and after the Johrei sessions. Ratings were obtained on more than one hundred givers and receivers.

We reported in a paper published in the *Journal of Alternative and Complementary Medicine* that responses from givers as well as receivers showed significant decreases in negative symptoms such as pain and stress, and significant increases in positive states such as alertness, empowerment, and gratitude. Moreover, the givers had a significantly higher overall positive state of well-being than the receivers. Both givers and receivers reported significant increases in perceived state of health as measured by the Arizona Integrative Outcomes Scale.

You may recall that Drs. Rubik, Brooks, and I have replicated such findings in Reiki practitioners who were not only giving Reiki to human beings but were even giving Reiki to *E. coli* bacteria that had been stressed by heat. And Dr. Ann Baldwin and I have replicated such findings in Reiki practitioners who were giving Reiki to rats stressed by noise.

What diverse groups like Johrei and Reiki on the one hand and Christian Science and Sufi healing on the other have in common is that they believe that they are not *generating* the energy per se but rather they are serving as a receiver, channel, or antenna for the energy. They believe that the energy is universal and comes from the Source itself and that the universal energy is itself intelligent. This universal energy pervades everything, and therefore everyone. Consequently it is available to you, right now, if you are willing to access it.

Let's assume for the moment that universal energy exists—as has been claimed by peoples all over the world throughout recorded history. Let's further assume that with our consciousness, we can help this energy serve its purpose of healing, creation, growth, and transformation.

Now consider the following. Imagine that you are closing your eyes, sitting still, with your palms gently facing forward, and you are inviting this universal energy to enter your body. Imagine that you are requesting that this energy pass through you and out your hands. Imagine that you are now directing this energy to a specific person or animal, perhaps in the same room with you, perhaps hundreds or thousands of miles away. Or, if you wish, you can imagine that it is your intention that the energy go wherever it is needed for healing and peace—to people, animals, plants, the seas—and that you are trusting that the universal energy knows best.

Yes, it is possible that doing this might help your loved ones or beings you have never met. However, this is not my primary purpose in sharing this vision. It turns out that contemporary research in positive psychology documents that people who do altruistic things for others, and experience a sense of gratitude in the processes, often have positive physical, psychological, and spiritual health consequences.

Let's focus our attention on what you're feeling as you gently allow this universal energy-healing process to occur, staying with the experience for fifteen to thirty minutes. What will you experience? What will be taking place inside your body, physiologically and energetically, as you enter this altruistic state of compassion and caring?

If you try this with an open heart and open mind, you will have the opportunity to experience a collective state of peace, joy, vitality, contentment, and even bliss beyond anything you may have imagined is possible. And if you choose to practice this daily, you will if nothing else be doing your body, mind, and spirit a great service.

Suppose that the explanation for this effect is not simply step 2 on the ladder of energy explanations (an expectancy or placebo effect) but includes at least steps 3 and 4 (classical and quantum physics) and potentially extends all the way to step 7.

With this in mind, now suppose that millions of people, perhaps even billions, are practicing this every day.

Also imagine if people who are incapacitated, hospitalized, and recovering, or even in hospice and preparing to die, instead of spending their time watching television or reading, for example, are spending part of their time every day engaging in universal energy healing and sending loving energy out to the world.

Even imagine a future world where every human being has been taught, as a young child, that energy is the fundamental reality of nature and the universe. And that it is in their best personal interest that they regularly spend part of each day engaging in whatever form of universal energy healing they find most appealing. This would benefit them, their loved ones, and the planet.

How may our world change? Will we naturally move toward love and peace? Will we evolve into a harmonious species? The work of Dr. Roger Nelson and colleagues initiated at Princeton University concerning the Global Consciousness Project (http://noosphere.princeton.edu) points to the probable quantum reality of this imagined possibility.

Thanks to twenty-first-century technology and the World Wide Web, there is an emerging world of possible training opportunities awaiting anyone interesting in developing their natural energy-healing abilities. For example, bio-magnetic touch healing—"bio-touch" for short, and playfully referred to as "just touch"—is a Tucson-based lay healing program supported by research conducted at the University of Arizona (http://justtouch.com/researchua.shtml) and the University of Texas

Health Sciences in Tyler (http://justtouch.com/researchtyler.shtml). Bio-touch tends to appeal to people who are secular, Johrei tends to be pre-ferred by individuals who are eclectically spiritual, while techniques like Christian Science tend to be practiced by persons who are devoted to Christianity. Energy opportunities from A to Z can be found on the Internet, and this is just the beginning.

Imagine that you and I are two of ten people holding hands in a cir-cle, and that this circle also includes an eleventh participant, a mechan-ical being whose left and right "hands" each contain an electrode connected to an EKG device attached to a computer. The computer is also attached to a projector displaying the resulting EKG signals on a large screen. What you, me, and the rest of the circle of people will see on the screen are our individual EKGs occurring all on the same single line: each of our individual heart energies is mixing with every one else's heart energies in the circle. By joining hands, we have created a complete circuit of circulating human energies.

Now imagine this on a global scale—not through people holding hands but through people consciously sending healing energy into the universe and receiving healing energy from others.

The implications of this await our emerging understanding and evolving application. It's worth remembering that for most of our exis-tence as a species on this planet, we did not know that we had a heart, or even a brain for that matter. It was not general knowledge that the heart pumped blood, for example, until Dr. William Harvey's work in the seventeenth century. We did not know that our hearts, brains, and every 60-plus-trillion cell in our body generated and received complex electrical, magnetic, light, and sound energies until the twentieth cen-tury. And we are only now, at the very beginning of the twenty-first cen-tury, learning that the energies associated not only with every biological living system, but all material systems, are in a continuous state of dynamic exchange, communication, and interaction. We had no idea that all systems, from subatomic particles to superclusters of galaxies, engaged in "wireless communication." We had no idea that the emerg-ing cell-phone technology, for example, was an expression of the funda-mental structure of all material/energy systems.

Can we join our brains with our hearts, increasing their connectivity not only physically, but also energetically, so that we may discover and manifest our true energy nature and live our lives as evolving energy healers?

If the science of the future continues in the direction described in this book, three conclusions are virtually guaranteed:

Our personal capacity to be energy healers—for ourselves and others—will grow over time.

Science and spirituality will become connected in a manner that fosters our capacity to promote health, peace, and vitality for the planet as a whole.

And we will witness the unexpected, discover the as-yet unimagined, and rejoice in the universal mysteries that await us.

Frequently Asked Questions

Though this book has officially reached its conclusion, you may still have questions about aspects of the content. I have included here a selection of frequently asked questions and answers, some of which have already been answered in the text but are repeated here for convenience as a reference. Additional frequently asked questions and answers can be found at www.drgaryschwartz.com.

What is energy healing?

Coming after the previous two hundred or so pages, you may be surprised to discover that I don't consider this a simple or obvious question.

In its most basic and limited sense, energy healing can be thought of as the application of energy techniques to medicine and healing. Whether the healer is gently touching the subject, placing her hands a few inches or a few feet away from the subject's body, or working with a subject who is hundreds or thousands of miles away, the focus is on the implicit concept and mechanism of energy as applied to medical treatment.

Examples include therapeutic touch, healing touch, Reiki, Johrei, Bio-Touch, acupuncture, Qigong, and aspects of yoga and Ayurvedic medicine.

This sense of energy healing can include the use of biomedical devices that generate electromagnetic fields—including light and sound, as well as electricity and magnetism—or material objects that transmit and receive fields of energy, including minerals, crystals, and homeopathic preparations.

But in a deeper and more comprehensive sense, energy healing can be thought of as being the role of energy in all healing processes. From this perspective, herbs, drugs, physical manipulation, and even surgery involve energetic processes in healing.

Finally, if we put on our metaglasses and envision energy as being the capacity to affect anything, then emotions, thoughts, and intentions can be thought of as energies that can have local as well as distal effects on the body, mind, and spirit. This definition can be extended to include spiritual healing approaches such as Sufi healing and Christian Science.

Whether you prefer a narrow definition of energy healing involving primarily steps 3 and 4 on the ladder of energy explanations, or a broader, more comprehensive definition of energy healing that includes steps 5 through 7, including spirits and even the Source, depends upon your comfort in envisioning the many levels implicit in the concept of energy.

How does energy healing work?

The leading theory that explains how energy healing works involves the concept of resonance—including what is called "sympathetic resonance" and "harmonic resonance." Resonance is a universal process typified by two tuning forks; if they are of the same size and structure, when one is struck, the other will spontaneously vibrate as well. The second tuning fork is said to resonate with the first. In sympathetic resonance, a small vibration in one system, over time, can foster an increasing vibration in a second system. In harmonic resonance, the vibrations can resonate over a number of frequencies that are harmonics, or multiples.

Resonance is the foundation of all energetic communication. It is the fundamental process of connection and sharing, and the basis for how antennas work. When two or more processes are in resonance, they are literally in tune with one another. Healers often talk about becoming attuned to energy and attuning to their patients.

New companies such as the General Resonance Corporation are exploring how resonance can be employed to enhance the effectiveness of conventional medicines as well as to create "energy medicines." Scientific books such as *The Living Energy Universe* and *Energy Medicine in Therapeutics and Human Performance,* and clinical books such as *The Healing Field* and *The Reconnection,* illustrate how resonance is the quantum-field mechanism underlying life, growth, evolution, and health.

How can I learn about energy healing?

With the advent of the Internet, there is now a vast and growing collection of Web sites that offer extensive materials: reading materials including scientific and self-help books and articles; audiotapes and CDs of healing exercises; videotapes and DVDs of lectures and demonstrations; and innovative devices, software, and other means of creating and measuring energies, including tuning forks and electromagnetic meters. A list of useful Web sites is presented in the recommended readings section.

Do some people have a natural gift for energy healing?

The answer appears to be yes. Just as there are natural musicians who can play music by ear, there are natural healers who can heal without training.

We don't need to be told that the better a jazz musician's techniques and skills are, the better is her or his ability to create music by ear. The same conclusion appears to apply to improvisational energy healing. The better a healer's techniques and skills, the better her or his ability to perform energy healing creatively and effectively.

I have witnessed a number of natural healers who had no formal training in healing achieve remarkable results. I have also heard accounts from credible people about natural healers at work—including young children—and their stories deserve to be taken seriously.

One example concerns my administrative assistant, Clarissa Sayre, and her son, Jake, who has cerebral palsy and has difficulty forming sentences when he speaks. Below is a section of the e-mail she wrote to me describing two instances where Jake healed her headaches:

> Last year Jake, [my husband] Ed, and I were at dinner at the Macaroni Grill. Dining was very busy because of the gem show in Tucson and there was the hustle and bustle of talk about it. It was a very eclectic crowd. Although I never develop headaches, one was brewing very strong. So strong, in fact, I couldn't even eat.
>
> Jake, looking concerned, asked, "What matter?" (His communication was improving.) I told him that I had a headache. He then verified, "Ouch?" I answered, "Yup!" He then proceeded to put his index finger and his middle finger on my forehead and in a matter of moments my

headache was completely gone. I sat there in amazement and said nothing, convinced that it was mind over matter and the pain would soon reappear. Five minutes passed and I continued to eat. I then told Ed out of earshot of Jake that there was no way that could have possibly happened . . . but it did. The headache did not recur.

This weekend I had a headache that would just not go away. I sat in the recliner massaging my head just hoping it would go away. I rarely get headaches, so the few I do get, I want them gone! Ed, who was on the couch, told me to come over by him and he would give me a massage instead of me doing it myself. As I made my way over to Ed, Jake asked, "What the matter?" I told him I had a headache. He reached up and grazed his hand from my forehead to my temple to the side of my face and continued in some sort of form. It was gone. I shook my head, to myself, and lay down in disbelief, thinking that this cannot be true, that once again he relieved a headache.

When Jake was born at twenty-six weeks' gestation (three and a half months early), he wasn't able to maintain his temperature, he was on a respirator, etc. etc. While in the NICU they allowed an experimental interaction called "Kangaroo Care." The theory and research showed that if you put a naked preemie onto the bare chest of its mother, that the mother's temperature would rise to compensate for the baby, that the mother's heartbeat would assist in regulating the baby's heartbeat and circulation as well as her respiration patterning the baby's in hopes of decreasing the need for oxygen from the ventilator and bringing down any carbon dioxide. Jake did very well with "Kangaroo Care."

To this day Jake, nine years old and soon to be ten, can sit on my lap, my temperature rises, and I will become immediately fatigued and fall asleep. I jokingly say that he is sucking the energy out of me! There may be more truth to that than I am aware of. Having CP, he uses a lot of energy having tight muscles, etc. He uses any reserve calories that he has just to maintain any muscle that he may build in strength and to fight viruses etc. etc. Could it be that he takes what he can to stockpile? Perhaps with my headaches, he is giving back some of what he has taken . . . hmmmmm.

Why are some people so skeptical about energy healing?

This is a complex and multifaceted question, and the answer is not simple.

First, some people were taught that energy healing is impossible, and they strongly believe that what they were taught is the final word. When they are confronted with solid scientific evidence to the contrary, and even have direct personal experiences, this may cause them extreme discomfort including anxiety, anger, and denial.

Some superskeptics suffer from I what I call PESD—posteducational stress disorder. The collection of symptoms are similar to, but typically much milder, than PTSD—posttraumatic stress disorder.

Second, there is wide range of economic implications concerning energy healing. Health-care professionals who have no background or skills in these techniques sometimes feel threatened because they lack the skills, and they may be concerned that their patients might seek other health-care providers, affecting the economics of their practice.

Another economic implication concerns potential threats to the bottom line of drug companies to the extent that patients may reduce or eliminate their use of medications following successful healing-energy treatments. Also, the economics of hospitals can be threatened because they perform money-making surgeries that may not always be advisable or necessary.

Medical researchers are typically supported by grants and contracts from NIH and drug companies. Because energy healing is controversial, there is an unfortunate built-in resistance to funding research if it occurs at the expense of conventional biomedical interventions.

Third, there are philosophical and spiritual implications to energy healing. If we are all interconnected by energy and consciousness, as proposed by Einstein and Planck, and supported experimentally by contemporary scientists such as Radin and Sheldrake, then there are vast implications for how we practice medicine as well as how we live our lives. Some of these philosophical and spiritual implications were discussed in chapter 19. There are people who dislike these implications and reject them out of hand.

Finally, superskeptics often point out, rightly so, that there are fraudulent and unethical individuals who practice energy healing as a scheme for taking advantage of people who are suffering. These practitioners may encourage patients to avoid conventional medical treatment when it is in fact warranted. What superskeptics do is overgeneralize from these bad apples and assume that if a few apples are rotten, then all the apples must be rotten.

What about experiments that appear to contradict some of our findings?

Experiments can fail to replicate for numerous reasons. Sometimes experiments fail because there is no phenomenon to discover, or the phenomenon is not very strong or reliable.

However, experiments can sometimes fail because the investigators did not take into account certain variables that are necessary to document or reveal the phenomenon. Some unanticipated variables may actually produce reverse or negative effects.

For example, a study was published in 1998 in the distinguished *Journal of the American Medical Association* (*JAMA*) that reported that healers could not sense the presence of an experimenter's hands. The authors claimed that their study was the first to have tested whether therapeutic touch practitioners could detect the energy of another person's hands (they were mistaken—see below). They further claimed that their failure to obtain positive results in this basic science study called into question numerous clinical studies (including double-blind studies of wound healing) that had shown positive healing effects.

However, my examination of their study revealed a number of potential problems: (1) the experiment was conducted by a young adolescent girl for her science-fair project, (2) she was the only experimenter, (3) the girl flipped a coin to determine which trials would be left-handed versus right-handed (an unreliable procedure), (4) one of the authors was a founding member of a skeptic's organization (www.quackwatch.org), and (5) the practitioners who were tested actually did significantly *worse* than chance. In other words, an unbiased analysis of the data revealed that the healers were correct less than what would be expected by chance when the girl's hand was above their left or right hands.

Though the authors (presumably the adults) reviewed—and discounted—dozens of clinical studies published in the literature, they failed to mention prior published basic science research conducted by my colleagues and me (described in chapter 4). Our studies included (1) adult experimenters, (2) multiple experimenters (more than twenty), (3) a counterbalanced order of trials (as well as a greater number of trials, making the experiment more sensitive), (4) a variety of experimenter beliefs about the possibility of energy detection, and (5) the finding that our subjects (who were not even trained as healers) did significantly better than chance.

As you may recall from chapter 5, our research (as well as research by others) indicates that sensing energy includes the capacity to detect conscious intention in addition to the ability to detect the presence of physical energy. Though school science fairs each year produce some surprisingly insightful experiments, no one expects an adolescent to understand the rigors demanded of a trained professional scientist. The mystery is what led *JAMA* to publish the experimental results of an unqualified adolescent—results that were then picked up by the media and reported widely, relying on the authority of that respected journal, with the unfortunate outcome that many people were left with false information that appeared on its surface to be authentic and reliable.

Are politics involved in the publication of energy-healing experiments?

Sadly, the answer is yes. At the present time, mainstream medical journals as a rule tend to publish negative studies, even if they are flawed, and reject positive studies, even if they are conducted pristinely.

I have substantial personal experience in this area. None of the editors of *Science, Nature,* or the *British Medical Journal* was willing even to send the Baldwin and Schwartz Reiki-sham rat experiments out for scientific peer review (chapter 14). Similarly, none of the editors of *Science* or *Nature* was willing to send the Creath and Schwartz plant biophoton imaging experiments out for scientific peer review (chapter 12). In fact, the editor of *JAMA* declined to publish a letter to the editor that we wrote concerning mistakes in the girl's energy-detection study and the fact that previously published experiments had produced positive results, on the grounds that "this was not of significant interest to their readers."

Editors have the prerogative to decide which papers are allowed to be reviewed and ultimately published. They are the gatekeepers. At a time when I was conducting mainstream mind-body research in the 1970s, my colleagues and I published a total of six papers in the journal *Science* because the editor at the time was open to psychophysiological research. I have firsthand experience in understanding the scientific and political aspects of research publishing.

This is the primary reason why less prestigious journals such as the *Journal of Alternative and Complementary Medicine,* the *Journal of Scientific Exploration,* and *Explore* have been historically the primary vehicles for communicating research findings on energy healing.

Are there any negative effects or undesirable side effects of energy-healing treatments?

Energy-healing treatments, when practiced carefully and wisely, create few, if any, negative or undesirable side effects. As a rule, energy healing is gentle, and ethical healers practice the "do no harm" philosophy.

However, people sometimes experience an increase in their awareness of their symptoms, and even an exacerbation of their symptoms, as the healing process unfolds. As people increase their energy awareness, they become more sensitive to energy sensations and therefore they will potentially become more aware of aches and pains as well as pleasures and joys.

In other cases, people may seek energy-healing treatments hoping to avoid conventional medical treatments and therefore potentially miss receiving essential medical diagnoses and treatment. As with any treatment modality, the key is discernment and wisdom—to know when and how to apply it.

Is healing energy "intelligent" and "alive"?

Many groups and traditions—ranging from shamanism and Reiki to Sufism and Christian Science—believe that the healing energy is intelligent, alive, and even conscious. Though some traditions express energy-healing effects in more spiritual and even divine language, the concept of energy is implicit in their logic and thinking.

Reiki practitioners, for example, set the intention that what happens in a healing session is for the patient's best and highest good, and then they leave it to the intelligence of the energy to determine what happens. They believe, for example, that the energy "knows best." They even believe that whether a patient receives symptomatic relief or not involves spiritual processes concerning the person's growth and learning beyond the physical.

Many cultures, including the Polynesians and the Hawaiians, believe that *"mana"* (their term for energy) is universal, intelligent, and the basis for life. Though it is beyond the scope of this book, the hypothesis that energy is both alive and intelligent is in principle scientifically possible and, moreover, can be tested in the laboratory. We are beginning to conduct research on what we term "implicit intelligence" to test our theory that even quantum fields have an intelligence that can be revealed under optimal scientific conditions. The challenge for all of us is to maintain an open mind, to not be lazy, as Richard Dawkins puts it, when it comes to imagining scientific possibilities, and to be willing to entertain these challenging possibilities as part of an emerging energy vision.

Has Gary Schwartz become a believer in energy healing?

I have conducted too many successful experiments, witnessed too many healings by gifted energy healers, and personally experienced too many healings myself as both a research practitioner and patient to justify sustaining an agnostic position regarding energy healing as a general phenomenon. At some point, there comes a time when the evidence is too great to be ignored. Also, I have come to understand that steps 3 through 7 on the energy-healing ladder are not only all scientifically plausible, but there is strong evidence supporting the conclusion that energy healing can operate at multiples levels of fields and processes simultaneously. Though this makes life more complicated, it describes a universe that is much more interesting and magnificent.

At the same time, I appreciate the responsibility to be cautious and humble about drawing conclusions, especially in specific cases. The history of science reminds us to keep an open mind at all times. To repeat once again the valuable Einstein remark quoted earlier, "The important thing is not to stop questioning."

How is energy related to spiritual healing practices like Christian Science?

I'm personally intrigued by the parallels between religions that focus on healing—in particular, Christian Science—and both contemporary physics and the emerging science of energy healing. Mary Baker Eddy, the founder of Christian Science, came to the conclusion that "Spirit is the real and eternal" and "the only true substance," while matter is "the unreal and temporal" and a "false belief or illusion."

Eddy's belief about spirit and the illusion of matter sounds curiously similar to Einstein's vision about energy being the basis of matter.

Christian Scientists who have researched and written about the history and impact of their religion have collected stories suggesting that Einstein visited the church's reading rooms on numerous occasions and was supposedly convinced about the ideas offered in founder Mary Baker Eddy's principal work, *Science and Health*. Books by church members attribute to him quotes such as "*Science and Health* is beyond this generation's understanding. It is the pure science" and "If everyone realized what is in that book, you would not have enough room anywhere to accommodate the people who would be clamoring for it."

Today we accept the existence of invisible fields of energy, the spontaneous emergence of fundamental particles in the quantum vacuum, and the zero point field as well as the existence of billions of galaxies in an expanding universe. If our scientific, medical, and religious institutions are to survive and evolve, they must be open to revising or discarding fallacious beliefs in the face of new evidence.

This includes the emerging possibility, mentioned previously, that energy may be intelligent and express consciousness. And it includes the emerging possibility that healings accompanied by profound transformation of consciousness involve more than mind-body effects. Whether healing energy is viewed from the Japanese perspective of Reiki or the American perspective of Christian Science, the belief in a universal intelligent force may be more than a superstition.

Though beyond the scope of this book, evidence supporting spiritual energy healing, enlightened by contemporary knowledge in physics and psychology, is leading us to an ever-expanding vision of nature and human possibility. There may a deep truth to the poetic phrase "It's not me, it's the energy; and it's not you, it's the universe."

Can energy healing take us to spiritual healing?

Every indication, as far as I can tell, points in the direction of energy healing leading to spiritual healing. What shamans and spiritual healers refer to as "spirit" overlaps what physicists and energy healers refer to as "energy." Shamans and spiritual healers see spirit as conscious and intelligent, essentially equivalent to what energy healers sometimes refer to as "conscious energy" and "intelligent energy." Conscious and intelligent energies become conscious and intelligent *entities,* and that takes us to spiritual healing and a larger spiritual reality. What religious people call the Great Spirit, Yahweh, God, or Allah energy and spiritual healers label as universal intelligent energy or infinitive intelligence. The late Dr. David Bohm used the term "implicate order," and Dr. Edgar Mitchell designates the "quantum hologram." All of these can be integrated with modern concepts in dynamical-systems and network theory and lead us to an evolving vision of a living-energy universe.

As Dr. James Levin put it, "Energy is the voice of spirit." This statement is worth pondering. It may be more than a metaphor. It may be a fundamental truth.

What's love got to do with energy healing?

The answer to this question is simple: everything. Love is the common denominator, the core intention, the foundational state of being that nurtures all healing, growth, and transformation. Just as Sir Isaac Newton envisioned the universal field of gravity to be a ubiquitous expression of God's love in the universe, we can apprehend the essence of unconditional attraction and caring as being the foundation of creativity, sustainability, and adaptability. When we put on our metaglasses and envision what "metalove" is, life, nature, and the unfolding universe become a seamless manifestation of an implicate and infinite Loving Source.

Can science address the question of the biophysics of love and meta-love? If we use the history of science as our guide, there is no justification for being anything less than carefully, yet enthusiastically, optimistic.

Some thirty years ago, I paid more than forty thousand dollars for a PDP-11 computer that took up an entire room. It required special wiring and air-conditioning. It came with sixteen kilobytes (thousand bytes) of memory—I paid five thousand dollars for an extra eight kilobytes of memory. The extra memory itself was the size of a suitcase. The computer was programmable primarily in machine language. It used a Teletype printer and stored programs on paper tape and reel-to-reel magnetic tape. It did not have a calendar, contact list, spreadsheet, word processor, or PowerPoint. I had to program the graphic display to put simple graphs on the screen.

Today I have a battery-operated electronic device that combines a cell phone and megapixel camera with a computer that has a calendar, contact list, spreadsheet, word processor, PowerPoint, and many other software packages. It has a two-gigabyte memory chip. It connects to the Web effortlessly. It plays digital music and displays video in real time. It connects wirelessly to a printer that produces gorgeous documents and pictures in millions of colors. The computer fits in my breast pocket. And it cost less than four hundred dollars.

The integration of theory and technology that has evolved mainframe computers into pocket PDAs illustrates the capacity of the human mind to discover how the physical world works, to create new opportunities for humanity, and to provide novel solutions that extend the implicit capabilities of our body, mind, and spirit. It is this power of mind that has allowed science to make the invisible visible and use this once-hidden mystery for greater and greater things.

Can science evolve to the point where it merges effortlessly with spirituality and in the process makes visible the as-yet-invisible force of love that is hypothesized to be the foundation of healing, life, and evolution? I listen to my PDA cell phone ring, I see Rhonda's picture come up on the screen, and I think to myself, *Why not!*

Recommended Readings

Books

There is a collection of books that should be required reading for anyone interested in energy medicine, energy healing, energy experience, and, ultimately, energy living. Readers of these works will discover that the experiments conducted in our research program complement and extend the body of science and clinical observations that have preceded it.

The first book that introduced general readers to energy healing was *Vibrational Medicine,* written by Richard Gerber, MD. Currently in its third edition, his book reviews the history of the field, including early bioelectromagnetic devices. A second book by Dr. Gerber is called *A Practical Guide to Vibrational Medicine,* with the subtitle *Energy Healing and Spiritual Transformation.* Dr. Gerber appreciates how energy can be viewed as the voice of spirit.

James Oschman, PhD, has written *Energy Medicine* and *Energy Medicine in Therapeutics and Human Performance.* These volumes cover some of the latest thinking in how energy healing works. Dr. Oschman has played a major role in shaping the work conducted in the Center for Frontier Medicine in Biofield Science. His books provide an essential foundation and comprehensive approach to understanding the findings and perspectives you have read in the preceding pages of this book.

A collection of books by Daniel Benor, MD, includes *Spiritual Healing: Scientific Validation of a Healing Revolution* and *Consciousness, Bioenergy and Healing: Self-Healing and Energy Medicine for the 21st Century.* In these books, Dr. Benor provides a wealth of published findings about how energy healing is integrated with spiritual healing. In addition, Dr. Benor has also written some popular books, including *How Can I Heal What Hurts?*, which provides useful how-to information.

Larry Dossey, MD, has written more books related to energy and spiritual healing than probably any other single author. His books include *Healing beyond the Body: Medicine and the Infinite Reach of the Mind* and *Reinventing Medicine: Beyond Mind-Body to a New Era of Healing*. I was transformed reading his classic works *Space, Time & Medicine* and *Healing Words*. Dr. Dossey is currently editor of *Explore*, one of the leading journals in the field.

In terms of contemporary biology and healing, one of the most important books is by Bruce Lipton, PhD: *The Biology of Belief*, with the subtitle *Unleashing the Power of Consciousness, Matter and Miracles*. Dr. Lipton's book in the biological sciences is complemented by a book in physics written for the general public by William Tiller, PhD, titled *Some Science Adventures with Real Magic*. Dr. Tiller's original book, *Science and Human Transformation: Subtle Energies, Intentionality and Consciousness* transformed me ten years ago when it was first published.

For a comprehensive review of contemporary quantum physics applied to extrasensory experiences, including effects of one person's mind on another person's body, I strongly recommend *Entangled Minds*, by Dean Radin, PhD, and *The Sense of Being Stared At* by Rupert Sheldrake, PhD. Dr. Radin's early book, *The Conscious Universe*, and Dr. Sheldrake's first book, *A New Science of Life*, were both transformative for me; they provided a scientific framework for viewing mind in the context of physics that incorporated what I prefer to term "energy sensory perception" (ESP).

Though there are numerous historic books on the subject of energy and spiritual healing, I would like to mention two in particular here because they were among the first to awaken me to these possibilities. The first was the classic *Mind as Healer, Mind as Slayer*, written by Ken Pelletier, MD, PhD, which focused on mind-body healing but included energy and spiritual healing as well. The second was the classic *Blueprint for Immortality*, written by Harold Saxton Burr, PhD. I learned of his book while I was a professor at Yale; it turned out that Dr. Burr had been an anatomy professor at Yale and had conducted pioneering research there on energetic communication, especially among plants.

There are books that discuss various levels of physics, from classical, quantum, and advanced physics to new physics, that are also well worth reading. A wonderful review of physics and field theory is *The Field* by Lynne McTaggart—in my opinion the single best introduction and overview to the contemporary physics concerning bioelectromagnetic and quantum fields and their applications to consciousness and healing. Her second book, *The Intention Experiment,* extends the physics of fields to consciousness and healing. The book written by Thomas Valone, PhD, titled *Bioelectromagnetic Healing* and the volume edited by Peter Moscow, PhD, titled *Energetic Processes* include applications of advanced and new physics to healing.

Books that integrate energy and psychology include *Energy Psychology* and *Energy Psychology in Psychotherapy,* by Fred Gallo, PhD, and *The Promise of Energy Psychology* and *Energy Psychology Interactive Self-help Guide,* by David Feinstein. These books will be of special interest to psychologists or people interested in the conjunction of psychology with healing.

The book *Infinite Mind,* written by Valerie Hunt, PhD, with the subtitle *Science of the Human Vibrations of Consciousness,* is of historic interest because it describes the research and healing journey of Dr. Hunt, whose pioneering work with distinguished healers, including Rosalyn Bruyere, set the stage for contemporary research in energy healing. Also of historic interest is the book *Primary Perception,* written by Cleve Backster, which reviews his remarkable research on biocommunication between humans and plants, foods, and cells.

Finally, there are numerous books written by healers that illustrate their personal journeys as well as the nature of their healing practices. My favorites include Barbara Brennan's *Hands of Light,* Rosalyn Bruyere's *Wheels of Light,* Donna Eden's *Energy Medicine,* Eric Pearl's *The Reconnection,* and M. T. Morter's *The Healing Field.* These five books present an inspiring introduction to the diverse conceptual world of contemporary healers and their techniques.

Web sites

Below is a small representative selection of Web sites of organizations that address areas of research and treatment discussed in this book.

Together they provide a useful entry to contemporary science and applications in energy healing.

http://lach.web.arizona.edu.

This is the Web site of the Laboratory for Advances in Consciousness and Health at the University of Arizona. The site includes representative research papers described in this book.

www.issseem.org.

The International Society for the Study of Subtle Energies and Energy Medicine (ISSSEEM) is an international nonprofit interdisciplinary organization dedicated to exploring and applying subtle energies as they relate to the experience of consciousness, healing, and human potential. The society publishes the journal *Subtle Energies and Energy Medicine* and holds yearly meetings.

www.scientificexploration.org.

The international Society for Scientific Exploration (SSE) provides a professional forum for presentations, criticism, and debate concerning topics that for various reasons are ignored or studied inadequately within mainstream science. SSE publishes the *Journal of Scientific Exploration* and holds yearly meetings.

www.psychotronics.org.

The U.S. Psychotronics Association (USPA) defines psychotronics as "the science of mind-body-environmental relationships, an interdisciplinary science concerned with the interactions of matter, energy, and consciousness." Their publications as well as their annual meetings bridge frontier science and energy healing.

www.bioelectromagnetics.org.

This is the Web site for the Bioelectromagnetics Society (BEMS). They define their mission as promoting "the exchange of ideas to advance the science of natural and applied electromagnetic fields in biology and medicine." They publish the journal *Bioelectromagnetics* and hold annual meetings.

www.energypsych.org.

The Association for Comprehensive Energy Psychology (ACEP) is an international nonprofit organization promoting professional energy psychology and collaboration among practitioners, researchers, and licensing bodies. They define energy psychology as a "family of mind/body techniques that are clinically observed to consistently help with a wide range of psychological conditions. These interventions address the human vibrational matrix, which consists of three interacting systems." (ACEP terms these three systems "energy pathways," "energy centers," and the "human biofield.") They, too, hold annual meetings.

www.justtouch.com.

This site offers an excellent self-help energy-healing system that can even be learned by children. Their videos and manuals are easy to understand and apply.

www.johrei.com.

This site covers the field of Johrei healing, including the Johrei Foundation, the Johrei Fellowship, and the Johrei Institute. Johrei can be learned by children as well as adults, is nondenominational, and integrates Eastern and Western approaches to spiritual energy and healing. They offer an online education course.

www.healingtouchcanada.net.

This site provides an overview to the practice of healing touch. It includes newsletters and annual meetings as well as course materials. The Canadian group is affiliated with Healing Touch International, which offers substantial research.

www.reiki.org.

This is the Web site for the International Center for Reiki Training. The site offers a Web store, free downloads, information about classes, and a newsmagazine.

What is truly significant is never seen by the eye:
the invisible golden thread of light that is woven
into the fabric of all life.

—JAMES LEVIN, MD

Appendix: Understanding Universal Energy

In this book, we have implicitly bridged physics, psychology, and medicine, with metaphysics, metapsychology, and, yes, even "metamedicine." It is worth pondering the most comprehensive and universal meaning of "energy"—and related scientific terms—in order to better understand humanity's expanding awareness of the universality of energy and its applications to literally everything.

In what sense is energy universal and reflective of a "meta" process in the universe? I use the term "meta" here not simply as in "metaphor," but more concretely, for example, as in "metamorphosis." Not a religious or new-age term, "meta" is a basic prefix with a precise and profound conceptual meaning.

Various dictionaries give the philosophical meaning of the prefix "meta-" as "more comprehensive" or "transcending." I want to apply those senses of the word "metalinguistics," turning it into what I would call a meta-concept: its meaning is sufficiently abstract and broad to be applicable to any concept or any thing. A metaconcept is a concept that is completely general and universal. A metaconcept is a universal concept.

The truth is, we can't understand the deep concept of energy and its application to energy healing without being able to think at least one level of description higher. We must examine physical concepts like energy and technologies like cell phones from a more comprehensive—and fundamental—perspective.

When I say that I am (1) putting on my metaglasses, (2) experiencing whatever I am looking at in terms of its implicit metaconcept, and therefore (3) seeing it with metavision, what I am doing is viewing the concept—whatever it is—at the highest, most comprehensive, and most universal level I can conceive of. When I suggest that you put on your metaglasses, I am encouraging to you shift your awareness from the specific to the general and therefore shift your consciousness from the particulars of a definition to the universal essence of an idea or concept.

Let's consider energy. As explained in this book, energy can be described at a physical level as the capacity to do work and overcome resistance. This is the conventional level, the level where physics typically operates. However, there is a higher level of description that provides a more comprehensive understanding of the lower-level meaning of energy. I describe this higher, more comprehensive, metadescription of energy as being *the capacity to do anything, whether at physical, psychological, or spiritual levels.*

Just as the capacity to do work at the physical level implies the existence of the term "energy," the capacity to do anything at any level—a universal or metalevel description—implies the existence of what might be termed "meta-energy."

Notice that the higher, more comprehensive concept of "meta-energy" is no more imaginary that the lower-level concept of energy. Both energy and meta-energy are inferred concepts, using the same logic and deriving from systematic observations that scientists make.

Also notice that hidden within the explicit meaning of the word "energy" is the implicit, more comprehensive metameaning of the word, which for clarity we are calling meta-energy. This higher, more comprehensive, more fundamental level of understanding reflects the implicit metalinguistic meaning of energy, in the sense mentioned previously of "beyond, transcending, or more comprehensive."

Most physicists—and most scientists in all fields—are not trained in metalinguistics and conceptual philosophy. Consequently they are often not aware that there are higher levels of implicit meanings embedded in the lower-level explicit uses of terms like "energy," "information," "fields," and "power."

It turns out that every fundamental concept in physics, including energy, information, fields, and power, has an implicit higher, more comprehensive, metalinguistic meaning in addition to its more limited, specialized meaning. Each concept has a more comprehensive metameaning that can be termed "meta-energy," "meta-information," "meta-fields," and "meta-power." Another more precise way of expressing this is to say that energy is actually a subset of meta-energy, information is a subset of meta-information, and so on.

Similarly, we can't deeply understand the concept of a cell phone, and more importantly a living cell phone, without being able to think at least one level of description higher about what a cell phone really is, and is becoming.

When I use the phrase "living cell phone," I'm speaking of a higher, more comprehensive and fundamental description of the cell phone. We can think of this as being a meta–living cell phone; for short, a meta–cell phone.

When you wear metaglasses, you have the power to perceive anything at any level in a more comprehensive and fundamental way. May you enjoy the opportunity for meta-exploration as much as we have.

Acknowledgments

From Gary Schwartz

Science can be thought of as the process of making the invisible visible. In a deep sense, my writing partner, William Simon, does this too. He appreciates not only the abstract and technical process of science, but the personal journey—often invisible to the reader—that inspires it. Bill is a musician with words, he is a special human being, and I cherish the opportunity to make music with him. I also thank his better half, Arynne Simon, for inspiring the two of us to play the best we can.

I began writing books for the general reader because James Levin, MD, a visionary physician, businessman, and advisor, called me one evening in the late summer of 1998 and said, "Gary, you must tell your story, you must tell your story now, and you must tell it from your heart as well as your head." Over the years, Jim has been, so to speak, an energy angel to me and the work. His wisdom, compassion, and humor are priceless. His statement, "May the story captivate us, the science awaken us, and the truth transform us" inspires me on a daily basis. His partner, Natalie Cederquist, is a multifaceted gem. Her creativity and enthusiasm are part of the invisible golden thread that is woven into the fabric of this book. I am blessed that together they are woven into my life.

The research described in this book was made possible by the support of various federal and private organizations, especially center and individual grants from the National Center for Complementary and Alternative Medicine (NCCAM) of the National Institutes of Health (NIH) and gifts from the Canyon Ranch Resorts. I'm especially indebted to Shan Wong, PhD, Stephen Strauss, PhD, and Margaret Chesney, PhD, of NCCAM, and to Mel Zuckerman, Jerry Cohen, and Tony Vuturo, MD, of Canyon Ranch. Without their commitment to fostering this work, there would be no energy-healing research program at the University of Arizona. Though they individually address the controversial nature of this work in different ways (and this book does not reflect their personal opinions or the positions of their respective institutions), they collectively champion that the work be done and that it see the light of day.

The energy-healing research was conducted primarily in the Laboratory for Advances in Consciousness and Health (formally the Human Energy Systems Laboratory) and the Center for Frontier Medicine in Biofield Science, both at the University of Arizona. The lab and center operate under the Department of Psychology in collaboration with the Departments of Surgery, Medicine, Neurology, Psychiatry, and Family and Community Medicine, and the School of Optical Sciences (formally the Optical Sciences Center). I especially thank Alfred Kaszniak, PhD, professor and head of the Department of Psychology, Lynn Nadel, PhD, Regents professor and former head of the Department of Psychology, Edward Donnerstein, PhD, Dean of the College of Social and Behavioral Sciences, and Richard Powell, PhD, professor of Optical Sciences emeritus and former vice president for research, for their commitment to academic freedom and their support of scientists pursuing important research even when it is challenging and potentially controversial.

I have been blessed to have had the opportunity of collaborating on the energy healing experiments with a diverse group of gifted basic scientists and research clinicians. You have met some of them in this book. They are, in alphabetical order, Mikel Aicken, PhD, Ann Baldwin, PhD, Iris Bell, MD, PhD, Audrey Brooks, PhD, Katherine Burleson, MD, Maureen Campensino, PhD, Melinda Connor, PhD, Katherine Creath, PhD, PhD (one in optical sciences, the other in music), Allan Hamilton, MD, Linda Larkey, PhD, Lewis Mehl-Madrona, MD, PhD, Cheryl Rittenbaugh, PhD, Beverly Rubik, PhD, and Linda Russek, PhD. They represent the fields of biophysics, biostatistics, cardiology, medical anthropology, music, neuroscience, nursing, optical sciences, physiology, psychiatry, psychology, psychophysiology, and surgery. Energy-healing research is inherently interdisciplinary and transdisciplinary, so that a principal challenge lies in integrating a diverse range of methods, theories, and findings. Though my colleagues—past and present—collectively endorse the general conclusion that energy plays a role in medicine, health, and life, the reader should appreciate that their endorsement of particular conclusions and speculations in this book varies at least as widely as the fields they represent.

The inspiration for our energy-healing research grows out of discoveries made by a diverse group of extraordinary scientists whose fields range from biophysics and medicine to quantum physics and parapsychology. I am especially indebted to Larry Dossey, MD, Richard Gerber, MD, Kim Jobst, MD, Joie Jones, PhD, Edgar Mitchell, DSc, James Oschman, PhD, Ken Pelletier, MD, PhD, Dean Radin, PhD, Glen Rein, PhD, Rustum Roy, PhD, Rupert Sheldrake, PhD, and William Tiller, PhD. In their unique ways, they have each not only informed and challenged my mind, but through our personal interactions at conferences, by e-mails, and over meals, they have touched my heart as well.

Students play many roles, probably the most important being as teachers. In the process of doing this research, I have collaborated with, and been taught by, a group of masterful former as well as current undergraduate, graduate, and postdoctoral students. They include Sheryl Attig, MA, Julie Beischel, PhD, Justin Beltran, Emily Cory, Vanessa Crawford, Mary Flores, Anastasia Gorbonov, Patti Harada, Shamini Jain, MA, Cecily Knepprath, Daniel Lewis, MA, Sabrina Lewis, Lonnie Nelson, PhD, Jason Patterson, Katie Reece, Shauna Shapiro, PhD, and Summer Stanwick. You are each a treasure.

Many others have contributed to this work from its birthing to completion in diverse roles as colleagues, healers, staff, and advisors who hold a special place in my heart. This group includes Henry Ajiki, Rosalyn Bruyere, Marty Hewett, PhD, Tomoe Lombard, Krishna Madappa, Shirley Maclaine, John Mack, MD, Suzanne Mendelssohn, PhD, Gerry Nangle, John Payne, Eric Pearl, Jeanne Renouf, PhD, EdD, Ernie Schloss, PhD, Willow Sibert, Clarissa Siefert, Susy Smith, Patricia and Robert Starrone, Linda Van Dyck, PhD, Catherine Yunt, Sam, and, more recently, Peter Moscow, PhD, and Kelsey and Camille Grammer. Though some of you are invisible, your energies are experienced and celebrated.

My father and mother, Howard and Shirley Schwartz, played a powerful early role not simply by tolerating a questioning child, but by nurturing my curiosity and encouraging me to speak up for the truth as I observed it. My parents, and their parents before them, had a passion for life and growth. The energy and courage to write this book comes partly from them.

Finally, I wish to acknowledge two special people who came into my life just as this book was being written: Marcia Claire Eklund and Rhonda Eklund. Every day one or both of you remind me, in countless ways, to celebrate the true miracle and magic of what scientists call "energy" and what spiritual people see as "spirit" and "divinity."

As Dr. Levin puts it, "Energy is the voice of spirit." It appears that science is leading us back to spirit in a revitalizing way that can be perceived, and received, by all. In the process, science is awakening within us a new vision of the cosmos and our role in it that is vibrant with healing and transformative possibility.

From Bill Simon

When some book collaborations end, even though the coauthors may have clicked with each other, they part and may never see each other again unless their paths happen to cross by chance.

My collaborations with Gary Schwartz haven't been like that. This is our fourth book together, and from the start we established a friendship based on mutual respect and admiration, bolstered by things we share in common—both refugees from the East Coast, both with Cornell undergraduate degrees, both with wide-ranging interests. What I thought was an assignment for one book has turned into what promises to be a lifelong friendship. Gary is that rarity: a scientist of inquiring mind who is willing to explore areas that make other scientists tremble for fear of being criticized by their more timid peers, and at the same time so open and engaging that he wins professional accolades and the admiration of a legion of fans. If any novelist ever wants to create a character who is the ideal writing partner, I nominate Gary Schwartz as the model.

The single word "thanks," like the words "I love you," cannot be said too frequently. I'm delighted to say and write both of those to my precious wife Arynne, so the world can know, and our children Victoria Simon and Sheldon Bermont can know, as well as our grandchildren Elena and Vincent Bermont, of Arynne's dedicated contribution to my success as a writer. As I sit here to write my acknowledgments, I have facing me on my desk a few of the anniversary cards my dear Arynne and I received yesterday, testimony that she has stuck with me all these years, helping me suffer through the dark moments all writers endure—especially dark when she frowns over a sentence, paragraph, or chapter. But she always comes through with a suggestion on how to fix the problem. I admit to often seeking the gratification of her instant approval but, in my heart, I know it's best to struggle a bit longer and get it right. I am a lucky man, indeed, to have lived and worked near this special woman. Many who know her understand how lucky I am.

As always, a humble nod of appreciation to my agent, the peerless Bill Gladstone of Waterside Productions, and to co-agent Ming Russell, for keeping me happily busy on engaging projects. Warm thanks as well to our editor, the ever-helpful Amy Tannenbaum, and to our publisher, the esteemed Judith Curr.

Index

About the Authors

Gary E. Schwartz, PhD, is professor of psychology, medicine, neurology, psychiatry, and surgery at the University of Arizona and director of its Laboratory for Advances in Consciousness and Health. He was recently named director of development of energy healing for Canyon Ranch Resorts. He directed an NIH-funded $1.8 million Center for Frontier Medicine in Biofield Science. He received his PhD from Harvard University in 1971 and was an assistant professor there for five years. He then served as a professor of psychology and psychiatry at Yale University, director of the Yale Psychophysiology Center, and codirector of the Yale Behavioral Medicine Clinic, before moving to Arizona in 1988. He has published more than 450 scientific papers and coedited eleven academic books. He is the author of *The G.O.D. Experiments, The Afterlife Experiments, The Truth About "Medium,"* and the coauthor of *The Living Energy Universe.*

William Simon has been writing professionally for thirty years and has credits on some eight hundred published and produced works. His own books include three bestsellers and have been translated into twenty foreign editions. His many national and international awards include ten CINE Golden Eagles, an Emmy nomination, and recognition from eight international film festivals including Belgrade, Berlin, and Venice.